PARANORMAL HERTFORDSHIRE

PARANORMAL HERTFORDSHIRE

DAMIEN O'DELL

AMBERLEY

The author and publisher wish to acknowledge that *Paranormal Hertfordshire* was substantially informed by *Haunted Hertfordshire* by Ruth Stratton and Nicholas Connell (Book Castle, 2006)

First published 2009

Amberley Publishing
The Hill, Stroud
Gloucestershire GL5 4EP

www.amberley-books.com

British Library Cataloguing in Publication Data.
A catalogue record for this book is available from the British Library.

ISBN 978 1 84868 118 7

Typesetting and origination by Amberley Publishing
Printed in Great Britain

CONTENTS

	Foreword	6
1	Royston's Restless Dead	8
2	Chilling Cathedrals, Churches and Chapels	19
3	Spooks Among the Books	34
4	Haunted Hertfordshire Hotels	50
5	St Albans – Fifth Most Haunted	64
6	Villages of the Unexplained	71
7	'Local' Haunts	83
8	The Stately Ghosts of Hertfordshire	97
9	Hertford and Ware Wraiths	111
10	Spectres of Stage and Screen	121
11	Uninvited Guests	131
12	North Hertfordshire Nightmares	145

FOREWORD

Paranormal Hertfordshire developed from my second book *Ghostly Hertfordshire*. It is a much more comprehensive account of the vast array of unexplained phenomena that have taken place in recent times across the county. Researching it has been an unforgettable, thoroughly enjoyable journey of discovery. In the course of this research I have learned a great deal about a diverse range of subjects which I gladly share with the reader. They include Britain's film and TV industry, the county's stately homes and its celebrated, famous residents as well as its highwaymen, villages, pubs, churches and hotels. I've never been an 'armchair researcher', content to pore over others' books to gain my information. I'm a firm believer in active research – meeting people face to face

Team APIS. *Left to right:* Jan, Linda, Rob, Damien, Julie and Brian.

and visiting sites personally, in short 'doing the legwork'. My APIS (Anglia Paranormal Investigation Society) research group has enabled me to share and to conduct some exciting 'ghost watches' at places known for paranormal activity, such as both Watford and Letchworth Libraries. These two investigations alone form an entire chapter of *Paranormal Hertfordshire*. In some cases I've been able to offer alternative explanations for alleged manifestations, to separate the myth from the facts and this, too, is an enormously satisfying aspect of paranormal investigation.

Hertfordshire holds a special place in my heart because I've lived here happily for over twenty years although I was born and raised in London. 'Trust and fear not' is the county's motto, it might also serve well as a ghost hunter's motto! This home county is much larger than Bedfordshire, which was the subject of my earliest investigations, as recorded in *Paranormal Bedfordshire*. Hertfordshire currently has a population in excess of one million. It is not short on its ghostly population either. According to the Supernatural Britain Report, St Albans is the fifth most haunted place in Great Britain, so it is most deserving of the chapter I have devoted to it. Royston also has a chapter to itself – APIS's investigation at Henrick's Hairdressers in that town was one of the most interesting that I've been involved in so far. Royston has featured in several television programmes about the paranormal. Some of the cases I came across must have been truly terrifying for the experients, such as the badly haunted cottage at Ashwell and the scary former post office in Weston. In the last chapter, 'North Hertfordshire Nightmares', the final story in this book concerns the infamous Stevenage Poltergeist, which is the subject of an ongoing APIS investigation.

Thanks, as always, are due to lots of people including the many friends of mine who are members of APIS, in particular Keith Ecott, for his superb photographs. It is due to Keith's hard work, patience and persistence that this book is graced by numerous fine illustrations. I hope that you enjoy the result of all our hard work.

Damien O'Dell
April 2009

CHAPTER ONE

ROYSTON'S RESTLESS DEAD

THE MOST HAUNTED HOUSE IN ROYSTON

Such is Royston's haunted reputation that two television programmes have been made about paranormal events in the town in recent years, *Ghostly Tales of the Unexpected* and *Derek Acorah's Ghost Towns*. Royston is Hertfordshire's most northernmost point, a small town with some 14,000 residents out of a total county population of one million. Lady Roisia (meaning Rose) gave her name to the town and she was the wife of Eudo Dapifer, steward to William the Conqueror. Eudo owned Newsells, the local manor house, and now there is a charming, 'hidden' hamlet called Newsells just outside Royston. A cross was erected by Roisia (or restored by her) at the junction of two prehistoric roads, Ermine Street and the Icknield Way. The foot stone of Roisia's cross is all that remains and it may be found at the bottom of the High Street. Crossroads, in ancient times, were considered sacred and early in the Christian era the practice of erecting crosses at crossroads was developed. Ermine Street was the Romans' Great North Road; it runs all the way from London to York. The Icknield Way runs from Salisbury Plain to East Anglia. The area around the cross became known as Roisia's Cross, and as the town grew up around it Roisia's Town eventually abbreviated to Royston.

A haunted hairdressers doesn't sound too scary a place, indeed it was the first time that I had been invited to investigate such an establishment. It was a warm day on the 10 July 2004 and I was in Royston to meet Mark Henrick, proprietor of Henrick's Hairdressers situated at Fish Hill not far from the market. The story he had to tell me was, indeed, hair-raising. Mark appeared to me to be a sensible, hard-working, level-headed young businessman who was totally unprepared for the plethora of paranormal phenomena which had beset the premises since he had first set up his business about a year before our meeting. His shop was in a Grade II listed building which had seen many changes, having been a pine furniture shop prior to Mark's occupancy. Originally the building had comprised two cottages and a barn and dated back to the sixteenth century. As I made my way upstairs I noticed that it was distinctly colder. My inbuilt 'haunted building detector' was confirming that I was in a seriously haunted place – my back felt distinctly cold. Normally you would expect a building to be warmer upstairs. I remarked about a space on one wall that I had noticed and was told that that a clock used to hang there. Every morning it would be found on the floor face up, working perfectly. This carried on for two weeks and so the clock was removed. At the end of my inspection the question that concerned me the most was why had there been no record of haunting activity prior to Mark's tenancy? It was a puzzle that was to be resolved during the course of the investigation.

Henrick's Hairdressers, Royston. The light in the upstairs window was not visible when this photo was taken. The ghost of William Armatage claimed responsibility for causing the light effect.

I interviewed both Mark and his staff; there were no inconsistencies in their stories. A whole range of anomalous phenomena, typical of genuinely haunted houses, had been reported at Henrick's. This included electrical problems, with fuses constantly being blown and as many as sixteen electrical problems experienced in one day including lights going on and off by themselves. Mark told me that sometimes 'something' will not let you flip the trip switch. Upstairs a 'cold spot' was felt in a corner of the beauty room by the couch. A mirror 'shot off a wall and smashed without harming a nearby member of staff'. Weird noises have been heard and Mark said 'there is always a feeling of someone else being present' when he is alone at the salon. Radio stations have been retuned by no human agency and heaters have also been turned on and off, seemingly by themselves. I spoke with Emma, a young employee who told me that she regularly had a variety of small items thrown at her by an unseen force. Even stranger was the fact that these items have not come from the salon, such as bottle tops, but have come 'out of nowhere'. I found this particularly interesting as apports (mostly small objects which materialise from thin air or transport through solid matter) are symptomatic of classic poltergeist activity. Interference with electrical equipment is similarly another hallmark of the poltergeist, so now I had some idea of what we were up against. Mark and I agreed that my group, Anglia Paranormal Investigation Society, would hold a 'ghost watch' on the night of Tuesday 28 September. I chose this night because the nightclub across the street would be closed, so it would be quite peaceful, and it was also the night of the full moon, which might be a good time for paranormal activity.

I had been preceded at Henrick's by a number of investigators but Mark was still anxious for some answers as to why he was being haunted. A psychic called Peter Foreman had visited Fish Hill after reading about the case. He used his dowsing skills to locate the ghosts of Henrick's. Peter, at eighty-three years old, was highly experienced at investigating haunted sites. He had travelled up from Hatfield and the journey was worth making. The ghostly impressions that he received were extremely strong. In the cellar he became most agitated, got red in the face and started shaking as he sensed that a fire had originated here. He also sensed the presence of a man in the far corner. On the first floor, in the shower room/toilet area, Peter picked up the spirit of another man 'with a troubled past'. He also encountered a female spirit by the sun cubicle area, and as he stood by a small cupboard on the landing its door inexplicably flew open. In the upstairs 'waiting room' Peter discovered 'a large energy mass' and his dowsing rods rotated wildly. Away from the room they stopped moving altogether and the psychic was left feeling dizzy. In total Peter detected the presence of twelve ghosts, eight men and four women, mainly haunting the upstairs part of the premises. He thought that some of these spirits may have perished in the fire that he had sensed

My good friend Martin Waldock and his team from Cambridge Paranormal Research Society carried out a vigil in the hairdressers in February 2004, four months before my initial visit. They identified 'a six foot mass of electrical energy' and in the treatment room they felt that 'someone was moving about and getting on and off the treatment table'. CPRS also detected the presence of twelve separate spirits haunting the place. They worked closely with the late Marge Kite, a medium from Ashwell village, not far from Royston. Marge had felt the presence of a man and a dog in spirit form in the toning table room upstairs.

I revisited Henrick's in August 2004 to confirm the details of the APIS investigation with Mark. Since my first visit a few weeks previously yet more activity had taken place. I spoke to Marta, the nail technician, and she told me that 'someone' had squeezed her in the back but when she turned around there was nobody to be seen. This was just one of at least four strange occurrences. An unexplained flickering and fusing light had also been reported along with the radio – its volume control had gone up and down of its own accord and a picture was seen to 'jump off the wall' before bouncing down the stairs and smashing.

On the day before the planned vigil I returned to collect the shop keys and was greeted with some interesting news by the excited hairdressers. Some mediums from Bedfordshire had recently held their own 'ghost hunt' at the hairdressers, along with a few of Mark's staff one evening, from 7.30pm till 10.30pm. It had been a productive few hours. A tape recorder left on in the salon had captured a child's voice. I listened to this tape later and, although I had to strain to hear the words at first (it was a bit like a bad phone connection from a foreign country), it definitely sounded childlike and the words could have been 'help me, help me'. The problem with EVP (electronic voice phenomena) is that it is rather subjective – you hear what you want to hear in many instances. It is also open to suggestion – someone thinks they can interpret the (usually) indistinct message and then convinces other listeners of the validity of their claim. Such was the case when I heard the Henrick's tape; other people had already told me what was on the tape thereby influencing what I thought I heard.

Gail Peacock, who led the Bedfordshire mediums, was seen, I was told by several witnesses, to transfigure (her facial features completely changed – to those of a man on this occasion). She seemed to be temporarily possessed by another entity. As she went up the stairs she 'froze' on the second step from the top. She started swearing, the shape of her chin seemed to change, her eyes became dark, a moustache was seen above her top lip and red wheals appeared around her throat. The medium's impression was that this man absolutely hated women, he was holding on to a little girl, who had somehow stopped him from making money. He had ended up committing suicide. Gail later told me that she had 'levitated up the stairs, without my feet actually touching them'. The two young members of staff that I spoke to were certain that they had witnessed the medium's face becoming dramatically altered. Transfiguration is a rarity amongst psychic mediums; I wished that I had seen it and been able to confirm it for myself. My viewpoint as a paranormal researcher is that mediums deserve a fair hearing and that it is best to approach their testimony with an open mind. APIS works with mediums because they are another useful resource, just as the electronic detection equipment that we use helps our search for the truth in paranormal investigations. Many other paranormal investigators refuse to work with mediums preferring to rely solely on scientific methods alone. That is their loss in my opinion, despite their oft-repeated mantra that to use mediums is to investigate one branch of the unknown with another. Unfortunately mediums have suffered a bad press, not undeservedly in many cases, because there are so many bad, fraudulent ones, whose main motivations are making money and self-glorification. We live in a celebrity culture, gaining fame as a medium is one way to become a celebrity with its attendant benefits. Others are merely lacking in self-awareness, are desperate to be noticed and have an over-inflated opinion of their own supposed 'powers'. My long experience has taught me two things about psychics, mediums or sensitives as they are variously known. Firstly that ESP (extra sensory perception) is not uncommon, indeed most of us can develop our innate ability to a greater or lesser degree. As with any gift, be it, for instance, sporting, musical or psychic ability, some people are more gifted than others. Secondly, the vast majority of mediums that I have encountered fall into the frauds and self-deluded 'wannabe' categories. The genuinely gifted and highly developed mediums I know of can be counted on the fingers of one hand. I have sat in development circles myself; indeed I was told that I had the makings of a trance medium. The idea of dead people speaking through me while I was in a trance definitely held no appeal. I do, however, have great respect for those who have some ESP and who devote much effort and many hours of development to make the best of their talent. In November 2007 I had the privilege of teaching paranormal investigation to mediums at the internationally famous Arthur Findlay College at Stansted Hall in Essex. I can, therefore, state with absolute conviction and total confidence that not all mediums are fraudulent.

Another fascinating insight into the Henrick's hauntings was provided by my friend Louise Morton, a gifted psychic artist, who at that time lived in Blunham, Bedfordshire. Louise was able to turn her psychic impressions into sketches. This lady was able to provide me with the details of the 'main protagonist' in the Henrick's case, as well as introducing me to some of the other eleven spirits that allegedly inhabited these particular Hertfordshire hairdressers. She was able to show us what he looked like, but she also received details of his name and the period that he lived in. He sounded like an extremely insalubrious character indeed, a suicide, a misogynist, possibly involved in smuggling and probably a murderer. His greeting to Louise was characteristic – 'Get my name right you bitch, Lord George Armatage'. I very much doubted that the leader of a gang of cut-throats would be a member of the aristocracy, but he may well have had an inflated ego when alive. Louise's drawings portrayed an extremely creepy-looking individual with hypnotic, staring eyes, strongly arched eyebrows and a droopy moustache, set in a thin face framed by shoulder-length hair. The overall impression was of a brooding, intense and cruel face. I strongly fancied that this man would show neither mercy nor pity, no matter the circumstances he found himself in; he had been a brutish, opportunistic villain. Louise was able to describe his clothing, his shirt had a ruffled front, he wore long black boots and he carried a cane with a brass top and bottom. He had lived in the reign of Charles I, during the 1600s.

On a later visit to the haunted hairdressers Louise was shown Armatage at the end of his earthly incarnation, 'My own demise' he explained to the psychic. His eyes were closed and his tongue was lolling out. 'I felt no pain; I was intoxicated when the knife cut my throat.' Visions and communications were received from some of the other entities inhabiting the building, one of whom told Louise 'George was a swanky yob who was going to stand trial at Newgate, that's why he took his life and many were glad of it. He was head of a large gang of cut-throats who aided and abetted their stealing. Where some got hanged for a loaf of bread he got away with murder, and more, for years.' The impressions came thick and fast, the building as it was in times past, of a side building for horses and staff, a horse tethered at the back wall, a kitchen lined with riding boots, it had been used as a tack room. In the salon the floor had been lower where there was a partition in the present shop. The psychic felt that a well had existed on the grounds. A young boy suddenly appeared, his face having superimposed itself on a poster in the shop window. He was about fourteen years old, his name was James, a sad boy 'who wanted to move on'. A date and name also came to the psychic's mind – 1672 and Betty. A man came through, a happy-go-lucky personality called Tom Skinner, who was from a later age. He described himself as; 'a justice of the law, with rouge a'plenty. I used to come a'courting and used to check this abode and its clientele.'

In the attic Louise encountered the spirit of a young girl called Millie or Mollie who wore callipers on her legs due to polio. This impression was shared by a number of other psychics who were with Louise at the time. They all felt an extreme heaviness in their legs as they walked up the stairs. An elderly lady named Betty lived in the attic once, she too had suffered problems with her legs, which had been ulcerated and eventually turned gangrenous. She was here when the house was 'used for letting to rough people. I stayed here and used to lock myself in at times'. Betty had welcomed death, she had been fed up with the cold, with poverty and hunger and she 'used to see like you (psychically) and I left before my body gave up. Betty's miserable room used to fill up with smoke from the lower chimney downstairs. 'I had a pauper's grave. I'm only the dogsbody and when ill no one to attend to me. Years of toil and sweat and graft for nowt, 'tis a trial this life o'mine, glad to break its bones and go.' A brief description of the former lives lived by five out of the dozen 'resident spirits' was interesting background material. What made it particularly noteworthy was that much of the details were corroborated by several different mediums.

On the night of Tuesday 28 September 2004 a team of eleven APIS investigators assembled at Henrick's. We familiarised ourselves with the layout of the building, checked our log sheets and discussed our plans. Next we set up and tested our equipment. This included night vision video cameras, temperature/humidity gauges, vibration detectors, electro-magnetic frequency meters, walkie-talkies, analogue tape recorders and digital voice recorders. Watches started at 11pm, in teams of two, for an hour at a time, followed by thirty minute breaks. At 12.30pm we began the second watch with a different combination of team members and a change of location (so that everyone got to work with everyone else and in every different location). The vigil carried on right through till 4.30am the following Wednesday morning. Louise Sassoon, a newspaper reporter for *The Royston Crow*, was our guest for part of the night, bringing our numbers up to twelve in total. Two of our crew were psychic mediums, Joan Dancer and Ian Edolls, but other team members had varying degrees of psychic sensitivity. All members had been trained by me in the skill of paranormal investigation. There is a right and a wrong way to conduct an investigation, as in any area of human endeavour, and some of our clients insist that investigators are both trained and experienced. The rest of my team were Andy Thompson, Andy Garrett, Carol Greenall, Mark Head, Moira Gray, Nigel Brockwell, Paul O'Dell and Ryan Chambers.

We didn't have long to wait for psychic impressions to be received and anomalous phenomena to be experienced. During the first watch (11pm-12 midnight) on the ground floor shadows were seen and Andy Garrett smelt the scent of roses. Upstairs, in the sunbed room area Joan, Paul and Louise all distinctly heard a loud exhalation of air. Joan received an impression of heat and believed that there had been a fire in this room in the past. In the nail room and beauty room Nigel and Ian witnessed an electric heater turning itself on and then off again after a flash photograph was taken outside the room. Ian picked up numerous psychic impressions; the name Penny, the years 1832 and 1879, as well as Leonora James, aged ten, and the year 1772. Ian asked Leonora if anyone 'bad' was there, but she left, saying 'Don't let him find me.' Half an hour later the sound of something falling/bouncing came from upstairs, this was followed minutes afterwards by the heater switching itself on and then off again. I had been on the top floor with Andy Thompson and we were sure that nothing had dropped on the floor while we were in there. We both saw a flash of light around the edge of the closed door. Andy felt cold and heard a shuffling noise from the stairs outside. The battery unaccountably drained down on our night vision camcorder, at this point both of us felt cold. Andy, who was nearest to the door, heard voices just outside the room, on the unoccupied landing.

During the thirty minute coffee break the strangeness continued. As my brother Paul waited to use the toilet in the salon downstairs, a large bottle of hair conditioner fell to the floor with a bang right in front of his startled eyes. He told me later that that there was absolutely no reason for it to suddenly fall off the shelf. One second it was there and the next it was on the floor. He was both mystified and adamant that nobody had been near enough to knock or push the bottle off the shelf; it hadn't been teetering on the edge but had been neatly and tightly stacked. I experimented, jumped up and down quite hard right next to the shelf to see if I could dislodge any of the bottles, perhaps there was a springy floorboard? Try as I might I couldn't make any of these bottles move, they were secure on that shelf. Nigel quietly informed me that he, too, had witnessed exactly the same thing as Paul. He had also been standing nearby and had been equally mystified by the incident. I have experienced this sort of thing before on vigils. Unexplained occurrences regularly happen when investigators are off-guard, often on a break between watches, so this was a typical example of this kind of phenomenon.

The second watch was quieter. Ryan and Ian were stationed downstairs. Shortly after 1am Ryan felt cold while Ian received a psychic impression of a middle-aged woman clutching her chest in distress. She was standing in the corner then fell to the floor before disappearing. The year 1873 was associated with this death. On the top floor Joan and Nigel were stationed in the attic room previously occupied by Andy Thompson and myself. At 12.45am Nigel noted in the log that a 4in vertical line of light had appeared on the wall opposite the door. It moved about a foot to the left then back again before disappearing. Joan felt that the present premises had originally been three dwellings converted into one. A vision came to her of the attic in past times, there was a double bed in the room and two children were playing with a train set.

Unexplained incidents continued into the third watch. Nigel and I checked the remote thermometers, which had been placed upstairs and they had unaccountably stopped working. In the first floor reception area Joan and Ian felt a coldness around their legs. Joan used her crystal pendant to do some dowsing, with interesting results. A man had committed suicide by the fireplace and a middle-aged lady had died of a heart attack. Ian then did some dowsing to determine the cause of the suicide's death. His throat became tight and he wondered if this was connected with poison. Joan then received a particularly strong and most unpleasant sensation in her throat, as if it had been cut. Ian used the EMF meter and received a high reading by the fireplace. High electro-magnetic field readings have been associated with spirit presences.

After our third watch we had our customary debriefing session while Ian returned upstairs alone. He was anxious to collect some final impressions from the spirits present in the attic room. Debriefing usually produces some incidents that may have been omitted from the log sheets and Joan recalled that 'something' had touched her hand after she had heard a 'clinking sound' upstairs. At another point it felt as though something was tugging at her hair. Another time she had heard music, like a military band at the front of the building. Ian rejoined us and reported that he had received a psychic impression of three people; a woman who had died of old age and two young brothers who had been hiding (playing hide and seek?) and had died from smoke inhalation when a fire broke out. The two incidents were just a year apart.

In an incident packed night the best phenomenon was saved till last, however, with an intriguing photograph taken at 3.30am by Mark, after we had left the building. He was taking some final exterior shots with his digital camera. I had locked up after turning all the lights off. When we saw the prints of Mark's pictures one of them showed a glow from the upstairs window. The photograph reproduced in this book shows an eerie glow from the upstairs window. It is not the kind of light given off by an electric light, but seems more like the glow that might emanate from a fire inside the place! It is also possible to make out a mysterious orb, floating at roof height. It definitely was not the moon, because that was positioned behind Mark's shoulder as we saw him take the photographs. Not only was I a witness to the circumstances surrounding this unexplained photograph but also Ian, Nigel, Joan and Andy Thompson. I later compared notes with psychic artist Louise Morton, who told me that she had received a communication from Lord George Armatage. 'I was responsible for the light in the photograph. Nobody knows the truth of my atrocities or it wouldn't be the perfect crime. Harbouring and abetting, I would have got away with it if it wasn't for that blackguard.' A chilling message indeed, we don't know who 'that blackguard' was but somebody seems to have spoilt Armatage's plans – if indeed that was his real name.

The APIS team were excited to see, just a fortnight after our investigation, a Friday night television programme, *Ghostly Tales of the Unexpected*. Medium Lizzie Falconer gave her views during her visit to Royston, when she investigated Henrick's. What particularly interested us was that Lizzie's main impressions tallied closely with those of the mediums that I had worked with and she seemed to make some kind of sense of the strange happenings. She homed in on the man who had slit his own throat. It was because he was so resentful that his former home had been turned into a hairdressing salon that the hauntings had begun. I had my answer, finally, as to why there had been no record of hauntings prior to Mark Henrick's tenancy.

This case seemed to revolve around Lord George Armatage (as the spirit identified itself) plus a number of supporting characters from a variety of eras. The change of use from a furniture shop to a women's hairdressers appears to have acted as the trigger for the manifestations of this principal, evil character, whose anger and malign influence has for so long been directed at womankind. It would account for the paranormal activity suddenly taking off since Mr Henrick's arrival. Before this there does not appear to have been this level of haunting experienced anywhere in the Fish Hill area of Royston. It is not uncommon with paranormal phenomena for there to be a trigger, a factor which precipitates a manifestation of some sort. Quite often, in my experience, the catalyst is building work, where alterations to the fabric of a property seem to stir up spirits which may have lain dormant for many years, sometimes centuries. It is as though the former inhabitants are resentful of modern day intrusions into *their* homes. What was noteworthy in this particular investigation was the fact that a number of mediums, working independently, without prior knowledge of either the case or each other's involvement, had received the same basic impressions of a principal, angry spirit of a dead criminal who hated women, a suicide who had slashed his throat in his own home some time in the seventeenth century. I would have to agree with my friends from Cambridge Paranormal Research Society, that there are indeed probably as many as twelve spirits that have been haunting the site at Fish Hill; many of them were children from different periods in history. As well as 'Armatage' there were the young people from 1743, one of whom identified himself as 'David Lawrence', who supposedly perished from smoke inhalation during a fire while he was playing with his brother. Several mediums felt strongly that there had definitely been a fire in the house. There was also ten-year-old Leonora James from 1772, Millie or Molly with the callipered legs and sad, fourteen-year-old James. There was a spirit lady identified as Penny, connected with 1832 and 1879 – the years of her birth and death perhaps? Other ladies included Rosemary and Bessie Edwards (with the gangrenous legs) and from 1833 the happy-go-lucky Tom Skinner. Real people or figments of the mediums' imaginations? It all depends on your viewpoint.

MORE ROYSTON HAUNTS

Curwen's Solicitors at 17 High Street is another famously haunted Royston landmark. In the Tudor Room upstairs a grey lady has been seen at night. This room is always cold and members of staff are always eager to leave it. At one time these premises were occupied by a hairdressers and a pile of sawn up bones were discovered on site. The manor house in Baldock Street is noted for paranormal sounds, both of breaking glass and doors banging. King James's Lodge is home to another spectral lady, this one tends the garden she once cared for on the site where King James's hunting lodge stood. In 1603 James VI of Scotland stayed at Royston en route to his coronation as James I of England. Evidently, he liked what he saw as he decided to have a country retreat here before he had set foot in London. The new king soon established a series of buildings for members of his court, his horses and his hunting dogs. Strict rules were created prohibiting anyone taking game within fourteen miles of Royston. James I regularly indulged in the royal sport of hunting in this locale as Royston combined the convenience of closeness to London with just enough distance to deter unwanted intrusion.

The nineteenth-century old magistrate's court and police station is now home to offices, but it has long been known as a place where paranormal activity has been witnessed. Reports in recent years have included the apparition of a policeman, said to have no feet, who has been encountered in the passageway. Office staff have seen a clock launch itself off the wall, a plant that jumped off a mantelpiece and smashed on the floor and a toilet door that slammed by itself. Several times taps have been turned on full at night down in the old cells whilst the building is deserted. Just a few years ago, when *Derek Acorah's Ghost Towns* was filmed in Royston, cast and crew visited the cells and had their own strange experiences. One of the presenters was pushed in the back by some unseen force. The sound engineer had a fright too when everyone present heard a fluttering sound, similar to fingers drumming against his radio mike. At the same time the lights on the sound equipment started flashing. Other phenomena encountered by various members of the crew included the strong smell of whisky and cold breezes. The medium's opinion was that the place was haunted by an angry spirit who had been a heavy drinker when he was alive.

THE MYSTERIOUS CAVE

The Celtic people had a word for it – they called them 'thin places', those countryside locations where the divide between this world and the next is at its most fragile. I have felt this 'other worldly' quality at only two places. One was on the top of Glastonbury Tor and the other was deep underground, in Royston Cave. The mysterious cave is man-made, cut out of the 60 metre thick layer of chalk that lies under the town. It is sited close to a 'sacred' crossroads and directly on a major ley line. This strange, beehive-shaped cave is unique throughout the whole of Britain. It is attributed to the secretive Knights Templar, some of whom were based at Baldock, not many miles away. The order was famous for its enormous wealth and occult rituals. Their cave itself remained hidden for over 400 years before its rediscovery in August 1742. Workmen improving the pitch, used by women selling butter in the market, discovered a large millstone under the surface of the road. Beneath this stone a shaft was found, leading straight down to the cave. Hundreds of cartloads of rubbish half-filled the cave and had to be removed before the interior was revealed.

My first visit here was about six years ago, as part of a group of sightseers. I found myself profoundly impressed by the oddly shaped interior with its numerous images of saints and other Christian symbols, which are carved into its chalk walls. They had once been painted, in various colours, but the paint is now long gone. Melbourne Street has an alley leading off it and the cave entrance may be found here, where a builder had his premises in 1790. On my second visit I was even more certain that this place was somehow special. I was privileged to be given a private guided tour, together with five friends, on a chilly Sunday afternoon in March 2005. Donning a hard hat and carrying a torch I made my way up the scaffolding that had been temporarily erected enabling me to reach the roof, some 30ft above the cave floor. This offered me an opportunity that the public don't get, to access a level where, hundreds of years before, a similar platform had existed. I had a distinctly creepy impression up there, as if I might not be alone. My intuition told me that the shelves, carved out high up in the chalk face, had once been used for storing offerings in ancient times. As I stood on the topmost, smallest platform my head was a matter of inches below the pavement of Melbourne Street. Flickering shadows through the grille told me when a pedestrian was passing by.

I made my way back down to the main platform where my friend Louise joined me. Louise voiced her impressions, and told me that she could clearly see an orb in what looked like a chimney carved into the wall in front of us. She shone her torch at the spot but I was unable to see an orb. This didn't surprise me since Louise was much more psychically sensitive than me and, in fact, she received some strong psychic impressions. She felt a young girl's presence; human sacrifices had been made here. Some unfortunate person was hanging from the roof, while their life's blood drained away into a chalice on the ground below.

There were more surprises when I reached ground level once more. My friends Andy and Sarah both distinctly heard a baby scream – it seemed to emanate from the rock walls. The other five people present didn't hear anything. Louise and Paula were certain that during its long history this cave had been used for both good and evil practices.

BARKWAY'S SPOOKY GARAGE

Barkway is a small, attractive village surrounded by open countryside yet it is not far from Royston. I was once a peripatetic youth worker and this was one of the North Hertfordshire villages that I used to visit. I remember that on occasion there would be unseasonable fog on the approach to the village youth club, lending the area an aura of mystery. There was also a graveyard which I used to pass by, and on the other side of the road, in the High Street, was Walsh's Garage and next to it was a house. There were stories that people were afraid to spend the night alone at the house or the garage. Children's voices were heard in the workshop. At first the sounds were playful but then they would change to frightened, panicky noises. What is known for sure is that in 1886 a girl called Ruth Mary Wilson drowned in just four inches of water, just outside the garages.

NUTHAMPSTEAD'S PUB PHANTOM

A few miles to the south east of Royston is another delightful village, Nuthampstead with its golf course and, not far away, a clay pigeon shooting range, which was sited on a former Second World War USAAF bomber base, constructed in 1942. American Boeing B-17G 'flying fortresses' used to leave here to attack targets in Germany throughout 1944-1945. Before the 'Flying Fortresses', during 1943-1944, it was used by American fighters, Lockheed P-38H Lightnings. It was decommissioned as a military airfield in 1959. Close by the former airfield is The Woodman public house which is haunted, possibly by a former fighter or bomber pilot. In 1980 the landlord reported an eerie experience when a chair pulled itself up to his table as though an invisible guest had joined him. He looked around carefully, for signs of trickery, but there were none; this 'something' sat in this chair to make itself comfortable for the evening. This is no isolated incident; people who visited the pub on their own often received the distinct impression that someone was watching them when in fact there was nobody else in the bar at the time. A picture of a B-17G bomber regularly fell off the wall, this particular bomber had returned to base badly shot up. There was a huge hole in the nose and the explosion which caused the hole also killed the bomb aimer. It is interesting to speculate if this crewman returned to one of the sites he visited before taking off on his final mission. Perhaps it was the last place where he had felt safe and happy in the company of friends.

THERFIELD TERRORS

A mile or so to the south of Royston the ancient village of Therfield may be found, also nearby is Therfield Heath which is a beloved haven for dog walkers, golfers and horse riders; it also has long barrows, which date back to the Iron Age. Therfield sits on a ridge of the Chiltern Hills, just far enough from the bustling A10 to retain its air of peace, order and rural charm. This is not my opinion alone; the village has won Hertfordshire Society's coveted Best Kept Village in Hertfordshire award on at least six separate occasions. Once upon a time Therfield boasted seven public houses, alas now there is only one, The Fox and Duck, which I have visited on numerous occasions. This out of the way hostelry hit the headlines in the local press, in 1975. Both the *Royston Crow* and the *Herts and Cambs Reporter* took up the story. Temporary managers had been brought in to run the pub and it seemed as though a former (deceased) landlord had taken exception to them. Lights switched on and off by themselves, lamps were turned around and one time the light on the dartboard was found turned to face the wrong way. Bottles were rattled by unseen hands, toilets flushed of their own accord and footsteps ran across the upstairs landing. Both bar staff and customers alike witnessed these strange events. In desperation the managers abandoned their bedroom and opted to sleep on a mattress in the lounge bar. Events culminated in a police investigation into an alleged break-in at the pub. The local constabulary also heard the footsteps overhead but upon investigation no trace of any intruders could be found. The sounds seemed to be coming from a room that had been used by the former landlord, but there was nobody there. Villagers remained tight-lipped about the weird goings-on at The Fox and Duck and no explanation was ever forthcoming.

CHAPTER TWO

CHILLING CATHEDRALS, CHURCHES AND CHAPELS

ABBEY APPARITIONS

The question 'What is the most haunted town in Hertfordshire?' is asked of me occasionally and I don't have to stop and think about it. My unequivocal answer is the City of St Albans. The successful ghost walks go some way to proving this point. Initiated in 1988, they rival anything that much larger cities, like London, Chester or York can offer. So numerous, varied and well documented are the St Albans spectres that an entire book could be written about them alone.

In this haunted city the most haunted building is undoubtedly St Albans Cathedral, built by the Normans as their Abbey Church from recycled Roman brick, between the years 1077-1115. The abbey and the city's roots, however, are much older, dating back to AD 303 when the first English martyr, Alban, a soldier in Diocletian's army, was beheaded by the Romans. In AD 793 a grand monastery was built in his honour, on the site where he was executed. Alban's Shrine became a centre of pilgrimage and many were the visitors who claimed that they had been miraculously cured of their disabilities after coming to the monastery, which was richly adorned with gold, silver and jewels donated by these grateful pilgrims. This sacred place has been a site of Christian worship for over seventeen centuries.

Like many before me, I was impressed by St Albans Cathedral's commanding presence and felt a sense of its long, unbroken history. Its series of twelfth- to thirteenth-century wall paintings remain unequalled in England. Extensive renovations, paid for by Lord Grimthorpe of Batchwood Hall, were carried out in the 1870s and soon afterwards the abbey was granted Cathedral status.

One eyewitness account of ghostly encounters at the abbey was revealed by a lady who had been born and raised in the city but wished to remain anonymous. 'For many years I lived near the abbey and one evening I was walking home along by the railings on the south side path and enjoying the last fingers of the summer sunlight, when from within the abbey I heard the sounds of the most beautiful music and choral accompaniment that I have ever experienced. When I decided to slip in through the main west door to hear more, I found the heavy oak door locked and as I pressed the knob the music ceased and the abbey stood in eerie silence.' This 'heavenly music' has been heard by numerous witnesses who have been passing by the abbey, usually at night. Here is another account; 'Again near the abbey one September evening, I saw four very tall monks approaching me, who swayed slowly from side to side, as they moved along the pathway from the great gateway to the west front of the abbey and again the atmosphere was very eerie. I stood for a while but nothing seemed amiss with the scene,

St Albans Cathedral. Invisible choirs and restless Benedictine monks are part of the fabric of this building.

those monks were definitely swaying like thin trees as they walked forward and between them was something which looked like a coffin – I turned and fled!'

Humphrey, Duke of Gloucester, died in 1453, in most mysterious circumstances at Bury St Edmunds. His body was rushed back to St Albans where a tomb had been prepared for him in Saints Chapel and he was buried at night. Could this scene have been re-enacted for this local passer-by? This same person saw, on several occasions, a gloomy figure in a grey habit, 'with head cowled and hidden', where the new chapter house is situated. This same apparition has been seen inside the building as well, in the Hudson Library.

One of the canons who served St Albans Abbey during the 1920s was Canon George Glossop, who lived at Romeland House in the town. Soon after the First World War, on a spring morning as he walked to the abbey he heard the organ playing. Curious to find out the identity of the organ player, the canon let himself in through the slype door and made his way to the organ loft. As he reached his destination the music stopped abruptly and there was no trace of any organist.

A few years later, in 1921, Willie Luttmann, the organist at St Albans Abbey, staged a performance of the Fayrfax Mass, in commemoration of the 400th anniversary of the composer's death. Dr Robert Fayrfax was born around 1470 and he rose to become a pre-eminent musician. He had been Doctor of Music at Oxford and Cambridge Universities as well as Head of the Royal Chapel's Music. He was appointed Master of the King's Music at Henry VIII's court. He not only composed many songs and the Missa Albanus (Mass for St Albans) but was also appointed organist and director of the Abbey Choir at St Albans in his later years. He died here in October 1521 and was buried in the presbytery of the church. Willie Luttmann received permission to transcribe Fayrfax's original manuscript, kept at Oxford's Bodleian Library, into modern notation. After hearing the performance Canon Glossop told the head verger at St Albans Abbey, John Watkins, 'this is the music I heard that morning'. After the Canon's death his widow revealed that her husband had heard the Fayrfax music on other occasions, one incident she mentioned happened late one night. As the Canon was working on his sermon he heard the music, which grew louder and louder until it faded away. Other witnesses, who passed the west front, reported hearing male voices singing in the night, music was even heard in the Brown Owl Café in George Street.

Canon Glossop was consulted about an ancient cottage near the abbey that was purchased by a London man, who entrusted the place to his children's nanny before the arrival of the family. Two nights in a row the unfortunate woman was shaken awake by a man in a black robe, who spoke to her in a strange language. She described the medal that the apparition wore around its neck and the canon was able to identify it as the medal of St Alban. A service of exorcism put a stop to the unwelcome visits and Dr Elsie Toms, St Albans' historian, pointed out that the house stood on the site of what had been the abbey charnel house (where dead bodies or bones would have been piled). An interdict from the Pope in the past had prevented burial services from being held at the abbey. If the phantom monk in black had died during that period he may not have 'gone to rest' with the last rites until the later exorcism service gave him the peace he desired. Another viewpoint was that the 'strange language' spoken by the monk was Latin and he may have been trying to impart the whereabouts of the lost abbey treasure.

Strange happenings in the vicinity of the abbey continued over the years. Dr Elsie Toms was told by Canon Glossop's daughter herself about an incident when she had heard mysterious singing outside the family home. She summoned her father and together they listened as an invisible choir passed by towards the locked abbey just across the road. It seemed to the witnesses as though the phantom singers continued on into the main entrance.

In the early part of the 1930s a man saw candlelight and heard singing coming from the Lady Chapel one night, 'it occurred to me that no ordinary choir sang so sweetly at 2am'. He was to hear it again, on several occasions. One day after Boxing Day, also during the 1930s, a couple heard organ music at 1.30am. They were told that it was impossible; the abbey and organ room were locked up as was the engine house which provided wind for the instrument. Again in the early hours of the morning a lady and five of her friends reported hearing 'simply heavenly strains' coming from the abbey.

A most spectacular sighting was made by the assistant verger, on All Souls' Day in 1931. Early one morning he saw a procession of monks coming towards him along the south side of the nave. They appeared to be solid and were wearing Benedictine dress. He moved aside, into the chairs, to let them pass but as he did so they simply vanished. Customarily the monks used to walk in procession around the abbey lands' boundaries on All Souls' Day and they were seen again by the curate just a few years after the verger's encounter.

Possibly the most famous ghostly experience reported at St Albans Abbey is the 'Firewatcher's Tale'. Sixteen-year-old ex-chorister Basil Saville was a member of the team of firewatchers whose job it was to check the whole building and its fire-fighting equipment, and to particularly look out for incendiary bombs during air raids. On the frosty night of Christmas Eve 1944 Basil was alone, waiting for another firewatcher to join him. The boy began his solo patrol by the feeble light of a hooded torch and he began to feel some unseen presence as he made his way to the loft. His first surprise was to discover two monks' habits lying on the floor. It is easy to imagine what it must have been like for a young lad with a duty to perform, alone at night in the vast emptiness of that venerable old building during the 'black out'.

The next anomaly was the peal of a single bell, which began tolling in the belfry. Basil knew that this was impossible because he had earlier checked the abbey's twelve bells which were safely stored on the ground floor, due to the risk of bombing. The steady tolling continued as he approached the belfry yet as he reached the door it ceased. He checked inside but the space was empty.

Next he made his way to the roof and took a brief look around in the chilly night air then made his way back downstairs when suddenly he heard the organ playing. The light from a nearby candle illuminated a book of music, whose pages were being slowly turned by an invisible hand. Now he heard singing from the high altar, so he hurried off in that direction. Monks appeared, carrying candles, led by their abbott. As Basil watched the procession passed through the screen doors into Saint's Chapel, where the doors closed behind them. The young watcher felt compelled to follow them yet upon reaching the chapel he found it empty and in darkness. He ran back upstairs to the organ loft where he found a spent candle and a large book with plain black covers and yellowing pages; it was entitled *Albanus Mass* and it was by Robert Fayrfax.

Eventually Basil's fellow firewatcher arrived and was informed about the mysterious events. The pair retraced the younger man's steps but this time there was no trace of the spent candle, the monks' robes or the book of music. Author Betty Puttick interviewed Basil Saville for her 1994 book, *Ghosts of Hertfordshire* and he stuck by his incredible story. 'I was stunned by it – overwhelmed,' he told the writer. 'I'm not psychic or anything like that and I've never seen anything like it either before or since. People may not believe me, but I know it happened.'

The phantom music was heard again in 1983 and it continues to be heard from time to time. There is also a ghost, affectionately known as 'Henry', who confines his appearances to the shadowy heights of the abbey. Perhaps he is reprising his role as guardian of the abbey treasures. Monks used to stand guard in the Watching Gallery in order to keep an eye on the pilgrims who visited the martyr's shrine.

Another phenomenon is the overpowering scent of incense, which can be smelt on the south side of the building on occasion.

These are many, but by no means all, of the paranormal phenomena reported at St Albans. Some people say that when unusual occurrences are due to take place the whole building seems 'switched on', somehow transformed, so that those 'on the right wavelength' sense it becoming a different place. Do experients encounter some kind of 'time slip' as, for brief seconds, the building reverts to times past when it was the country's premier Benedictine ecclesiastical establishment, a centre of excellence and a seat of learning?

A TALE OF TWO CHURCHES

Students of the paranormal sometimes ask me 'Is there any equivalent in Hertfordshire to the atmospheric 'Black Magic Church' (Old St Mary's) at Clophill in Bedfordshire

St Bartholemew's church, Layston, where phantom bells have been heard to ring.

which I wrote about in *Paranormal Bedfordshire* and which aroused the most interest amongst readers. I can think of two possible candidates, one is at the quaintly named Cold Christmas and the other is on the edge of Buntingford, in Layston. The Layston church is reached via a country lane and it is a 'brooding' site, high on the eastern bank of the Rib Valley (the Rib is an East Hertfordshire river). It is medieval in origin and it is called St Bartholemew's. After the eighteenth century fewer and fewer churchgoers made the journey from Buntingford up to Church Street, Layston, and they attended St Peter's, which was much more conveniently sited in the centre of Buntingford. With the decline in attendees it became uneconomic to maintain St Bartholemew's and after the Second World War the dilapidated nave roof was finally removed. Only occasional services were held in the covered chancel in connection with the neighbouring cemetery.

The remote setting and the atmospheric ruined condition of flint-built St Bartholemew's makes it comparable to Old St Mary's at Clophill. St Bartholemew's is a natural backdrop for ghost stories and it does have one of its own. During the nineteenth century the people of Buntingford often heard the peal of bells coming from the abandoned church at Layston. It was well known that it had become an empty ruin. One night the bell-ringers of Buntingford gathered together and descended on the site. They were determined to catch those responsible for playing a practical joke. The shocked party found the church to be brightly lit, while the bells continued their tolling, as if for Evensong. The bell-ringers approached cautiously then, summoning their courage, they entered the church. With that the bells stopped ringing and everything plunged into darkness. The bellringing in the ruins at Layston remains completely unexplained.

Hertfordshire's other contender for spookiest church may be found at the end of Cold Christmas Lane in Thunderidge, not far from Ware. The Church of St Mary and All Saints was erected in the fifteenth century and it was pulled down in 1853, now all that remains is the ruined tower. The new St Mary's church was built that same year on a hilltop south of the River Rib. It was paid for by wealthy philanthropist Robert Hanbury at a cost of £9,000. The old church ruin is in a most atmospheric setting, isolated and surrounded by trees, set in a field that is moated on two sides. In the 1940s a lady passer-by claimed to have seen Roman soldiers near the old church tower ruins. More recent visitors have commented on the number of children's graves in the overgrown cemetery to the east of the tower. Unsurprisingly there are rumours of phantom children associated with the site. I climbed the narrow stairs to the top of the tower during my visit to the ruins, but would caution that it is not for the faint hearted. Care should also be taken as the place is crumbling and not at all safe. Some acquaintances of mine who also looked over the site in recent times played me a digital recording made in the crumbling tower. There are the group's own conversations about the church but during a pause in their chat it sounded to me as though a chirpy young cockney boy's voice chimed in briefly. The group were shocked as they hadn't heard this voice at the time of their recording.

St Mary's and All Saints', Thunderidge. Roman soldiers and ghostly children are associated with this site.

The vicarage, St Lawrence's church, Abbots Langley. Scene of the haunted fireplace and the spirit of Mary Anne Treble.

THE CURIOUS CASE OF THE HAUNTED FIREPLACE

In May 2005 my wife Vicki and I took a trip out to Abbots Langley to see the Church of St Lawrence for ourselves. The site was well known to us for the ghostly housekeeper associated with the church, churchyard and nearby vicarage. We found a charming, tranquil old vicarage with a verdant lawn set in the middle of an attractive, well-kept garden and there was plenty of shade to be found beneath several large trees in the foreground of the house. The nearby country church, built in 1150, is pretty, small and square. I hadn't seen a vicarage before that was so close to its church; they are merely yards apart, most convenient for its vicar.

In 1914 rumours surrounded the death of Mary Anne Treble at the rectory and there were allegations of her mistreatment by the vicar's wife, Mrs Parnell. It was rumoured that the tragic servant had been murdered by her mistress. It was variously suggested that she had been shaken to death while in her sick bed or that she had been pushed down the stairs. Others thought that she might have committed suicide. Mary had been a popular figure in the village, notable for handing out sweets to the little children. What made the subsequent haunting unique was that Mary Anne's spirit seems to have focused her angst on the fireplace in her former bedroom in the vicarage. It was mysteriously damaged on several occasions and repaired, but it would then be found damaged again soon after being restored.

Ghost hunter Peter Underwood personally investigated this most unusual story. In his book *The A-Z of British Ghosts*, first published in 1971, he tells how he tracked down a former rector who recalled consulting a local builder about alterations to the Queen Anne period vicarage. The builder had pointed to the damaged fireplace which was sticking out from the wall in the haunted bedroom and said, 'Not much use repairing that; it will be out again within six months'. When the vicar asked what he meant the builder explained, 'Annie it was; died a horrible death in this room and the place will never be free of her'. The fireplace was, however, repaired but within a few months it was out again. This was the second occasion when the vicar's attention had been brought to the fireplace. Soon after he moved in he met a parish priest who had been assistant curate at St Lawrence's church. The parish priest told him that during Mass on All Souls' Day ten years previously he had seen a stranger, a woman who vanished as he turned to give the Invitation, a woman that his wife did not see at all. The curate gave a full description of the mysterious lady, a description that was subsequently found to match that of Mary Anne Treble. After the service the curate and his wife accompanied the rector back to the rectory, where they discovered the fireplace had been freshly cracked.

Following Mary's death, villagers who lived in cottages on the other side of the road from the rectory confirmed that they had seen the former housekeeper's ghost looking out of the window of her bedroom. She was also seen walking from the vicarage to the graveyard. Another assistant curate was praying alone in St Lawrence's church on Hallowe'en night when he heard footsteps approaching from the west end of the church and then clothing brushed his face, but he couldn't see anyone. The ghostly footsteps continued to echo on towards the east end before ceasing. The ghost was seen several times on All Souls' Day and a year after the curate's report it was seen again on this day. An Irish vicar saw the same mystery woman in the congregation and he also witnessed her abrupt disappearance. Concerned about this supernatural phenomenon, the Irishman reported the matter to his bishop. The result was that Bishop Michael Furse conducted the full Service of Exorcism. Things quietened down for a while, apart from an unexplained broken grate. The succeeding vicar's wife heard some 'unaccountable noises' emanating from the haunted bedroom, which caused her to keep this room locked.

Writer Betty Puttick carried out her own enquiries for her 1994 book *Ghosts of Hertfordshire* and she discovered new information from the Reverend Andrews, the vicar at that time who had come to the parish in 1979. He was convinced that Mary Anne Treble had fallen downstairs and died as a result of that accident, possibly of pneumonia. His sources did not hint that she had either been pushed or had committed suicide. The Reverend Andrews did admit that there had been some strange incidents soon after he moved in with his wife. An electric toothbrush had switched itself on one night as they were going to bed. An electric kettle had also switched itself on in the kitchen.

At the local antique shop, owned by Mr Dobson, Betty Puttick managed to trace a photograph of Mary Anne Treble. The shopkeeper had come by it via a (deceased) close friend of the former vicarage housekeeper. This friend had been certain that there was a mystery surrounding Mary's death.

So why did the spirit of Mary Anne single out the fireplace for special attention? Why was there persistent village gossip and rumour that she was, at least, an ill-treated servant and at worst, murdered? Why was her close friend convinced that mystery surrounded her death? Could it have been a coded message to the living from the dead? There is an old adage 'There is no smoke without fire'. Was this the ghost's way of telling us that her death had been the result of foul play? If so, the perpetrator, most likely to be Mrs Parnell, would appear to have got away with murder – or did she?

Abbots Langley hit the headlines of the national press in 2008 when Manuel Almunia, who had moved here, claimed that his house was haunted. The Arsenal goalkeeper and his wife were frightened by a variety of paranormal phenomena. The Spaniard discovered that his property was built on the site of an old psychiatric hospital. This could have been the Leavesden Mental Hospital, which was known as the Imbeciles Asylum prior to 1920. Construction work began in 1868, on the north side of what is now College Road, and after many delays the asylum was ready for occupation in 1870. From 1920 onwards it became known as Leavesden Mental Hospital, which finally closed its doors in 1955 and the site was redeveloped for housing. Only the admininstration block, chapel and recreation hall were retained, as most of the original buildings were demolished. Almunia said, 'When we first moved in we heard a lot of strange noises, like chains being dragged around. Then, when we were sleeping the stereo came on at full volume. One night my wife suddenly woke me up with a shout. She said there was this figure with a candle in his hand. She was in bed, next to me. I didn't see him but I was s*** scared.'

TEWIN TALES

St Peter's church at Tewin is reached via a long straight driveway at the bottom of which may be found the small, squat, flint and brick-built place of worship with its great clock face which dominates the square tower. Inside the church there is a marble tomb in commemoration of General Sabine, former Governor of Gibraltar, who died in 1739. A figure wearing a black cloak with a hood is reputed to haunt the vicinity; it is thought to be the spirit of Lady Hester Sabine, who was the general's wife. During the 1980s two visitors to St Peter's spoke of hearing crinoline skirts rustling in the aisle and of feeling a female presence in the bell tower. The church stands on a small rise which affords panoramic views over miles of open countryside. A great variety of trees have been planted in the churchyard, some in remembrance of those people who lie buried here. I saw oaks, acers, firs, a red chestnut and a tulip tree amongst them. Many once-prominent and influential individuals rest in this graveyard, among them are members of that famous aeronautical family, de Havilland. St Peter's churchyard is one of the most attractive and peaceful final resting-places that I have ever visited.

Behind the church one particular grave, with its wrought-iron fence, stands out. It contains the mortal remains of Lady Anne Grimston, who was said to be a Sadducean. The Sadduceans were an ancient Jewish priestly sect which flourished for around two centuries before the destruction of the Second Temple of Jerusalem by Roman legions in AD 70. Lady Grimston was a non-believer in the Resurrection of the Dead but the vicar felt obliged to make an attempt to save her soul by making her recant her heresy. When Lady Anne lay dying, in November 1780, she refused to change her beliefs and wouldn't even let the priest administer the last rites. 'If, indeed, there is a life hereafter, seven trees will render asunder my tomb,' she is reputed to have challenged him. My visit to her grave confirmed that several trees have, over the years, sprung up through

Lady Anne Grimston's grave, St Peter's churchyard, Tewin. Proof of a life hereafter?

the tomb, causing it to lift slightly and breaking off large pieces of mossy masonry onto the nettles and brambles inside the wrought-iron fence which guards the unrepentant Sadducean's final resting-place. The ghost of a lady has been seen at night by church bell-ringers on a number of occasions. She wanders alone amongst the gravestones and it is assumed that this is the shadow of Lady Anne Grimston.

Curiously, there is another, very similar, tale attached to St Mary's churchyard in Watford, where there is a grave known as the Fig Tree or Witch's Grave. Legend has it that a certain lady buried in a vault in St Mary's churchyard was an Atheist. On her deathbed, so it is said, she expressed a wish that if there were a God a fig tree might grow from her heart; there certainly is a grave in this churchyard that has a fig tree growing out of it!

DATCHWORTH'S CHURCH

Datchworth has long been regarded as 'Hertfordshire's most haunted village' and All Saints' church stands at the highest point of this small community. It is a small, plain edifice that can be seen for miles around. Its churchyard is reputed to be haunted by strange chattering sounds and shadowy figures have been seen among the gravestones. All Saints' church is situated at the top of narrow, unlit Rectory Lane, which has a

All Saints' church, Datchworth. The highest point of Hertfordshire's most haunted village.

spooky reputation, with reports of both phantom footsteps and manifestations of a cart carrying the dead.

This cart sighting is thought to be a grisly replay of an incident in the 1760s. A family named Eaves infamously starved to death in the ruined poorhouse at Datchworth Green during the famine of 1762. Their final journey was made in a cart that took their remains up Rectory Lane. The family was buried together in a mass grave in the churchyard there. James Eaves, his wife, his son and daughter 'perished from want of food, raiment, attendance and a habitable dwelling'. Mrs Eaves was last seen crawling to the village pond for water but was too weak to carry the filled kettle home. When the family's bodies were found they were 'emaciated beyond any conception, lying on a very small quantity of dirty peas straw spread on the bare earthen floor.'

In 1998 Carlton Television came to Rectory Lane to make a feature film for its programme *London Tonight*. The presenter confessed that he found the atmosphere there 'most unsettling'. Rectory Lane was also investigated one autumn night in the 1970s by journalist Evelyn Hall-King and psychic Eileen Ison, when they visited in search of material for a magazine article about Britain's most haunted places. At the end of their findings Evelyn and Eileen concluded that Datchworth was the second most haunted location in the UK – I would like to know which location came out top! The women were walking down Rectory Lane in the dark and rain when the psychic suddenly started moaning as she bent over like she was receiving invisible blows, which indeed was what she was feeling. She received a particularly intense psychic impression of being viciously beaten about the head and shoulders. She called out, 'The horses they're coming, can't you hear them?' The journalist surmised that her friend might be receiving the 'psychic echoes' of a killing carried out some two hundred years earlier, when highway robber Walter Clibbon met his end in the neighbourhood. His grave is half way along the Datchworth to Bramfield road, just a few miles from where the ladies were standing, and it is marked by a plain wooden post. Clibbon had terrorised the neighbourhood over many years and his death was the occasion of celebration for local people when his body was brought to The Horns public house, where it stayed overnight.

Walter Clibbon was dubbed 'the murderous pie-man of Hertford'. He was a vicious criminal of the late eighteenth century; his gang preyed on traders returning from the four annual fairs and regular Saturday markets held at the county town of Hertford. What nobody could understand at the time was how the robbers were always able to select their victims from the most successful farmers and peddlers who were carrying the most money on the day. The answer was simple; gang ringleader Walter Clibbon led a double life. By day he blended in with the crowds, he was a local, from Babbs Green, Wareside. He attended all the fairs and markets since he was a pie-man by trade. This provided him with the ideal opportunity to mix with the people, to see and hear about who was making the most money, while he sold his pies. Clibbon's real business, however, was robbery, which he carried out under cover of the night, with the aid of his two sons. As darkness fell these footpads dressed themselves up in anonymous smock-frocks, homemade linen garments worn by Hertfordshire farm labourers right up to the end of the nineteenth century. They blackened their faces with soot to further disguise themselves. With their expert local knowledge they were able to carefully choose the best ambush spots. One of their many victims was a comfortably wealthy farmer, Mr Kent, from Bennington. He put up a fierce resistance when attacked by the Clibbon gang, so they murdered him. His badly battered body was unceremoniously dumped in his own cart and his horses found their own way home.

Trade began to decline at Hertford and traders took to leaving before dark and travelling in groups, but the robberies continued until the night of 28 December 1782. That evening the robbers ambushed a young man named Whittenbury in some woods to the west of Hertford, and he prudently offered no resistance. When they had taken their ill-gotten gains Whittenbury drove his cart hell for leather to the nearby Queen Hoo Hall, to seek help from his uncle, Benjamin Whittenbury, who was at home. Young Whittenbury's father had been visiting but had just left with another uncle so Benjamin and his nephew set off after them. They decided to take Ben's servant, George North, as well as a dog, and they armed themselves with a stout stick and a gun. The three men were then ambushed themselves by the Clibbon crew, in dense woodland at Oakenvalley Bottom, before they could meet up with the other Whittenburys. The younger Whittenbury was knocked down but his uncle was a powerful man who put up more of a fight. He was, however, outnumbered and overpowered so he called on his servant to shoot. George North fired at almost point blank range, felling one of the gang and scattering the other two. The badly injured Walter Clibbon was then tied to a horse and dragged to Bull's Green where the angry locals bludgeoned him to death. One of his accomplices escaped but the other was caught and hanged at the next Lent Assizes.

As a murderer, Walter Clibbon, like suicides (and the insane), was denied a burial in consecrated ground. Such was the anger and hatred aroused by the deceased that he was given the very worst of burials. His body was interred at the side of the road where he had been shot in Oakenvalley Bottom. In accordance with the superstitions of the day his body was 'staked', 'to keep it down' and stop his unquiet spirit from roaming the area. 'Clibbon's Post', a simple, stout piece of wood with the felon's name carved on it, may be seen to this present day. The original has long since rotted away but it has always been replaced when necessary, usually at the expense of the resident of Queen Hoo Hall. Was it successful in 'laying the ghost?' There are those who say that they have seen the dim shape of a horse pulling a writhing body along the lanes and others have heard the sound of hooves or ghostly moaning. As in the much earlier case of notorious highwayman 'Black Tom', who was hanged in Bedford in 1607 (see *Paranormal Bedfordshire*) the traditional stake through the heart only works in vampire movies.

MYSTERIOUS MINSDEN

South of Hitchin, on the B651, is an inn called The Royal Oak, a useful landmark if you are searching for Minsden Chapel. There is also a small car park on the B651, at the junction with Hitchwood Lane where you should leave your car as Minsden's isolated position means that it can only be accessed on foot. Turn left onto the B651 and 200 metres or so along the way you will see a footpath sign on the left. Follow the footpath across the fields to a small copse of trees, which partly obscure the remains of Minsden Chapel. It can be a muddy trek in bad weather and be prepared for signs of occult rituals, which I have seen. They have been carried out on the track and in the woods. Little is left of Minsden Chapel now save a few crumbling walls and an archway; long gone are the roof, tower and windows. Take care as flint can still fall from the decaying ruins. This is a very ancient site, dating from the fourteenth century, when it was a small chapel-of-ease, named after St Nicholas, protector of children and the poor. It is said that Minsden was once the property of the Knights of St John of Jerusalem, what is known for certain is that the Knights Templars were located at nearby Temple Dinsley. Presently the site is occupied by Princess Helena College, Preston, where the Knights Templar are rumoured to have kept a great treasure. This order was associated with the Church of St Ippolitts, also in the neighbourhood; the church was dedicated to St Hippolytus, patron saint of horses. Legend has it that the knights had their horses blessed here, before setting off to the Crusades. Minsden Chapel served the farming communities of the local villages and provided a sanctuary for travellers and pilgrims en route to St Albans Abbey. During the Reformation (from 1538) worship declined and between 1690 and 1725 the chapel was systematically pillaged. Some 400lbs of lead were stolen as were stone and oak fittings, the font, painted glass windows and in one daring robbery the chapel's three bells were looted. The romantic rustic appeal, however, continued to attract weddings. The moss and ivy adorned shell set amidst elm trees and cooing doves had a strong allure. The end to these ceremonies came in 1738 when the curate's service book was knocked from his hands by a lump of falling masonry during the marriage of Enoch West and Mary Horn. The Bishop of Lincoln thereafter refused permission for any more weddings to be conducted at Minsden. This highly atmospheric place is one location that has good reason to be haunted because it had a guardian who swore to protect it, even after death. His name was Reginald Hine, a Hitchin attorney, writer and historian who became quite obsessed with Minsden Chapel. He visited the

Minsden Chapel, near Hitchin. An ALP (anomalous light phenomenon) appeared on this photograph taken at Minsden Chapel by a member of APIS. None of the many other photographs taken that day showed anything out of the ordinary.

site whenever he could and eventually obtained a lifetime lease of the building from the vicars of Hitchin. He completed one of his books there, *Confessions of an Uncommon Attorney* in 1943. Reginald Hine was passionate about protecting 'his' Minsden. He went so far as to make this chilling promise: 'Trespassers and sacrilegious persons take warning, for I will proceed against them with the utmost rigour of the law, and, after my death and burial, I will endeavour, in all ghostly ways, to protect and haunt its hallowed walls.' Some people believe that he carried out this solemn vow after his death. The manner of his passing (in 1949) was most strange. He had retired from the legal profession and was talking with friends at Hitchin Railway Station. When the train approached he casually said, 'Wait a minute' and with that he walked into the path of the train and died instantly. He left a note, which was addressed to the local coroner. His remains were cremated at Golders Green in North London and his ashes were later scattered at Minsden. His wife made the ruins his memorial; she kept the walls and arches safe from the invading creeper, ivy and brambles. A memorial stone was erected at the site, but it was damaged by vandals in the 1980s and consequently was re-laid in its present grave-like horizontal position. Rumours that the site was haunted began around 1907. This was when a local professional photographer, T.W. Latchmore,a friend of Hine, took a remarkable photograph of a ghostly monk. The photograph was reproduced on page ninety-two of volume II of *The History of Hitchin* by Reginald

Hine. The 'Latchmore photograph' caused great excitement at the time. Sadly, for the cause of paranormal investigation, it turned out to be a fake. In 1930 Latchmore confessed to Elliott O'Donnell, the ghost hunter and writer, that the 'Minsden Ghost' photograph was a hoax. It had been achieved by deliberate double exposures. My strong hunch is that Latchmore's friend Hine was dressed up as 'the phantom monk'. The hoax could have served two purposes; firstly it might scare off the trespassers that Hine so detested. Secondly it probably would have helped sales of *The History of Hitchin*. This scheme badly backfired because the very idea that the site might be haunted has attracted curious sightseers and thrill-seekers in their hundreds over the years. What might have remained a forgotten and lonely ruin is now a new place of pilgrimage – for all those with an interest in the paranormal.

All Hallows Eve is the night when Minden's ghosts have traditionally been most active, with a number of stories concerning horses and dogs behaving as though they have seen or sensed some invisible presence as they approach the ruins on that particular night. A host of legends have sprung up like the weeds around the chapel. They include the apparition of a ghostly monk, not surprisingly, after the hoax photograph of a monk! The tale has become embroidered over the years. The 'lost bells of Minsden' are supposed to toll, preceding the appearance of the phantom monk, who walks, with head bowed, up invisible steps under the south side arch, before disappearing. Another legend mentions the existence of a tunnel linking Minsden to the Brocket Arms pub, but this is obviously untrue as the distance involved would be too great and what purpose could such a tunnel possibly serve? It has been said that the chapel is situated on the site of a former hermit's cell but is this also a rumour without foundation? Another spirit reputed to haunt the ruins is 'Dame Margerie'. She is alleged to have been a local resident and benefactress of the chapel, who lived in the fourteenth century. Once again this is completely unsubstantiated, but Minsden is traditionally associated with Alice Perrers, mistress of Edward III (1312–1377). She was charged with stealing her lover's rings when he was on his deathbed. Alice infatuated the old king by using occult spells manufactured by her physician who was regarded as a mighty sorcerer. He was eventually arrested on a charge of confecting love philtres and talismans. Then there are the tales of two other ghosts who are supposed to haunt the ruins, one is of a murdered nun, the other is of a small, flute-playing boy, aged about seven.

Many people claim that they feel as though someone is watching them as they approach Minsden Chapel. Elliott O'Donnell visited it at Hallowe'en on several occasions and he wrote about feeling 'extraordinarily uncanny' and conscious of something scrutinising him although he saw and heard nothing out of the ordinary. He discussed the case with fellow paranormal investigator Peter Underwood and told Underwood that on one occasion he had 'heard sweet music' and thought he had glimpsed 'a white-robed figure standing in one of the archways'. Peter Underwood met with Reginald Hine and obtained his permission to investigate the site, together with Peter's brother and a friend. During their preliminary visit both Peter and his friend heard a brief, unaccounted snatch of music, but Peter's brother heard nothing. I, too, have seen and heard nothing which could be regarded as unexplained, despite a number of night visits to this fascinating location.

CHAPTER THREE

SPOOKS AMONG THE BOOKS

WATFORD WEIRDNESS

It all started with a phone call, out of the blue on Friday 24 August 2007, from Toby Friedner of BBC Three Counties Radio. He was inviting my society, APIS, to investigate persistent reports of hauntings at Watford Central Library, which the radio station would publicise as part of Family Learning Week. I was both flattered and honoured to be chosen as *the* paranormal research society, out of so many in the country, for this exclusive piece of research. The next six weeks were to be a blur of activity as I interviewed the library staff, studied the library's history, put an investigation team together and planned the event, agreed for Wednesday 10 October. It felt like something out of the movie *Ghostbusters*, to be checking out a haunted library!

Watford Central Library is situated at the top of Hempstead Road, close to a busy roundabout in the heart of Watford Town, which is Hertfordshire's largest town, with the biggest population in the county. The library building was constructed in 1928 and it is located on the site where a natural pond used to be, in an open area of land not far from a large house (no longer in existence). The library is directly opposite The Horns public house which was standing when the library site was still open land containing a pond. This pub still exists on its original site.

I pored through the eyewitness accounts, which dated back over thirty years and they make interesting reading. Gordon Morrison, a library assistant, was one day passing through the 'stack area', which is out of bounds to the public, when he decided to ask out loud for the ghost to come and see him. As he got close to the door at the reference library end he felt a tingling sensation 'as if some sort of energy force was passing through my body. I did not feel scared, but I will never forget this strange experience.' Alison Smith, the assistant library manager, was touched by the ghost. 'I was sitting in the work room, with my back to the door, when I felt someone tap me sharply several times, on the shoulder. When I looked round there was no one there and I was alone in the room, but I was not near enough to the door for anyone to have left the room without me seeing them.' Sue Brandon, another library assistant, said, 'The automatic doors at the front of the library often open on their own, for no apparent reason, because no one comes in or goes out.' Reader Development Librarian Carol Humphries recalls, 'When I first started working at Watford Central I was shown around the stack by another member of staff. We heard a noise like a book falling to the floor, but although we searched we could not find anything that might have made the sound. We were standing next to *The Book of the Dead* when this happened.' Staff member Sarah Costello also had a strange experience as her

Watford Library. Location of a fascinating APIS ghost watch.

introduction to Watford Library. 'Not long after I started work at Watford Central myself and a colleague were called upstairs to answer the panic alarm that had gone off in the stack. We raced up but there was no one there. We then heard a door shutting at the far end of the stack, so I went one way and my colleague went the other, but when we met in the middle neither of us had passed anyone on the way.' Iris Oakley, district librarian, North Herts and Stevenage, used to work at Watford and she saw an apparition. 'I remember an incident when I saw an apparition in the stack. A ghostly presence floated along the walkway and hovered above the back copies of the electoral roll and *The Illustrated London News*. It was wearing a black suit and a badge saying 'Borough Librarian'. Whilst not malevolent, I got the impression that it was unhappy.' Just a week before my vigil was due to take place another incident occurred. Assistant Pat Denton told me; 'I was at the counter side when I heard my name called but when I turned round there was no one there. The counter area was quiet and there were no staff or customers behind me.'

Francine Millard now lives in Edinburgh but she, too, was employed at Letchworth Library and was in no doubt about its eeriness when she wrote the following, 'I worked at Letchworth Library for a few years and loved it there, it would not take any specialised equipment to convince me it was haunted. The hairs used to stand up on the back of my neck in some areas, books were found placed on the floor and on several occasions I heard a weird shuffling noise when I was alone first thing in the morning!'

Letchworth Library. Haunted by its former caretaker?

Before the APIS ghost watch at Watford Central Library began our dowser, Keith Paull, remotely dowsed a plan of the building that I had received from the staff. Keith returned the plan to me with his notes and markings. He had detected three active paranormal 'hot spots'. Of these the stairwell was the most affected and the reference library store (aka 'the stack') and the staff room were the other two areas. I now had all the information needed to deploy the team most effectively around the large premises.

There were twelve APIS members in the investigation team plus myself as team leader when we assembled at Watford on Wednesday 10 October 2007. Three of the team were local girls, the O'Neil sisters, Roisin, Katrine and Liadain, my friends from Garston Manor. The team was divided into six units of two people in order to cover the most promising locations (as indicated by Keith's dowsing in conjunction with reported activity by library staff, past and present. I therefore allocated the team to six separate locations. These were (upstairs) the reference library store (known as 'the stack') the lecture hall and the local studies room. Downstairs were the staff room, work area and the district librarian's office.

We were in for an interesting night. Three members of the team had various degrees of psychic development and we had the usual electronic investigation equipment with us. This included video cameras and monitors, sound recorders, temperature/humidity gauges and EMF (electro-magnetic field) meters to measure any observable or audible anomalous phenomena. Watches of forty-five minutes duration interspersed with fifteen-minute breaks, were held throughout the night. APIS undertakes investigations with an open mind, combining both psychic impressions as well as the more scientific approach. Team members were not briefed on reported phenomena so as not to prejudice any experiences and information received during the investigation. Log sheets were left in the designated areas of investigation within the library. These were to record sightings, sounds and feelings experienced by the watchers.

We arrived at 8.30pm in order to set up our equipment, to familiarise ourselves with the layout of the building and to get some initial impressions. The most spectacular phenomenon happened before we had even set up our equipment or assigned team members their roles/locations. At 8.35pm a book suddenly flew off the library reception desk and landed on the floor about 5ft away. This was witnessed, from different angles, by Steve Webster and two other APIS team members. Unfortunately one of the excited investigators picked up the book before I could reach the scene. I was in the car park checking new arrivals and directing other members of our group into the library. One of the problems of running a paranormal investigation society is that you often miss out on the most interesting events of the night as you are too busy organising things! It was a lost opportunity for me to record the displacement of the book with my tape measure and thereby work out the angle of movement. It would also have been interesting to see the pages that fell open to see if there might have been a message, as the investigator who picked up the book recalled that it was open at a chapter concerning poltergeists! All three investigators present were adamant that nobody could have staged the incident and all saw the same thing at the same time – a book flying off a desk by itself.

Steve Webster, who lives in Hemel Hempstead, is an experienced APIS investigator and the following is directly quoted from his written statement about the night's events.

> I was the first APIS member to arrive. The front door was closed to the public and the ground floor was empty save for the few members of staff about. I went to the counter area with one of them, collected a parking permit and then went out of the building immediately to place it on my car. I rang for re-entry, was ushered in and then made my way alone to the counter, stopping a few feet away from it to assemble the take-apart pocket dowsing rods which I carry with me and use on these vigils. I was putting these together when a book flew off a display of paranormal books from a tabletop next to the counter and landed face down and open near to me. I saw it move. So did two other witnesses from an aisle between two rows of books opposite. It didn't fall vertically nor did it roll or otherwise cross any distance on the floor. I was alone and out of reach. All the lights were on. Do I think this was paranormal or just a fluke? Of all the hundreds of thousands of books, pamphlets, posters and notices in the library, one 'fell' near me as I was on my own, the first APIS member to arrive and just as I was putting my dowsing rods together. Perhaps it was a coincidence. But, it hadn't seemed just to fall. It travelled a little distance. I'm left with the thinking that perhaps this was thrown to make some sort of statement. After all it had come from the paranormal book display. The book's title was *Paranormal Sources*. Perhaps a statement was being made, 'Here I am' or 'Just to let you know that someone is here'. Another APIS member looked inside the book, opening it at random and discovered pages about poltergeists. She closed the book and re-opened it on exactly the same pages.

The next shift (in the local studies room) comprised Liadain and me. My dowsing rods had crossed three separate times in the same spot in front of the stage (in the next door lecture hall) and to the right. We felt nothing in the room and retired into the local studies room where we formed the hypothesis that perhaps there was more chance of experiencing something if we were out of the room. Why would this be? Could it be spirit children? We decided to try this out. In turns we went to the door of the lecture hall, spoke into it and encouraged any children there to play and make a noise. As our forty-five minutes were due to run out two female members of APIS did this consecutively, the last one saying we were leaving soon and 'they' had one minute to play a trick on us. At the end of that minute we went to the doors to look inside and see if a trick had been played. We couldn't do it. The doors had become locked. Was this the trick?

A non-public area is what is known as 'the stack'. This is an area with no windows. Whilst the lights within the library were turned out for our vigil, some emergency and exit lights stayed on in the building and of course there was the light from the street outside through the windows. Not so for the stack which was as dark as it could get. First I descended the small flight of steep steps to the bottom and walked around it with my dowsing rods. By one particular area the left rod was vibrating. I didn't know what to make of this. Later we discovered that this is where a massive ancient tome was called

The Book of the Dead whose contents were about ancient Egyptian funerary rites. A piece of paper with coins on top was placed there as a trigger object and it was moved at an early stage in the vigil. Above the lower ground level is 'the bridge', beyond which is another office. At one point Roisin and Katrine, on the lower ground level, heard a sound like breath being exhaled right next to them – or a gasp – and felt spooked. Some of us took the view that this might be the somewhat disapproving reproach towards women from a (spirit) male member of staff from the early period of the library. Mick and I went down in their place and Damien stood on the bridge above us. We heard recurrent knocking moving around us, which seemed interactive, giving us two knocks for 'yes'. Roisin and Katrine joined us a little later and it continued. The impression that I formed was that the spirits there may have had a curiosity about us but might also have experienced our visit as a bit intrusive and, therefore, kept just out of reach. Be this as it may, the fact is that our vigil was not long enough and we did not cover all areas. Watford Library clearly has secrets that are still to be revealed.

The more psychically developed members of the team received numerous impressions. All three psychics independently sensed children. One gave a description of a fair-haired child around ten years old with long hair, wearing a smock. There follows a sample of their various comments.

> I got the feeling of being chased off it (the stack bridge) and also being told to leave, but as he came to the door (the presence) stopped as if he could not go any further. The gentleman in question was called Tom; he was about 5ft 7in in height, greying dark hair, moustache and on the plump side. I was told by him that he died on the gangway of a heart attack; he gave me an image of himself being spread-eagled across the gangway where he fell. He also told me that he suffered from vertigo and this was the last place he would want to be, his job was a cleaner. The feeling is that as people walk across there, they would get the feeling of his fear and unsteadiness, illness and the feeling of vertigo. The energy in the library is stronger upstairs than it is downstairs and it is mainly of despair.

Kevin was also strongly affected in the district librarian's office.

> As I sat down the energy in the room seemed to increase rapidly and the temperature dropped like a stone. Felt really buzzy, I could hear the spirit children running in and out of the room giggling, they were playing a type of hide and seek. Then I could see the outline of a small boy who was standing in front of me, he was about 3½ft tall with a slight build, dark hair, blue eyes, his clothes were a bit ragged and his name was Patrick. There was also a little girl, with the name of Emmy. There was also a man that came in to tell them to be quiet, and as he walked out of the room I could hear his footsteps. Then all of a sudden I heard the sound of a chair rattling, as if the children brushed past it, so I then asked them if they would make some more noises for me. There was the loud sound of a ruler or a book being slammed on the table, which was clearly picked up by my tape recorder. As it went on the noises increased, every time I asked there was a response, also breathing in my ear, but mostly books being dropped or pens being flicked. As other investigators entered the room the energy level dropped and the noises stopped, as if the children were shy! So I left the room and came back again a few minutes later when the other investigators had gone. On my own again it all started once more even louder than ever, with the sound of running and very large bangs.

Another investigator commented,

> Whilst conducting one of the EMF meter readings I happened to be walking down the aisle directly opposite a small table situated at the right hand side of the reception with a number of books on display, Steven was conducting a search with his dowsing rods. As I watched, a book flew off the display. I knew Steven couldn't have been responsible because at the time he was a good way away from the display. The book was replaced and remained in its place for the rest of the vigil. Shortly after 11pm Roisin and I were allocated to the local studies room for our vigil. After we had conducted all the usual baseline tests we sat at the table nearest the main doors (that lead from the hallway into the room). We had been in the room for approximately fifteen minutes when I clearly saw what I can only describe as the solid shadow of a male walk across the doorway leading to the lecture room; it went from my right to my left. My team mate and I went to the lecture room but the team members there were sitting on the stage and hadn't moved from there since the watch began. While we were discussing my experience we heard a bang from the passageway, like a door slamming. We went, as a group, to check things out, but the passage was empty.

As for the team leader's experiences the best was saved till last. I was pretty tired and was getting ready to leave the investigation. It was about 3am and I was in the stack, on the bridge with Steve and Mick when we all heard a distinct tapping noise from the walls of the room. The taps moved from wall to wall, encircling us, with at least twelve taps in all. We then experienced tapping on request. From 3.15am till 3.30am I stood below the bridge with Steve while Mick stood above us. My team-mates reported the energy level building up and knocks in response to questions were heard by us all, on numerous occasions. If we take the statements of many Watford Library staff members and add this intelligence to the events witnessed by a number of trained APIS investigators on the night of our ghost watch, there can be no doubt in my mind that the place is haunted. I will leave the last word on the matter to my good friend Michael Lewis, who is APIS's investigations co-ordinator. Michael is highly experienced, has been investigating the paranormal for forty-three years, and commented,

> The library is one of the best locations I have been to. The auditory phenomena in the stack (which I did not personally witness), the wide range of phenomena in the librarian's office and the events in reception, backed up by verifiable data obtained by mediums convinces me this is an excellent case. Part of the answer is that we now have much better equipment (e.g. to record orbs) plus access to good mediums and we are much better placed to investigate hauntings than we were in the past. The library gave us access which in the past has been rarely forthcoming. We know such cases as this are out there, but because of the attitude of the materialistic western culture, public officials feel constrained when confronted by phenomena. The problem is not lack of good cases but lack of access. I think a public body running a promotion and inviting us in is a first of which Watford Library can justifiably be proud. It displays cutting edge thinking and a modern attitude which is in line with public interest.

Before we leave the Watford area there are a few more 'strange but true' stories from this part of the county. The Garston area of Watford made the pages of the local press in 2003 when the story of two families living on the Bramfield Estate was revealed. A series of unexplained incidents left the families with the conviction that the events were paranormal in nature. Worst of all was the pervasive stench of urine. A little historical research revealed that the site of the houses had previously been occupied by some garages. Some ten years previously a tramp had been burned to death at a fire in these garages.

The offices of the *Watford Observer* made their own news when it was revealed that they were haunted. The canteen has been the focus of unpleasant paranormal phenomena where canteen staff arriving early for work have been pushed and prodded by an unseen assailant. One woman was knocked to the ground by the force of this ghostly onslaught. A man working alone late one night heard something banging on the window, but on checking could find nothing to account for the noises. The banging sounds continued and in addition a strange whistling noise invaded the room as well. The badly frightened employee's response was to turn up the volume on his radio in order to drown out the unexplained sounds.

Copperfields was a restaurant in Watford which was subsequently converted into offices in a High Street building that dates back to the fifteenth century. An employee who arrived early for work one morning was greeted by the ghost of a man in Elizabethan dress which promptly disappeared. The restaurant owner, Albert Fiedler, didn't see the phantom for a number of years but one day as he was working in the kitchen he became aware of someone in the restaurant. He went out to see who it might be but there was only a grey mist to be seen. Some days later there was a scream from the restaurant and a frightened young worker ran into the kitchen. She said that she had seen something like a grey mist moving across the room and she didn't want to go back there. Mr Fiedler hadn't told anyone about his own previous experience. On another occasion he was alone and the business was closed when he saw the grey mist again, but this time it shaped itself into a human form. Fiedler was able to give a detailed description of his sighting, 'a man wearing a tight-fitting tunic with puffy sleeves and a ruff around his neck.' Mr Fiedler's father-in-law also saw the 'Elizabethan'; the figure ascended the stairs and moved through the restaurant before vanishing near the outside wall. The restaurant eventually closed and the premises were used as offices, with the installation of an alarm system the ghostly attentions were renewed. Office workers detected a strange atmosphere about the place. One time the alarm sounded and no one was able to switch it off. Computers seemed to be adversely affected and members of staff arriving early in the day were greeted by a spooky 'good morning' from an unseen presence.

The most outstanding paranormal event associated with Watford took place, funnily enough, in France in 1901. In fact it has been described by some as the most famous ghost story of all time. One of the principal witnesses was Eleanor Jourdain, headmistress of Corran School for Girls, in Langley Road, Watford. Miss Jourdain was born in 1863 and was one of the first women to go to Oxford University. She studied modern history at Lady Margaret Hall. This was at a time before sexual equality was achieved in education; females were not allowed degrees and were only permitted to attend lectures if no one objected, as long as they were accompanied by knitting chaperones! Eleanor Jourdain was nearly thirty and had taught for six years before she established her school at Langley Road in 1882, with just six pupils.

Miss Jourdain continued to improve Corran School for Girls. New classrooms were added, playing fields were purchased and two boarding houses were built. This establishment quickly achieved the local education board's approval and by the turn of the century there were over 100 students and 18 members of staff. As the school prepared girls for Oxford its headmistress kept in touch with the women's colleges, where she came to the attention of Miss Annie Moberly, principal of St Hugh's, who was seeking a deputy. That summer of 1901 Eleanor invited Annie to stay at the flat she had acquired in Paris, so that they could get to know one another better.

On 10 August 1901 they decided to visit Versailles as neither of them had been there before. Eleanor and Annie were like any other tourists, neither had any particular interest in Versailles, or French history in general, and they displayed no interest in, or knowledge of, the supernatural. The two Englishwomen looked around the main building before heading for the Petit Trianon, the small palace in the grounds that was a gift from Louis XVI to his wife Marie Antoinette and which had become a favourite place for the Queen. The teachers soon realised that they were lost and felt that something was not quite right when they met two men that they took to be gardeners. The men gave the women directions but the ladies thought the gardeners' attire was odd – long grey-green coats and tricorn hats. As the ladies continued their walk a strange feeling of oppression stole over them. Eleanor wrote her account later: 'I began to feel as though I were walking in my sleep'. The friends both felt that their surroundings seemed flat and lifeless and the atmosphere was intensely still. Ahead of them, surrounded by trees, was a small bandstand or garden kiosk and on the steps stood a man, wearing a black cloak and a large hat. There was something disturbing about him, his dark skin had been ravaged by smallpox; there was an evil and unseeing expression to him. Suddenly a running man approached, Eleanor observed that he was young, agitated and red in the face, he had long dark hair and he wore buckled shoes and a cloak. He directed them towards the house before hastening away. Eventually they reached the Petit Trianon and were about to join the tour when Annie noticed a woman drawing in the garden, but Eleanor did not see this woman. Later Annie described the lady as wearing old-fashioned clothes, including a white hat on top of her mass of fair hair. Annie and Eleanor entered the Petit Trianon and saw a wedding party in the distance. After they had toured the building they went back to their hotel for tea.

It wasn't until the following week that Annie wrote a letter home describing her visit when she suddenly felt the same 'oppressive feeling' return. When she asked Eleanor if she thought the Petit Trianon was haunted it began a discussion about what, exactly, each of them had seen. It was the first time they had compared notes and they were in agreement that something mysterious had occurred on the afternoon of their visit to Versailles.

That November Annie Moberly invited her future deputy head to Oxford to compare notes again on the strange experience in France that the two ladies had shared. Miss Moberly undertook the task of thoroughly researching the history surrounding the French Revolution. Miss Jourdain then set down the details of her own version of events and asked her French mistress, Mademoiselle Menegoz, for any details relating to the haunting of the Petit Trianon. Mme Menegoz told her that on a certain day in August Marie Antoinette and her courtiers could often be seen in the gardens.

One cold and rainy afternoon in January 1902, Eleanor Jourdain returned alone to Versailles. It was another strange experience for her – 'It was as if I had crossed a line and was suddenly in a circle of influence'. Two labourers in brightly coloured tunics and hoods were loading a cart. When she looked back again there was no sign of them yet there was a clear view in all directions. Around her she could hear voices and the rustling of silk dresses but could see no one. Later that year Miss Jourdain took up the post of vice-principal at St Hugh's, Oxford and handed over the management of her Watford school to Miss Wishaw, her fifth form mistress.

Three years later Miss Moberly and Miss Jourdain returned to the gardens at Versailles and were shocked to see that everything had changed. Trees, a rustic bridge, a kiosk, a ravine and a water cascade that they remembered from their first visit, had all vanished. The teachers were now certain that the surroundings they had formerly seen belonged in the period of Louis XVI and Marie Antoinette. After studying a multitude of history books they became convinced that they had seen real, historical, pre-Revolutionary figures. Annie Moberly's 'sketching woman' was, in all likelihood, Marie Antoinette herself. The teachers had a book about their unexplained encounter, titled *An Adventure*, published in 1911, under the pseudonyms of Elizabeth Morrison and Francis Lamont – it was to become a sensational bestseller. It fired the imagination of the general public and intrigued academics, believers and sceptics alike. Readers were as puzzled as the experients themselves as to what it all could possibly mean. After publication several people who had lived in a house overlooking the park at Versailles confirmed that they too had witnessed similar scenes so often that they had come to accept it. With Eleanor Jourdain's death in 1924 the authors' true identities were revealed. This aroused further public interest when it became known that the witnesses were women of impeccable character and solid social standing. Miss Jourdain's Watford school was eventually demolished but an educational link is maintained at Langley Road through West Herts College's presence there.

I was sad to learn that the remarkable book, *An Adventure*, is now out of print, but the writers never altered their story. The two teachers' researches satisfied them that they had been privileged to see the park as it had been in 1789. That year the French Revolution reached its climax with the fall of the Bastille on 14 July and the aristocracy's agreement to surrender all feudal rights on 4 August. After years of painstaking research Jourdain and Moberly worked out that the exact date in time which they had travelled to was August 5, 1789, Marie Antoinette's final day spent at Versailles. The 'running man' was the messenger who brought the news of the mob's advance, while the 'gardeners' were two Swiss guardsmen on duty that fateful day. The 'smallpox marked man with the black cloak and large hat' seen at the kiosk was identified as the Compte de Vaudreuil. He was a pock-marked Creole actor and a friend of Marie Antoinette. In all probability every one of the ghosts encountered by the two English ladies at Versailles, died a horrible death at the hands of a French mob.

On 10 August 1789 the Tuileries was sacked, the King and Queen arrested and their Swiss guard murdered. In her final days at Versailles, with bad news of the ever-worsening crisis developing, Marie Antoinette must have been anxious and frightened. The King and his courtiers would have shared that fear – enough to produce a kind of group terror so strong that it left its psychic imprint which was picked up by a sensitive over a hundred years later? Miss Jourdain was certainly psychic with powers of second sight, as attested by Miss Moberly, but her friend refused to develop her abilities. She disapproved of occultism and considered it morbid and dangerous, a view shared by Miss Moberly herself.

In 1938 an English psychical researcher named R.J. Sturge-Whiting reinvestigated the case. He claimed, after much research, to have located all the places the two teachers had described in their account. He concluded that they had followed the paths that were still in existence on their first visit and failed to find them on their subsequent visit. Further fuel was added to this particular fire when Philippe Jullian published a biography of Count Robert de Montesquiou describing how this dandy took a house near Versailles in the early 1890s and often spent whole days in the park. His friend Mme de Greffulhe organised a fancy-dress party in the dairy. Philippe Jullian surmised that the two English teachers possibly mistook some costumed guests for 'ghosts'. It was pretty damning stuff at the time and continues to influence some modern writers on the paranormal, who dismiss the whole amazing Versailles adventure as 'explained'. I am not convinced by this rather glib explanation and find it rather insulting to the memory of two remarkable educators. I do remain convinced that they did not suffer from over active imaginations, selective memories or mistaken identity. These were two highly intelligent, respectable ladies in full command of their faculties. They were certain about their experiences, sure of the details and with no motivation to concoct such an amazing story.

If we leave aside the characters of the witnesses, the theorists didn't attempt to explain the dramatic changes in the physical features of the locale. What happened to the kiosk, the ravine, the bridge and the small water cascade, all of which were seen during the first visit?

During 1903 and 1904 Miss Moberly, the one time Watford headmistress, returned many times to Versailles. She became quite familiar with the layout of the park but always found it 'modernised' in contrast with the 1901 visit. It should also be mentioned that the fancy dress theory didn't hold up as the Compte de Montesquiou moved to Versailles in 1890 and moved to Neuilly in 1894. Any fancy dress party rehearsal would have happened at least seven years before the English ladies' visit.

There can be no doubt that this particular adventure remains both a classic case and a great rarity in the annals of modern psychical research. It continues to fascinate readers who discover it for the first time. It has been the basis for a great British television adaptation which was also shown in the USA in 1983 and 1984. It has been described as an experience in retrocognition of the past. Certain parapsychologists have labelled it an 'immersion timeslip', where the percipients are immersed in another era yet remain able to physically interact with their environment. The Versailles case defies explanation; it is a deeply puzzling and strange incident that will continue to be debated for many years to come.

LETCHWORTH GARDEN CITY GHOULS

Success breeds success and after the Watford Library investigation it wasn't long before APIS was asked to look into another haunted library but this time it was in the north of the county rather than the south and much closer to home, in Letchworth Garden City. Some eight months after the Watford ghost watch I was approached by staff at Letchworth Library. News had reached them about APIS's findings at Watford and they wanted us to conduct a similar investigation at Letchworth. As at Watford there was a considerable haunting history that stretched back to at least the 1970s and it was still paranormally active. Library workers would come in to unlock the building of a morning to find books out of their shelves, sometimes standing upright, well away from where they have been stored overnight. On Wednesday 18 June 2008 at 6.30pm I visited the library with my APIS friend and fellow investigator John Wickham. We were there at the invitation of Gill Clements, one of the senior librarians. While John and I were given a guided tour we made notes and made observations. At the end of the meeting Gill and I agreed that APIS would conduct two investigations at the library that September. My next priority was to try to get a vigil organised in the Letchworth Museum next door to run concurrently with the Library vigil. I had heard reports that the museum was also haunted, so it seemed sensible to organise for their investigation to be held on the same night. I got permission to conduct an investigation for one night only, on Friday 12 September but it was only for three hours, from 9pm till midnight.

As well as producing our customary written report for our clients I would also give a lecture to the public at the library in October to explain our investigations. Gill provided me with a plan of the library layout and APIS's Dowser, Keith Paull got to work. At his home in Bedfordshire he remotely dowsed the plan with his pendulum. I kept his findings confidential until the end of the investigation in order that proceedings should not be influenced by his information and Keith's report makes interesting reading.

> It looks as though you may have quite an interesting vigil as not only is there a strong green line[1] running through part of the building but there are no less than three hot spots (rather more like areas really) where I am getting a good signal.
>
> The green line runs across the ground floor only and two of the hot spots sit along this line whilst on the first floor there seems to be a strong green area in the room above the lending library.[2] I have tried a bit of an experiment which may or may not work out but if it does it might prove useful on future vigils.
>
> I have tried to gauge on a scale of one to ten what the likelihood is of some paranormal event occurring at each of the designated positions during that night. As you can see from the notes on the plans, there is a 9/10 chance of something on the energy line and in the stack room but only a 4/10 chance in the junior library. On the first floor there is a 3/10 chance in the museum but in the room over the lending library the chances are 9/10. In actual fact the pendulum indicated a 10/10 chance but that would be sticking my neck out a bit further than I feel comfortable with!

I was armed with Keith's report (which was to turn out to be uncannily accurate), and the diary of paranormal events logged by library staff, I had assembled an investigation team so we were now ready for our first vigil. I was trying a new experiment of my own. For the first time APIS was working with no less than four other paranormal investigation societies because my watchword has always been co-operation, not competition. The Association for the Scientific Phenomena (ASSAP) was represented by

1. For readers not familiar with advanced dowsing techniques, energy line colours denote different characteristics – green always indicates haunting energy.

2. This was particularly useful information because this 'room above' was the lecture room, so I would give it special attention.

Dr Simon Sherwood who is a fully qualified parapsychologist. Cambridge Paranormal Research Society was represented by its founder, my good friend Martin Waldock. Marq English, another friend of mine, and Al Piddington were from Spiral Paranormal. Finally Richard Court, with whom I had worked before, of Renegade Paranormal, was also with us. Working alongside our five guests were six highly experienced APIS members, medium Margaret Rolph, investigators Michael Lewis, Linda and Rob Rothwell, John Wickham and myself.

Letchworth Garden City Library was built in 1938 and first opened in 1939. As the museum is adjacent to the library it looks as though the two form one building. The museum was, however, built earlier, in 1914, for the specific purpose of housing the collection of stuffed birds contained in glass cages which were owned by the Letchworth Naturalists' Society. Before this the collection had been on display in the Skittles Inn. Being that Letchworth was a Quaker town, however, the Skittles Inn was an unlicensed public house which sold Cydrax (a non-alcoholic apple wine) as well as Bourneville's drinking chocolate, tea and Sarsaparilla (a root beer soft drink). The original village of Letchworth stood just under a mile south of where the library and the museum now stand in Broadway. Also in this area are St Mary's church, Plinston Hall and the Letchworth Hall Hotel (formerly the manor house). For hundreds of years the village remained small, with a population of about one hundred, without any shops or pubs. Then, in 1899 Ebenezer Howard founded the Garden City Movement. He wrote his book *Tomorrow* in 1902 which outlined his ideas for the future. These included restricting the unregulated growth of industrial cities and creating towns based on a combination of aspects of both the town and the country. This would, he hoped, avoid the problems of overcrowding, pollution and poor living conditions. Work on the construction of Letchworth Garden City began in 1903. It was done so that every other house had its own plot of land, all factories were outside the city whilst amenities were in the centre and the whole was surrounded by a 'green belt'. All of this can be seen in the maps of the county, in 1901 there were just fields yet in the 1922 map the town had been developed.

On the night of 12/13 September Martin was in charge of the museum investigation while I concentrated my main efforts on the library. During the two watches carried out next door Martin recorded no paranormal activity. Three hours was felt to be too short a time for a full investigation. A strong energy was felt by the team when Margaret, our medium, was present and when she left the energy seemed much lighter. Margaret herself felt a presence, upstairs, in the archaeology gallery. This is the area where an apparition has been reported. One cleaner, in particular is nervous about going into the gallery alone. The figure of a woman, all in black, has been seen on several occasions. On an earlier inspection of the archaeology gallery I noticed amongst the many exhibits an ancient skeleton in a glass case. The skeleton is that of a female. I was reminded of Danny Ward's comment made in Bedford back in the 1970s (as described in *Paranormal Bedfordshire*) 'If disturbing bodies upsets the dead, who knows what being put on public display will do?'

Things were more active in the library, which we manned from 9pm till 3am the following morning. The watches were of one hour's duration with a thirty-minute break in between. I teamed up with Margaret Rolph, one of the very few genuinely gifted psychic mediums that I have ever met. We began our vigil in the stack room and it wasn't long before Margaret was receiving psychic impressions. She visualised a woman from the earliest days of the library, describing her as short and stout. On checking Margaret's description with Gill Clements we discovered that it matched the woman who opened the library back in 1939. Communications at the library were disturbed at an early stage, a common occurrence at haunted locations. Margaret had to take the battery out of her mobile phone because she was having so much trouble with it. My walkie-talkie warbled as though someone was trying to contact me, but on checking with the other teams no one had called me. As we were chatting (21.45 hours) just outside the stack room the entrance door in front of us, to our right, unexpectedly opened and closed, seemingly of its own accord. As I returned to write this up in the log sheet, located in the stack room, it happened again. A minute or so later both of us felt cold, Margaret's hands and arms were very cold and my back felt chilled. I went to check the outer doors of the library to make sure that nobody could have got in to set off the automatic inner doors, which are activated by movement sensor. The outer doors were securely locked.

During the second watch (10.30pm–11.30pm) in the stack room, when Michael and Simon were on watch the EMF meter crashed and had to be reset. The children's library produced some activity on the second watch, soon after it began. A heavy roll of carpet (which had been leaning against the wall) suddenly fell with a loud thump as Richard was moving away from it. This was close by the rear door which leads out to the church (St Mary's) car park. Later on I returned the carpet to its original position, it took quite a bit of effort to move it as it was heavy.

The most interesting anomalous phenomenon was reserved for the library staff who had agreed to stay with us for the duration of the vigil. Gill Clements and Daniel Crutchfield sat well apart from the APIS team, in the librarian's office. Between 11.08pm and 02.16am they heard loud, quite distinctive footsteps, on at least half a dozen occasions, approaching their refuge along the short corridor that leads to the office. On one occasion the footsteps stopped right outside the door. At another time the footsteps passed by, went next door and then there was the sound of books being moved and a thump on the wall. When Daniel opened the office door to check outside there was nobody there. As far as I was able to ascertain none of the APIS team were in the area at these times. I went so far as to check upstairs but when I walked about the lecture hall directly above the librarian's office, my footsteps could not be heard below.

We concluded from this initial investigation that there was no conclusive proof of a haunting at the library but there were enough unexplained events occurring to warrant further investigation. We had statements from library staff, trained APIS investigators and highly experienced investigators from other respected research societies. Parapsychologist Simon Sherwood commented, 'It was good to see a number of different investigation groups co-operating towards a common goal rather than competing against each other.'

At this point I should mention some of the paranormal phenomena reported over the years at Letchworth Library, which led to our investigations. One spring day in 1975 the library floor was being varnished and the building was closed to the public. Some members of staff were in the workroom and two members of staff (including Sue Marina) were sitting on the stairs overlooking the library. The foyer was glass fronted and the entire library could be seen from the vantage point of the stairs. Something was seen, moving from the back of the library through and left to an exit door. Both members of staff shouted a warning, 'The floor has just been varnished, please get off!' One of the ladies went to the door but nothing was seen and no footprints disturbed the newly-varnished floor. Both women clearly saw the same thing. Sadly one of them, Pat, has since died. Another report, from a different staff member, is as follows, 'Whilst closing up the library one night, I went down to the fiction section to close down the lights. After doing so I ambled over to the fire exit and stared into the garden. As I turned around a book came flying off the shelf and landed at my feet. It was a large print book. I wasn't scared, I think it was more of a telling off for being in there after lights out!' Some of the library staff think that they know who the ghost is, and it is their view that it is the restless spirit of Phillip Kane that haunts 'his' library. He was the caretaker at the library from 1939 until his 'official retirement' in 1974 (being the irreplaceable sort he carried on for a while afterwards until he reached retirement age). I was fortunate enough to meet his daughter, Sylvia Lewis, who joined us at the library on Wednesday 3 September 2008 when several mediums were invited in to give their impressions. Margaret Rolph was among the mediums and it turned out that her mother, Rose Gladden, the famous psychic healer and medium, who lived in Letchworth, had met Phillip Kane when he was taken seriously ill. The other mediums present were Andrew Grant, Alan Bennett and Jean Cheffin. All agreed that there was a male presence and great energy present in the library. A major ley line runs through Letchworth Library so this could account for the energy that the group sensed. Sylvia's father, Phillip Kane, had been a Letchworth institution. As a local newspaper cutting revealed, 'He was acquired with the new building in 1939'. He wasn't there long before he had to leave for war service but he resumed his library duties in January 1946 and continued working there till the end of his life. Not only did Mr Kane (as he was known to all the library staff) work at the building he also lived there in a large flat upstairs which he nicknamed 'the elephant'. He was a fit and energetic man who would run up and down the stairs. He was always on the go, an early riser yet also able to stay up till the early hours and always kept his library spotlessly clean. He could be heard singing 'The Rock 'n' Roll Waltz' as he buffed the floors with his electric floor polisher. He had a reputation for cheering up the library assistants and seemed to possess the secret of eternal youth. It is a matter of public record that on the day of Phillip Kane's funeral Letchworth Library's electrical supply went wrong, the heating and the lighting failed completely and the building had to close for half a day. There were those who felt that the place had, of its own accord, decided to come out in sympathy.

APIS began the second ghost watch on the night of Friday 19 September. This time there was a much smaller team as we did not need investigators for the museum and this was for APIS members only. Once again I led the team and joining me were Judith Basil, Keith Blackaby, Aaron Hardy, Jasmine Jenkins, Michael Lewis and John Wickham. The librarians were Gill Clements and Janice Brooker. We began at 9pm and located ourselves in the lecture room upstairs as well as the stack room, children's library and the large print area. It was fortunate that Gill Clements allowed APIS to conduct a second vigil because it added considerably to the information that we gathered together for the investigation as a whole. This second vigil was also more productive in terms of anomalous phenomena recorded. The team in The stack recorded a definite mechanical click from the main library and later on various creaks, including a loud one from the ceiling, were heard. On the third watch a faint, distant and intermittent thudding was logged. Of course, these noises may have had natural causes, such as the building cooling down, but they hadn't been apparent on our 12/13 September vigil. In the large print room a sharp noise was heard at the start of the first watch, it came from a back shelf and it was quickly followed by another noise from the ceiling and again at a point above the bookshelf, at the same time a movement was detected in the corridor. Next, two clicks were logged, followed minutes later by two creaks. Shadows appeared through the middle bookshelf then footsteps were heard in the corner. An eventful first watch! The second large print room watch was taken by Judith and Michael and both noticed a novel's tasselled bookmark moving as though in a breeze but the investigators could find no draught to account for the movement. Aaron and I had an uneventful third watch here, but during the final watch, with Sonia and John, blue flashes of light were seen reflecting off the neighbouring church wall. Both witnesses were certain that they had not been made by a passing emergency vehicle's warning lights. We expected activity upstairs in the lecture hall, given that our dowsing report had indicated a high probability of paranormal phenomena occurring there, and we weren't disappointed. It was on the third watch in the lecture hall that things really kicked off. On Jasmine and Keith's watch, their two-way radios were affected and a message that sounded like 'Let me out' was heard at 12.28am. At 12.58am a loud clattering broke out, both Jasmine and Keith went to investigate and they found a pencil had appeared on the window ledge and another had appeared on the floor yet the noise that had alerted them was too loud to be just the movement of the pencils. Nobody in the APIS team that night could recall the two stray pencils but we did remember seeing a pot of pencils at the opposite end of the hall, on the stage. As the two investigators checked on the two pencils there was another loud sound from the stage end of the room but when they retraced their steps nothing was found to account for the noise. We cannot rule out for certain that the pencils on the floor and window ledge were overlooked by everybody at the start of the investigation. To the best of our knowledge, however, this was not the case.

The most noteworthy event of the evening occurred, most unexpectedly, in the children's library. At 11.10pm Jasmine and Keith heard a double thump and were sure that something had landed on the floor. They had been sitting together and the sounds had come from behind them. On investigation they discovered a book (one in the *My Little Pony* series) lying on the floor. Sensibly they left it exactly where it was and reported the incident to me at the end of the watch. I questioned one of the librarians, Janice as to where the book had come from and she was able to tell me precisely. I used my tape measure to calculate the angle of trajectory. This book had travelled horizontally, in a 27 degree angle from its bookshelf. It had not fallen vertically, as might have been expected. The double thump heard by Jasmine and Keith was most probably the sound of the book first hitting the shelving on the back wall and then hitting the floor.

The strangeness at the library continued after our two vigils. When I returned to give my talk to the public on Saturday 11 October, the ghost was still making its presence felt. The lecture hall was packed to capacity with sixty-four people in the audience. It was 2.30pm and I had just started to speak when a pot of pencils that had been standing on the window ledge flew across the room. Members of the public and two librarians witnessed this and it caused a nervous ripple of laughter to flow amongst the audience. Nobody had been standing next to the window and it was not a windy day, so no strong puff of wind could have dislodged the pot. I questioned Gill Clements after the talk and she told me that books were still being moved about in the night, as reported by library staff arriving first thing in the morning. Is Phillip Kane still keeping an eye on his beloved library? Tom Corbett, a famous psychic medium in the 1960s, had this to say about why ghosts haunt a particular place. 'Ghosts are just people who have died and bound themselves, because of great happiness or great tragedy, to a spot on earth.' If that is the case Letchworth Library is in good, if incorporeal, hands.

While I was busy conducting the library investigation I learned that Plinston Hall, which is also situated in Broadway, just the other side of Kennedy Gardens from Letchworth Library, has its own ghost. The figure of a woman has been seen from time to time, flitting about in the main hall and she has been spotted by several staff members. This seemed entirely appropriate as many of APIS's meetings are held in Plinston Hall!

CHAPTER FOUR

HAUNTED HERTFORDSHIRE HOTELS

FANHAMS HALL

Fanhams, on the outskirts of Ware, was known as Brandefanhams in the thirteenth century, when it was no more than a cluster of farm buildings. In the Middle Ages 'brande' described blighted or infertile land or crops. 'Fan' is also Old English and was used to refer to fen or marshland. 'Ham' was commonly a contraction for homestead. In 1651 John Nash, yeoman of Ware, was recorded to be in possession of the property. On his death in 1663, William Weld, a 'gentleman' of Widberrry Hill, Hertfordshire, purchased the estate. When he died, in 1699, Fanham sold for £1,810.15*s.* 0*d.* a small fortune in those times. The new owner was John Evans, cloth maker and citizen of London. The Queen Anne house that he had built here stood for almost 200 years. Little remains of this original house now, save for the elegant White Hall staircase and an old metal bell-pull in the courtyard. As the house took shape, a garden and orchards were planted, the garden still exists, dominated by quince and medlar trees, varieties that are quite rare these days. There are also figs, peach, nectarine, walnuts, mulberries and morello cherry to add colour and variety. The paths that wind through the garden were only added last century and pleached lime alleys were set out around what became the croquet lawn. The Evans family and then their cousins the Phelps owned the property till 1771, when it was sold for £4,000 to the immensely wealthy and influential William Plumer of New Place, Gilston. 'One of the most opulent country gentlemen in the kingdom besides possessing the most extensive property of any gentleman in this country, his additional estates in Essex, Middlesex and Suffolk make up a clear income of fifteen thousand pounds per annum' was how *The English Chronicle* described Fanhams Hall's latest owner. He did not spend much time here however, as he was a busy Member of Parliament and spent much of his time at his Gilston home. The next occupant, in 1822, was Samuel Adams, barge owner and banker, of Ware. His grandson put the house on the market again and in 1859 maltster Thomas Page bought it and let it out. Page made some improvements to Fanhams in the 1870s, for his daughter, Anne Elizabeth. She was married to Lieutenant Richard Benyon Croft, a bluff, outspoken Royal Navy officer, who had seen service in the West Indies and China. Croft could trace his family back to Croft in Hertfordshire, mentioned in the Domesday Book. After his 1869 marriage he resigned his commission to join his father-in-law's malting business, and eventually to run it as its head. Croft was a local celebrity, who wholeheartedly involved himself in local affairs. He became an Alderman and High Sheriff of Hertfordshire and enjoyed living at Fanhams Hall until his death in 1912. During the Crofts' residency Anne Elizabeth Croft set about the complete rebuilding of Fanhams Hall. Mr W. Wood

Fanhams Hall, near Ware. A wide variety of manifestations have been reported from this haunted hotel.

Bethell was the architect and Mr Thomas Hunt was the builder chosen to undertake the transformation. Bethell's design was in the Jacobean style with extensive alterations and additions to the structure of the property and its complete encasement in stone. One of his hallmarks was minute attention to detail; he even drew up the designs for individual hinges, door latches and grates in the building. Most of the interior work, including the Italian walnut panelling with inlaid mother-of-pearl in the lounge, the oak panelling in the Minstrel's gallery, tiled fireplace in the great hall and the elaborate plaster ceilings, as in the long gallery are the work of Lawrence L. Turner.

As the house was taking shape (in 1901/02) Anne concentrated on the redevelopment and improvement of the landscape and was about to create the most unique gardens. She was particularly interested in Japanese culture and entrusted a Mr Inaka to draw up designs for a traditional, beautiful and delicate Japanese Shin garden. This is one of the three main types of Japanese garden designs. His plans set out an elaborate and undulating landscape, with hills, waterfalls and lakes. Each physical feature had some intrinsic significance in its relationship to the others. Mr Inaka called the garden Koraku, after a famous Tokyo garden. Koraku recalls the Japanese saying, 'Start worrying before others, and afterwards rejoice in the advantages of foresight!' Professor Suzuki and two professional gardeners were given responsibility for creating Mr Inaka's vision. Every year before the start of the First World War they came over from Japan to spend the summer months in the 'Jap Cottage' tending and expanding their horticulture, much of which may still be seen today. This includes the tea-house, Sei-shin-tei (house of the Pure Heart) sent over from Japan and erected in 1900; Kitsune-ike (Fox Lake) crossed by Shin-Kyo (Spirit Bridge), the mound known as Fuji-Yama and the 'Small House', which represents a Shinto shrine. The Queen Anne Garden was restocked and the shape of the lime alleys was improved by the addition of numerous young lime trees. An Austrian house was added and an Italian garden planted containing fine specimens of roses. Once the house was completed and the garden alterations were well under way Mrs Croft moved on to the furnishings, illustrated Dutch tiles were imported and William Morris's stained glass windows and tapestry curtains adorned the interiors. Eight Croft children, two sons and six daughters, were brought up at Fanhams Hall. The second son, Henry Page Croft, inherited the estate. Educated at Eton and Cambridge, he entered the law then became a Conservative MP and was eventually created the first Lord Croft. Lord Croft's third sister was Anne Page Croft, who married the Liverpool brewer, Charles Alexander Nall-Cain, First Baron Brockett of Brockett Hall. She lived for many years at her husband's ancestral home near Welwyn but was determined to return to her roots at Fanhams Hall after Lord Brockett's death in 1934. Anne inherited her mother's passion for the gardens and took great pleasure in opening them to the public on certain summer days, so that all could enjoy their beauty. During the Second World War Lady Brockett shared her home with many young people. The Cheyne Hospital for Children evacuated its charges to convalesce at Fanhams Hall, under the care of Matron Miss E.M. Price, SRN. The military also had a small presence at the hall; the Royal Army Service Corps had a supply depot and administration unit sited in the basement of one wing of the great house. Anne Page Croft remained at her childhood home until 1949 and with her death the days of Fanhams Hall as a private residence effectively ended. The cost of running a building of this size was prohibitive and Anne's heir, Major R.A. Page Croft decided to sell the property and auction the contents, which were sold in 1950. In 1951 Fanhams Hall was bought by the Westminster Bank and they used it as their Staff College. In the 1960s a number of alterations were carried out, including the demolition of the old stables, harness room and loose boxes in 1965. This was to make way for a new two-storey accommodation block to include syndicate rooms and study bedrooms. In 1971 the bank sold the hall to the Building Societies Association. They, in turn, sold out to J. Sainsbury Plc in February 1986. Sainsburys also used the house as their training centre as well as hosting meetings for outside companies. They substantially modernised it after taking ownership and stayed on until 2004. It was subsequently sold twice before being acquired by Exclusive Hotels, the present owners, who renamed it Fanhams Hall Hotel. It is a four star hotel with 73 bedrooms set in 27 acres of Grade II listed gardens.

THE GHOSTS OF FANHAMS HALL

What makes the ghosts at Fanhams Hall so interesting is the variety of their manifestations; they are sometimes seen, at other times heard, they may make their presence known by touch – or even by smell! In addition they number partial as well as full-body apparitions. One bitterly cold February day in 2005 I visited the site to talk with some of the staff who were working there at the time. Many of them had worked at Fanhams Hall for many years and none of them were in any doubt as to the authenticity of the hauntings. Christine worked here for sixteen years as a cleaner and she was something of an authority on the many ghostly activities. In Christmas 2004, after a party, she was staying the night at the hall with some friends. The friends complained about the noise, 'a lot of running about, up and down by someone in high heels'. Nobody occupied the rooms above them in the almost deserted Hall at that quiet time of the year.

Christine went on to explain that one of the 'hot spots' for the hauntings seemed to be centred around rooms 205 to 212. About three years previously a lady called Joyce Lyons was staying in room 207, whilst attending a pre-retirement course. She heard music next door and thought that someone had left their radio on. It transpired that the next door rooms were unoccupied, but in times gone by, directly above 207 had been the music room. In the corridor outside 205 to 212 a cleaner and a conference delegate had reported seeing a reflection in the mirror of 'something' that wasn't actually there. Christine herself has heard talking when nobody else was in sight in this same area. It's always indistinct and the words can't be made out, except for one – Christine's own name called out quietly, in an otherwise empty corridor.

Some years back at the time of an eclipse of the moon, Christine had an eerie experience in the drawing room while she was on her own. At first she felt someone behind her, and the next instant she felt freezing cold hands around her neck. She turned around to face an empty room. Another cleaner, Betty, had an odd encounter when she clearly saw an apparition reflected in the mirror on the main staircase. She described it as being reminiscent of Guinevere, with a long flowing dress and a tall, pointed hat. In this same area Christine recalled that she had heard the sound of children crying. 'It seemed to come from under the stairs, near the library.'

Shirley has cleaned at Fanhams Hall for a long time and although she has witnessed some fascinating poltergeist phenomena she remained quite phlegmatic about them – they didn't frighten her in the slightest. Eight years before our meeting she had been working in the Hitchin Conference Room when she noticed her polish sliding across a perfectly level table, all by itself until it finally fell on the floor. She replaced it only for the same thing to be repeated a second and then a third time! When she had finished cleaning the room she was locking the door when her hair was pulled, hard, from behind, by an invisible hand. She span around but there was no sight nor sound of anybody else but herself. The long gallery is another place where weird things happen, Shirley observed that they seemed to be more likely to occur when she was feeling a bit down or unwell. The partial apparition of a man haunts the long gallery, and observers only ever see the top half of him. He wears a waistcoat and seems to gaze out into the gardens. James, who was a manager at Fanhams Hall, was always dismissive of the cleaners' reports until one day he, himself had a strange experience in the long gallery. As he entered the gallery he got quite a fright. 'It felt as though people were rushing towards me,' he said later. Ghostly aromas are smelt in the long gallery too; a strong smell of tobacco smoke has been noticed in this non-smoking building, both here and in the Knebworth and Welwyn Rooms. On one memorable occasion Shirley had been preparing a room for a meeting, when she turned back to check that all was in order. On the large u-shaped table all the notepads and pens were crazily spinning around! An even more spectacular encounter with the ghosts of Fanhams Hall happened early one evening, about 7pm. Shirley had laid out a dining table for fifty-eight guests. She heard a tinkling sound and returned to the room to witness all fifty-eight glasses hovering about 6in above the table! She also felt an extreme chill, 'like a cold blanket around me.' Shirley is one of many people who have seen the 'grey lady' who haunts the main staircases. The lady wears a short, grey cap and a long grey dress. She is known to lean over the banisters as though looking for someone or something. In fact, Shirley had several sightings; the most recent one was the year before our discussion. Another female apparition seen by Shirley happened by as she was wheeling her trolley along to room 15. 'A dark-haired lady passed me; she was wearing a cream coloured dress with brown markings. I followed her as she went into room 15 but when I checked I found the door locked. I opened up the room but it was quite empty.' This incident had happened in broad daylight, just last year. Shirley also told me that radios often got switched on and off by themselves and she too has heard her name called when she's been alone, usually in the long gallery or the Hitchin room. Joyce worked in the coffee area and we managed a brief chat together. When I asked her if she had had any strange experiences she recalled one in particular. 'One morning, as I was putting the cups away I stepped backwards – onto someone's foot. I felt a foot and two hands on my back, as if to stop me falling over and my whole body went cold at the same time.' She turned around to apologise but no one was behind her. The only other person present was Audrey, busy cleaning the floors and quite some distance away. The ghosts of Fanham Hall seemed to know all the staff's names. Joyce was the third person I interviewed who had heard her name called in the Atrium. There was definitely nobody else about this time, which was two years previously. Joyce was extremely matter-of-fact about her experiences but not so Adam, a waiter. Early one December evening last year he had insisted that Joyce accompany him to the cellar as he had to fetch something and he seemed extremely nervous. She went with him but, 'it was freezing cold down there and the hairs on the back of my neck stood up'. Adam confided in Joyce, 'I saw some stranger walking through the basement'. Joyce thought it peculiar that all the fuse boxes were left open. On checking with the maintenance man she found that when he had last been in the cellar all the boxes had been firmly shut, there was no reason for them all to be open.

Sarah Murphy, a duty manager, told me of her own weird experience at Fanhams Hall. It was in December 2004 and she was working in the Atrium Bar. She clearly heard the sound of breaking glass, as did her colleague. They made a thorough search of the bar but could find no breakages. Minutes later there was a phone call. The guest in room 40 was calling to say that on entering his bedroom he found broken glass all over the place. The glass was found on its tiled shelf, it hadn't fallen at all, it was as if the glass had just 'exploded' into tiny fragments in an empty room. Sarah's scariest moment was reserved for Christmas 2004. She was alone on duty at the reception desk. The duty manager knew that there were no guests booked in at the hall, yet she could plainly hear doors opening and closing in the otherwise deserted old house. It freaked her out quite badly; she admitted that she had unlocked the heavy front door, in case a quick exit became necessary.

A few days after my visit I learned from Steve Lomas, another duty manager, that one of the night porters, who preferred to remain anonymous, had only recently managed to build up his courage to return to taking his break in the drawing room. He had, on numerous occasions, heard the sounds of laughter coming from behind the sofa, so he stopped going in to that room for some considerable time.

THE WHITE HART

As St Albans is the most haunted place in Hertfordshire it comes as no surprise that it is also home to an authenticated haunted hotel. The White Hart is a fifteenth-century coaching inn at Holywell Hill, an area notorious for haunted houses. Formerly known as Halliwelle Street, this is one of the oldest streets in St Albans and one of the most interesting if your hobby is ghosthunting! Ghosts haunt numerous locations at the 600-year-old building – even the car park is haunted. Some people have reported seeing a headless woman's apparition, believed to be that of Elizabeth Wilson. It is claimed that this unfortunate lady was decapitated when her horse-drawn carriage thundered under the low hotel archway. I have heard a similar story attached to the Sun Hotel at Hitchin and wondered why there might have been so many careless coachmen recklessly speeding along the streets of Hertfordshire in the era of stagecoach travel.

The 2001 White Hart investigation by a paranormal research group was of more interest to me. They set up a camera in the cellar, as it was reputedly haunted by a former landlord of most dubious reputation. When the group's control room monitor screen went blank they rushed to the unmanned cellar only to discover that the wires had been wrenched out of the back of their camera, which still stood on its tripod. Another ghost hunter is said to have captured 'an unearthly face', also described as 'fierce-looking, an evil face' of what may have been the landlord who was allegedly found hanged from a ceiling beam (it was conjectured that he was murdered). The stairwell is another focus of paranormal activity, where guests have encountered the spirit of a young girl, said to be about seven years old. This 'child' kicks out at anyone who might be walking up the stairs and whispers in the ears of unwary women who visit the ladies. Other guests have seen the ghost of the little girl by the fireplace in the bar. Legend has it that a former landlord's daughter died in 1803, the tragic casualty of a fire which destroyed many of the hotel's outbuildings. Her father was suspected of paedophilia, preying on his daughter and other very young St Albans' girls. His spirit is the one that supposedly haunts the cellar and it was he who died at the hands of one of his victim's vengeful father.

The attic corridors in the White Hart have been described as gloomy and claustrophobic, and the attic as eerie. The ghost of a prostitute, described as grey-haired, is also associated with the attic rooms. As recently as June 2008 a shaken guest reported feeling icy hands clutch his neck while he was sitting on the end of his bed. A chef who used to work at the hotel woke in a sweat after the impression that the ghostly prostitute had tried to strangle him as he slept. Sue Pearce is another ex-employee, who worked here in the late 1990s. She recalled feeling a cold breeze, as if someone had passed by, and sensing a strong presence when she laid out the breakfast tables on her own. Jon Woolard worked here and remembered strange happenings below stairs. Heavy barrels, which were difficult even for a strong man to handle, would move about the cellar at night. They were left, carefully stacked at night only for them to be found scattered all over the cellar the next morning. Lights would also switch themselves on and off and the cellar door would lock itself despite the absence of a key.

A guest received unexpected company one night when he saw a stranger, a man, sitting on the edge of his bed. Next thing a message formed on the mirror – 'Meet me in room 7 at 7.30'. The shaken guest told Evie Scully, landlady at the time, about his weird encounter. Evie promptly went upstairs to check for herself. Later she said, 'The writing was big and bold, sort of childish and written in a chalky substance.' The landlady erased the message and returned to her guest. He then went back up to his room but reappeared minutes later to say that the writing had returned! Other guests using this room (room 8) have told of waking in the morning to find towels strewn around the floor. Next door (room 7) people have seen the fireplace engulfed in flames, despite the fact that it has been bricked up for many years. Well-known medium and psychic artist Marion Goodfellow attended a séance at the hotel some years back. She encountered the spirit of a child who perished in a fire that broke out in 1803 and her parents were called John and Elizabeth. Subsequent research revealed that there was a John Rudnan-Heywood, married to Elizabeth, who had been landlord at the White Hart in the early 1800s. Marion also received the impression of a young Georgian woman whom she associated with the date 1830 – could this have been Elizabeth Wilson?

BROCKET HALL

One of the most attractive hotels in Hertfordshire is Brocket Hall, situated at Lemsford, a village that lies just to the east of Welwyn Garden City. It used to be the country seat of Lord Brocket, of television's *I'm a Celebrity Get Me Out of Here* fame. Strikingly attractive, Brocket Hall stands opposite Lemsford Church. The house was built in the late eighteenth century. A square mansion set in immaculate grounds with an artificial lake spanned by a picturesque bridge set directly in front of the house. This has been the country retreat of two of Queen Victoria's Prime Ministers. Lord Melbourne (William Lamb) was one, a favourite with the monarch as he guided her in matters of state and had been her mentor during her earliest days on the throne. Melbourne's wife was the notorious Lady Caroline Lamb, a beautiful, highly-strung rebel who fell madly in love with the 'mad, bad and dangerous to know' poet, Lord Byron. Unfortunately Byron tired of this particular mistress. She was to learn of her former lover's death in the

Brocket Hall, Lemsford. A phantom lady's presence has been felt here.

most terrible circumstances. As she was driving out from Brocket Hall one summer's day in 1824 she saw a funeral cortege and enquired as to whose it might be. She was told it was Lord Byron's; his cortege had been travelling back to his old family home in Nottingham. In 1948 Lord Melbourne himself passed away. Legend has it that he died in the billiard room after engaging in vigorous sexual intercourse! The other Victorian Prime Minister who lived at Brocket Hall was Viscount Palmerston (Henry Temple) who was famous for his 'gunboat policy', using the suggestion of military force when British overseas interests were threatened.

At the present time Brocket Hall is used as a conference centre, hotel and golf complex. I visited in 2002 and talked to one of the maintenance staff, a down-to-earth young man who confirmed that he had personal experience of the unexplained at his place of work. Alone one night, it was his task to secure the mansion and just as he was leaving he distinctly heard someone cough close to him, in a house that he knew for certain was empty apart from himself. He had also smelt perfume when there was no one else about and he told me that some people were convinced that the ghost of Lady Caroline was making its presence felt. He told me about some of the many celebrities who had visited Brocket Hall. These included Nicole Kidman, John Thaw, Michael Winner, Ronnie Corbett, Timothy Dalton and Kim Wilde. The mansion was used for filming on occasion, particularly for period dramas. Back in the 1950s a cult black and white horror film, *Night of the Demon*, was made here. It was based on *Casting the Runes*, one of the great M.R. James short stories. As a horror film fan I was familiar with the movie, particularly the scenes where the invisible demon stalks its prey through the woods, leaving smoking footprints in its wake. My favourite horror movie of all time, however, would have to be *The Exorcist*.

In 2001 the pop group Steps shot a video in the mansion and were spooked by sudden temperature drops in certain places and objects seemingly moving about by themselves.

In 2003 permission was granted to carry out a vigil to a Hertfordshire-based group of investigators. Ghost Hunters UK reported several unexplained incidents. Perfume was smelt on leaving the Prince of Wales Room. In the dining room a medium said that she felt someone touch her side and then her lap. Another ghost hunter claimed to have seen 'a broad-shouldered silhouette'. In the library a camera set to 'on' was found with its manual switch turned to the 'off' position, but not by anyone in the team. A tape recorder picked up an indistinct voice, which sounded as though it had spoken very close to the microphone. A minidisk recorder seemed to have suffered battery drain. Finally one of the mediums allegedly conversed with both Lucy, a fair-haired six-year-old girl, and her brother Phillip.

THEOBALDS PARK

Theobalds Park in Cheshunt has a chequered and fascinating past. In 1762 George Prescott MP bought the estate and built the red brick and white stone mansion that lies at the heart of the present day hotel complex. It remains an imposing edifice, from its entrance hall with ornamental arches, Etruscan painted ceiling and beautifully curved staircase with iron railings. Some reception rooms have Jacobean wood panelling and moulded and plastered ceilings abound. In 1820 the Meux brewing family leased the property and later bought the freehold. Their improvements include the Italianate tower and domestic quarters, which

Theobalds Park, Cheshunt. A ghost that scratches...

were added to the south end in the 1880s. In 1910 they built the ballroom wing at the north end. Admiral of the Fleet Sir Hedworth Meux, who died in 1929, was the last private owner. Thereafter the house became a hotel until 1938 when Middlesex County Council acquired it. The Army requisitioned Theobalds Park during the Second World War. From 1951 till 1969 it was used as a Secondary School. From 1973 till 1989 it then became a college under the London Borough of Enfield. In the 1990s it was completely restored and sold to a conference centre. The present owners are De Vere Heritage Hotels.

At the end of September 2008 a lady named Janice Allgood, representing a group called Petals in the Wind, approached me about an event that she was staging in Theobolds Park. It was to be a ghost hunt for members of the public and Janice wondered if APIS would help out. We would guide her guests around the old manor house part of the hotel, use our recording equipment and make notes about the evening. Occasionally APIS gets involved in public affairs so we have plenty of experience in dealing with the general public. I accepted the challenge as I wanted an opportunity to do some investigating of my own. I had visited the hotel a few months before, when I had attended a conference, but had seen very little of the place. A small APIS team assembled here on Sunday 5 October, comprising of Jude Basil, Aaron Hardy, John Wickham and myself. The hotel management had allowed almost full access to the mansion. This included the boardroom, Lambton Room, Portland Room, Burley Room, Carpenter's Landing as well as three bedrooms – 104, 209 and 219. It was an enjoyable night; each member of the APIS team was responsible for nine members of the public as we had a total of thirty-six people in our care. Some areas affected the visitors more than others. Some table turning was tried in the boardroom and it did rock quite violently at one end. When Aaron and I were in the room on our own later we found it easy to lift the table using just our knees. We suggested trying the experiment again and we moved the participants around so that they sat in different places. This time the table didn't move at all. People felt and sensed different things in the boardroom. Some heard a tapping noise from the fireplace, chimes and rustling sounds were noted by others and some sensed a presence at the end of the room but it was all very subjective. The most interesting area was the Carpenter's Landing which many group members instinctively did not like, sensing that someone had died there. Danielle, one of the psychic mediums, felt that a woman had committed suicide by throwing herself off the balcony. As one group, led by Jude, left the landing and started down the stairs Jude yelled out. 'Something' had scratched her. She was absolutely certain that it could not have been one of the group that she was escorting. Nothing like this had ever happened to her before although she has been in more than her fair share of very haunted locations. I checked her and on the lower right hand side of her back was quite a vicious scratch. The puzzling thing for me was how was she scratched? She was wearing three layers of clothes as it was a cold night; a fascinating ending to a most unusual evening.

I had not told the party of visitors about the haunted history of Theobalds Park so I was particularly interested in their spontaneous reaction to the Carpenter's Lounge and lobby areas because this is where ghostly footsteps are most frequently heard. Could it have been the shade of Lady Valerie Meux that badly scratched Jude Basil? Valerie is said to regularly wander the main staircase. Lady Meux had formerly been a barmaid, who was plucked from obscurity when she married the wealthy and powerful brewing magnate Sir Henry Meux in 1878. Their marriage had created a scandal in high society at the time. The most interesting story surrounding Lady Meux concerns her avid collection of antiquities. One of her possessions was an Egyptian mummy in a sarcophagus. A curse was inscribed on this sarcophagus, which when translated read, 'Any person who shall move this coffin shall die a childless death'. Legend has it that this curse was fulfilled, on more than one occasion. Eventually the sarcophagus was sold to an overseas collector, and shipped out on... the *Titanic*. There is now no possibility of anyone ever moving the mummy again. I was also intrigued by the fact that the hotel management hadn't let us near the most haunted room – 221 – during our 'ghost hunt'. Guests have asked to be moved on numerous occasions from this room, indeed so powerful are the psychic impressions for certain people that a 'sense of unease' has oppressed them on entering room 221. What is on record is that guests have reported the feeling of some unseen force pulling their bedding off them in the middle of the night and the sounds of male whisperings. Perhaps its reputation now precedes it, but many members of staff do not want to be in this room unaccompanied. Disappointingly we were also not allowed access to bedrooms 215 and 216, some other paranormal hot spots. Apparitions have been seen in both of these bedrooms. One terrified lady was in bed with the light on when she saw her clothes being moved across the floor. The hallway connecting rooms 215, 216 and 221 is also notorious. Strange things happen with the mobile communications used by managers and security guards. One manager was called on his radio four times and told to leave the area during a single night, yet no living person had radioed him. Another trouble spot is room 107 and the adjoining hallway, where things can jump out of people's hands for no good reason. A security guard was making his rounds one night when he was suddenly grabbed by the shoulder; he quickly turned around to find an empty corridor.

A footnote to the weird goings-on in the grand old house concerns the grounds of the estate. In 1887 Sir Henry Bruce Meux and Lady Valerie Meux created a new entrance and also decided to purchase Temple Bar. In the eighteenth century the heads of traitors were mounted on pikes and exhibited on the roof of Temple Bar. This ancient monument had been one of the old gateways to London and it was relocated, from the City of London to Theobalds Park. It was, rather incongruously, sited in a clearing in a wood on the estate. Eventually it was returned to the City of London, in 2003, where it can be seen today, at its new home in Paternoster Square. Before its removal a member of the hotel's staff had an eerie experience when driving past the monument. She felt as though she was not alone in her car and looked into her rear view mirror to see the outline of someone sitting in the back. When she reached her home she got out of the car and as she was walking up her pathway somebody rather forcefully pushed her. She turned slowly around, only to find that she was completely alone.

BANYERS HOTEL

I visited Banyers Hotel in Melbourn Street, Royston, on several occasions to speak with the friendly and helpful staff there. They were in no doubt that they had some non-paying guests, who were not of this world. My first meeting was in July 2003 with the manager, John Guisberg. He told me that he had stayed overnight more than thirty times but one night was to prove particularly memorable. John was alone when he awoke to hear a baby crying. It was past midnight and around midweek. Puzzled, he turned off the television and noticed that the sound seemed to be coming from near the window. He opened it but finding nothing outside he wondered if the sounds might be coming through the vents in the windowsill. The crying was persistent and he decided to get dressed to search the rooms. He found nothing but the sounds of distress, which John described as high-pitched and definitely female, continued. As he was, by now, thoroughly awake, he thought that he might as well search the rest of the premises, both inside and outside. It was about 3am, there were no cars outside and no lights were on. The security light, which would be triggered if anyone came within five yards, remained off. While he was searching outside there was a final, louder burst of crying, which abruptly stopped altogether. 'It was so frightening that I nearly went home,' John admitted candidly. The incident had occurred only some six months prior to our meeting. He went on to say that he had been roused from slumber before, by other noises. He had heard loud heavy hand raps on the front door in the middle of the night on several occasions. The knocking might be repeated but stopped when he got downstairs. When he opened the front door there was nobody to be seen. At other times, when he was alone in the hotel, he heard conversation in the bar, but once again, upon investigation, the place was empty. John kindly showed me the notorious room 1. Some accounts have erroneously reported room 4 as being the haunted bedroom. Room 1 was a solid, oak-panelled chamber which is listed. It was maintained in its original condition despite refurbishments to other parts of the hotel. The ghost, affectionately known as Henry by the locals, is dressed as a Cavalier. He is obviously a gentleman among ghosts for he takes off his cape and bows to any hotel guest he meets.

A year later I met another manager, Dawn Adams, who also treated me to a conducted tour of Banyers. This time I visited some parts of the hotel that I hadn't seen before. The conversation turned to room 1 and I was told that many guests had reported that the room was very cold, but when checked the radiators were found to be hot. When I attempted to investigate the cellar's alleged tunnel I was thwarted when all four lights down there refused to work. This was strange because they were on different circuits and when we checked the mains switch it was in the 'on' position. 'He' had known that I was coming, 'he' being the Reverend Banyer, who was vicar of Royston from 1739 till his death in 1751. The hotel was named after him and it appeared that he did not like me. As a seasoned paranormal investigator I am used to this sort of thing. My medium friends tell me that often the ghosts know when I am coming, or when a vigil is going to take place and act accordingly. Dawn felt that the Reverend Banyer's presence could be felt strongly down in the cellars. When the hotel had been his vicarage a tunnel had linked the vicarage to the church.

Back in the bar upstairs Dawn related to me an interesting incident that had occurred just four weeks before my visit. Dawn had been in the bar with the hotel's owner, Delia. The two women were sitting near the TV, enjoying a quiet drink together. Out of the

Banyers Hotel, Royston. Haunted by a crying baby, a Cavalier and a reverend.

corner of the eye a figure could be seen behind the bar, by the Pepsi dispenser. Both Delia and Dawn saw the same thing. 'It was a man, he was all in white, white hair, white jacket and trousers and he appeared to be about forty-five years of age.' His image was only briefly glimpsed and then it was gone. This is fairly common in my experience of ghosts. They are often seen in the observer's peripheral vision, for the briefest of moments, so Dawn's account had a ring of truth about it.

Bernard Lee had been chef at Banyers for many years. He clearly recalled a night seven years previously when he had been enjoying a pint in the same bar with a couple of friends when suddenly, 'the clock just flew off the wall, about 8ft across the room'. It scared the trio of drinkers, who hurriedly finished their drinks and made a quick exit from the bar. Was this the Reverend Banyer 'calling time'? Was he making his displeasure at late night drinking be known?

Another incident had happened in the bar, only three weeks before my visit. Stacey, the barmaid, told me that a drip tray, 'flipped out and landed on the floor for no reason'. A bit later, when she went into the ladies' toilet, 'it just went all cold in there'.

SUN HOTEL

The Sun Hotel, in Sun Street, is both notorious and interesting – Hitchin's own haunted and historical hotel. From medieval times Hitchin's principal lodging and

Sun Hotel, Hitchin. Lord Havisham's haunt, a ghostly game of bowls and a suffocating presence.

meeting place was the Angel Inn situated in Angel Street. The Angel burnt down in 1523 when Henry VIII was a guest; he escaped 'with not so much as a shirt on his kingly back'. The Angel was rebuilt but the tenant of the adjoining tithe, owned by Trinity College, Cambridge, used the opportunity to build a rival – the Sun Inn. By the reign of Charles I the Sun had overtaken the Angel as the leading inn of the town. Its importance continued to increase, to the extent that Angel Street became Sun Street. During the English Civil War the Sun served as the headquarters of 3,000 parliamentary soldiers quartered in the town and the Council of War met here regularly. The coaching era began for the Sun in 1706. By 1741 the London to Hitchin and Bedford service was established and it lasted for 100 years. In 1792, when the Hitchin Directory was printed, some fifteen coaches passed daily through the town as well as many stage wagons and village carriers. The south wing of the building, which backs onto the Conservative Club, dates back to the middle ages and much of the original Elizabethan and Jacobean building work survives. The present front buildings were constructed circa 1717 and the great ballroom in 1770. Further bedrooms were added as a second floor in 1870. John Loudon McAdam, inventor of macadamized roads and Samuel Whitbread, of brewing fame, were two famous friends and regulars at the Sun Hotel, where they would dine and deliberate together. During the nineteenth century Hunt Balls and Easter Balls were regularly held here. The place was a hive of social and intellectual activity. By the turn of the century the Sun Inn had become the Sun Hotel and the property was purchased by Trust House Limited in 1933 and in 1961 Charrington became the new owners and it was transferred within Bass to Toby Hotels. The rivalry between the Sun and the Angel finally ended in the late 1950s when the Angel was demolished. The Sun Hotel is currently owned by Greene King as part of their Old English Inns group.

Guests at the Sun have heard disembodied voices in the night outside their windows, around the archway. Coach drivers in the sixteenth and seventeenth centuries would call out 'Mind your head!' as they thundered under the low archway. Apparently, one day, someone didn't take that advice, and was decapitated. As discussed earlier The White Hart Hotel, St Albans has a similar story attached to it.

At the opposite end of the building, near the car park, some ladies reported being struck on the shins by ghostly wood and the distinctive sounds of clacking woods have been heard in this vicinity. This used to be the site of an ancient bowling green which was used by local clergymen. As far as I know it is the only example of anyone experiencing phantom bowling balls!

Psychically aware people have refused to sleep in room 10 as soon as they have entered it. It has become known for stories of the ghost of a woman, whose body is felt, lying across the faces of sleepers and almost suffocating them.

The most famous apparition is that of Lord Havisham and it doesn't carry its head under its arm but a fish! This former aristocrat was a contemporary of the Duke of Bedford, who at that time was Lessee of the Sun under owners Trinity College. Bedford would pay off his friend Havisham's gambling debts until one day he decided that enough was enough. Faced with debts that he could not possibly repay Lord Havisham committed suicide and now his ghost is said to wander the hotel. The phantom of a monk has also been reported either crossing the bar or behind the bar (presumably he prefers Abbott ale). Other strange things have been observed, like the dumb waiter that goes up and down by itself, or the invisible presence that moves things around after functions have been held in the ballroom.

APIS investigated the Sun Hotel on Sunday 17 September 2006. We concentrated our efforts on five locations: bedrooms 8, 10, 25 and 27 (the Lavender Room) as well as the ballroom. Everybody loved the feel of the place; it is a rambling old building with uneven, creaky floors in the corridors, low beams and plenty of character and charm. We had an interesting night, soon after we had set up around midnight a tea urn was heard rattling in a room behind the ballroom but on investigation there was nothing to account for the noise being made, the room was empty. Around the same time, in bedroom 27 (the Lavender Room) two team members, Annette and Jack, observed two indentations suddenly appear in the 'trigger object', a tray of sand with small pebbles laid on top of the sand. The indentations appeared as if two fingers had pressed the stones into the sand. Three minutes later 'something' rushed, like a wind, between the couple, making a whooshing sound and both of them felt very cold. As is sometimes the way with vigils, most of the interesting activities occurred early in the watch and as the night wore on it became quieter. The exception was the Ballroom, where, at 2.51am Dave Minney and I heard what sounded like footsteps, followed shortly afterwards by loudly clinking glasses. On checking the corridor behind the ballroom we found a stack of trays filled with empty glasses and this would account for the sounds we heard, as though the trays had been disturbed, but, again, there was nobody but ourselves in the vicinity.

CHAPTER FIVE

ST ALBANS – FIFTH MOST HAUNTED

ST PETER'S STREET PHANTOMS

You are more likely to encounter a ghost in St Albans than in any other part of Hertfordshire. According to The Supernatural Britain Report, conducted by my good friend Lionel Fanthorpe, a leading authority on the paranormal, St Albans is the fifth most haunted place in Great Britain. Lionel examined reports of supernatural activity in forty cities across the country and compiled a list of the ten most haunted places in the UK. Within this most haunted of cities a strong contender for most haunted street would have to be St Peters Street, one of the main city thoroughfares, once described as 'the most beautiful main street in Europe'. A famously haunted house in this location is the Ivy House. It was built as his own residence by Edward Strong, Chief Mason to Sir Christopher Wren during the construction of St Paul's Cathedral. The ghost that haunts the Ivy House is believed to be that of a tragic young chambermaid called Meades. She was walled up in the chimney of a house that previously stood on the site occupied by the Ivy House. Her 'crime' was to become pregnant by a member of the household. She is known as 'the cleaning ghost' since she is responsible for cleaning the handrail of the elegant staircase believed to have been made by Grinling Gibbons, and she also tidies the cellar. A St Albans resident, Martin Oliver, wrote to me to say that his mother-in-law lived at what was a doctor's house, next door but one to Ivy House, in the 1920s. She often talked about the mysterious staircase in the Ivy house that never needed cleaning. This sounds like the sort of ghost that we would all welcome into our own houses! This ghost, however, was known to frighten some people. In more recent times, when major renovations were carried out, despite there being dust everywhere else the handrail remained remarkably dust free. Ivy House was for many years occupied by an electricity company, Northmet. It was also used as the offices of solicitors Turner and Debenhams, whose staff refused to enter the building after dark and nobody wanted to be the last one to leave on winter evenings. On a dark and windy Friday night in 1975 a manager returned alone to collect some important papers. As he entered the building he saw a stranger, a young, blonde-haired woman dressed in white standing at the top of the stairs. She glanced at the man and then continued on up the stairs. The manager turned around and hurried away again, without his papers. The apparition of the sad serving girl was also seen at Christmas, by staff who had come in to decorate the tree. Her pale form was seen staring down at them from the top of the stairs. It wasn't only staff members who had spooky encounters in Ivy House. Cleaners and visitors have heard footsteps on the back stairs and other odd noises when unaccompanied. Taps were known to turn themselves on and doors were seen opening and closing as though someone had just walked through, but nobody was visible. The staircase handrail, apparently, continues to remain highly polished.

St Peter's church, on the other side of the road, 'feels uncomfortable' for solitary workers, who say they sense a presence or feel overlooked in this ancient place of worship, which is over 700 years old. The Grange is another St Peter's Street property with a reputation. Mayor John Osborne had the house built in 1763; it was acquired by the council in the 1940s and used for offices where typists and caretakers were frightened from time to time. A new caretaker in 1975 had an unpleasant experience when he was alone in the cellar. 'I got this awful feeling there was someone else with me and there was an eerie, icy atmosphere, so I turned on all the lights and the presence disappeared.' The restless spirit of The Grange was thought to be that of Dorothy Osborne, daughter-in-law of John Osborne. The story is that 'Sad Dorothy' committed suicide after discovering that her husband had a mistress. A former Town Clerk, Miss Betty Entwhistle, claimed that this was the case but although her family are mentioned in the register at St Peter's church there is no mention of Dorothy Osborne herself. Mallinson House, in the same street, has been known as the head office for the National Pharmaceutical Association for many years. This was where a builder had a peculiar meeting in 1977. He was working late one evening when the partial apparition of a man passed him on the stairs; it was partial because the builder saw that it had no legs. Following this sighting staff reported that files and other items of stationary had gone missing. It was concluded that this was probably the same spirit that was first reported as far back as 1872. In those Victorian times Mallinson House was known as Donnington House, the home of Dr William Russell. His home was, briefly, the most famously haunted, with the largest number of witnesses, in the land. One Sunday evening (at 7pm) in 1872 a crowd of some 200 people gathered in front of Donnington House. The incident began when a passer-by saw a ghostly figure, tapping at an upstairs window. The figure wore a silver-buttoned butler's livery complete with white wig. The passer-by attracted the attention of other people until a sizeable gathering amassed. The story was reported in the *Hertfordshire Advertiser* that year. The newspaper's editor decided that the policemen, who had later entered and examined the house, believed someone had got in via a back door of the late surgeon's house 'for a lark'. What is known is that Dr Russell's butler did kill himself in this upstairs room after being sacked. He had been caught red-handed drinking his master's brandy and had been unable to live with his shame. My correspondent, Martin Oliver, was a technician at St Albans' Abbey Theatre and he and the other technicians could only work on stage after rehearsals, maybe 11pm or later, so they often drove through the streets of the city late at night. They noticed, on many occasions, a light shining through the middle window upstairs and remarked on it among themselves. They must have wondered, did an insomniac live here? They thought no more about it until reading about the paranormal phenomena associated with Mallinson House.

HOLYWELL HILL HAUNTS

Formerly known as Halliwelle Street, Holywell Hill is one of the oldest streets in St Albans and one of the most interesting if your hobby is ghost hunting! To respect the residents' privacy, their lovely old Georgian house must remain anonymous, but it is situated in Holywell Hill and there is an intriguing story to tell. One night the wife was alone in bed when the heavy bedroom door opened of its own accord. Later on, some neighbours, accompanied by the police, turned up on their doorstep. They had been concerned to hear bells ringing and to see every light on in the house. Electric bells had been fitted to every room in the house. The police duly investigated but could find no signs of an intruder, so the lights were turned off and the house securely locked as the police departed. In the morning all the lights were found on again. At another time the husband was also at home when the couple's son came into the bedroom in the early hours of the morning. The boy complained that he couldn't sleep because he felt the presence of someone else in his room. His father offered to swap bedrooms and went to sleep upstairs. He said later, 'I had only been in bed a little while when suddenly I had a premonition that all was not normal. I knew immediately that there was a presence in the room with me; I felt no alarm for it seemed to have a soothing effect on me and I spoke to it and shortly afterwards I fell asleep and awoke in the morning quite converted to "There are more things in Heaven and Earth than are dreamt of in our philosophy".' Although the house was early eighteenth century the cellars and foundations date back to the twelfth century. A passage down here used to lead to the tomb of St Alban, but it had been filled in many years ago. It was thought that the pilgrims held services in the cellars before going on to visit the tomb.

The daughter of the household never liked going upstairs on her own and a sceptical family friend happened to express his disbelief in poltergeists. As he made his comments a door slowly opened, but there was nobody behind it and the friend left rather hurriedly, never to return. After an extra staircase was installed there was no paranormal activity for several months. (It seems that building work involving structural alterations may either set off poltergeist activity or quieten it down for a time). The husband continued his story, 'After about a year I was working on some odd jobs in the cellar when suddenly I felt his or her presence, it was so vivid that I exclaimed, "Good heavens, poltie, where have you been? We have missed you," – and a feeling of contentment filled me. Frequently after that we felt the presence with us – in a room, on the stairs or in the cellar.' The wife commented, 'He or she was very naughty really but never spiteful, although it had me up in the night many times ringing bells, turning on lights and leaving doors open, particularly in the cellars. I wonder where poltie is now and whether it missed me when we moved away.'

'Granny Sheldrake' is the ghost that haunts another house in Holywell Hill. Her presence is felt and sometimes her heavy footsteps are heard, mainly by young people rather than adults and she, in turn, seems to take more interest in the children living in the house.

Martin Oliver told me of a story from Holywell Hill that happened to him in the late 1980s, when he used to work at Fernau Avionics at the bottom of Holywell Hill, the firm was sited adjacent to the river, where Latium Close is now situated. One lunch time he decided to pop into town. He was just crossing Belmont Hill when he became conscious of a rather eccentric lady in front of him, dressed in decidedly Victorian clothing. She was wearing a flowery, ankle-length skirt which was rather wide. This lady had on brown boots, wore a woollen shawl, her head was covered by a cloth hat with a floppy brim and on her left arm hung a large wicker basket. Martin was unable to overtake her on the pavement and had to wait for a break in the traffic so that he could step into the road. It occurred to him to turn around and get a good look at her face. He was staggered to see that there was no one in sight on the length of path from where he was down to Belmont Hill.

FISHPOOL STREET… ANOTHER CURIOUS PLACE

Once it was the main coaching route into St Albans but Fishpool Street suffered a decline in fortune when Verulam Road was built in the late nineteenth century and it became a notorious slum area for a time. In its coaching heyday nearly every other building was an inn, now they are all long since gone, The Angel, The Blockers Arms, The Crow, The Cock and Flowerpot, The Queen, The Royal Oak, The Rule and Compasses and the Welclose Arms.

Nowadays Fishpool Street is a quietly prosperous old street in a middle class city. 'The lady in blue' is one well-known ghost associated with this street and she is rumoured to have suffocated her daughter by accident, back in the eighteenth century. She turns up at 3am in her long blue dress, looking suitably anguished as she wanders between her former home and the street, wiping her tears away with her handkerchief. Another house in the street is allegedly the site where someone was strangled to death. In one particular bedroom people awake in a panic, after feeling invisible hands around their throats. A former shop in this area is home to the spirit of 'Charlie', who shifts phantom biscuit tins around the floor. In another property the grey figure of a man has been seen at night by the bedside. A window fitment mysteriously disappeared from this room only to turn up again weeks later. The unwelcome attentions of this phantom are reputedly the cause of some owners moving out after only a short period of residency here. Another ghostly visitor to Fishpool Street is 'Old George' who appears, complete with top hat, and 'welcomes' new arrivals to his former home. 'The Crow', a former coaching inn, is now a private residence with four unwelcome visitors. A family with three daughters who lived here between 1959 and 1969 admitted that they had invisible lodgers. In a small room at the rear of the building doors would have their latches lifted noisily and would then be opened by unseen entities. These presences were invisible to human eyes but pets were able to follow their progress around the room indicating that they, at least, could see them. Popular opinion was that Tom Baker was the haunter; he had been landlord at The Crow Inn before the First World War. He used to travel up to Sloane Square in London in the early hours of the morning to his other business. He was Blacksmith to Edward VII. This hard-working man would then return to serve his customers at The Crow in the evening. Two other ghosts that haunt this former inn are a mother and daughter. The mother is heard rather than seen; she was an invalid who was nursed by her daughter. She would constantly rap on the floor to attract her daughter's attention and tapping on a partition wall continued to be heard long after her death. The daughter died before her mother and she has been seen wearing her nurse's uniform. Furniture has been regularly moved around in the dining room by paranormal forces. The oddest story connected with this house is that of the man woken up one night by the apparition of a young Boer War soldier by his bedside. 'What do you want?' the man asked. 'I am Charlie Rowley and I have come to see my mother,' answered the phantom soldier. 'Well, she's not here,' came the reply. With that the soldier politely shook hands and left. The startled witness observed that the soldier's hand was 'ice cold'.

VERULAMIUM VISITATIONS

Remnants of the Roman city of Verulamium, such as part of the city walls and a hypocaust, can still be seen, near the River Ver, in the parkland situated to the south-west of the modern city of St Albans. Verulamium had been the third largest city in Roman Britain before it was razed to the ground and its garrison slaughtered by Boudicca, Queen of the Iceni, in AD61. Before the Romans arrived Verulamium was known as Verlamion (meaning settlement above the marsh) when it was the capital of the Catuvellauni tribe.

In 1970, at Christmas time, two young lads out cycling in the park encountered the ghost of a Cavalier. Their description was fairly detailed: the soldier wore a silver-buttoned tunic with tassels, his loose fitting trousers were tucked into high boots, his long hair was curly, he carried a sword and appeared to be 'floating in a silver mist'.

In the summer of 1985 another young man was walking home through Verulamium when he was confronted by a Roman Centurion on horseback. The panic-stricken lad fled the spot in such a hurry that he tripped and injured himself badly enough to need treatment at the local hospital.

'Ginger' Mills was a local character who lived for a time in a caravan parked by the lakes at Verulamium. It was his custom to stroll around these lakes in the early morning. On one of these walks he heard the tramp of marching feet behind him and instinctively moved to one side to let the marchers through. He turned to see... nothing, but he felt the passage of this unseen phantom army and was shocked by a distinctly chilly breeze as it passed him by.

BERNARDS HEATH TIME SLIP?

One of the participants in St Albans' celebrated ghost walks told the party her own story of a spooky encounter at Bernards Heath. This lady's daughter and a friend were passing St Peter's church late one night when they heard the sound of hoofbeats which passed them and travelled on in the direction of Bernards Heath.

One of my favourite true ghost stories comes from well-known St Albans resident and author Betty Puttick, who wrote *Ghosts of Hertfordshire*.

> Bernards Heath is a stone's throw from my own home and from time to time while exercising my dog there I have picked up small, completely round stones and idly wondered if they could be stone shot from the battle (the second battle of St Albans in 1461). One day I had a curious experience there. As I walked towards the wooded part of the Common I noticed something odd about the trees. They were completely still, with no movement in the leaves and branches, appearing to resemble a painted backdrop and everywhere seemed unnaturally quiet. I walked on into the trees and suddenly all hell broke loose. I could feel movement, violent movement, all around me. I felt that horses were rearing up almost on top of me and I could hear neighing, shouts and the clash of metal so close that I threw my arms over my head to protect myself from I knew not what, as there was absolutely nothing to see. As I whirled round to get away, there in front of me with his back to a tree sat a man. He was wearing a leather cap and jerkin, boots and some sort of leggings and he had a bow and arrows. He was holding his head in his hands and I could tell he was wounded and in pain. As I looked at him he began to fade and I realised that I could see the trunk of the tree through him and seconds later he had vanished. Somehow I found myself out of the trees with the feel of the breeze on my face and the sound of birds and the traffic on the Harpenden Road just as usual. My dog came running towards me and we walked home, as I tried to come to terms with what

> had happened and find some rational explanation for it. Nothing like that has ever happened again and I visit Bernards Heath often, but I have never forgotten the day when I really believe I may have walked into a re-enactment of part of that Shrove Tuesday battle so long ago.

A remarkable encounter with another world, which I am convinced was a rare 'time slip'. Betty was somehow transported back to Bernards Heath as it was in 1461. It is reminiscent, in many respects, of 'time slips' as described by other people, the famous case of Jourdain and Moberly at Versailles (described earlier) for instance. The fact that she was in a relaxed (and therefore receptive) frame of mind while walking her dog and 'idly wondering' about the second battle of St Albans is most interesting. Betty's observation that the scene wasn't quite right somehow, with 'the painted backdrop of the trees', and the 'unnatural quiet' have a certain resonance. 'Retrocognition of the past' would seem to be an appropriate category in which to fit this particular experience.

ST ALBANS SCHOOL

The Abbey Gateway in Romeland is part of St Albans School and the Gateway was once the site of a prison (for some 500 years). At least one schoolboy has heard strange sounds, including screams, from this vicinity. More recent ghostly sounds have been linked to a long dead caretaker who served the school for much of his life. When the old biology department was closed down, prior to its demolition, the distinctive sound of hobnailed boots was heard on the stairs by the master who locked up the place for the final time before its closure. The teacher was certain that he was alone yet it was as if the caretaker's ghost was returning to say goodbye...

A MEDLEY OF MANIFESTATIONS

We have seen many reports that St Albans Cathedral is haunted and in a later chapter we will look at haunted pubs, when it will be clear that the city has a host of haunted hostelries as well. This contributes to proving that the city of St Albans is deserving of its number five position in the top ten most haunted towns in the UK. As well as the Cathedral and the many pubs (and ex-pubs) there are many other buildings in charming, history-steeped St Albans which harbour 'uninvited guests'. The new City Hall, the Alban Arena, is built on land that once formed the garden of the Grange, previously mentioned. In the 1980s at the City Hall, following a mayoral banquet, a manager was working alone when he heard someone pass by his office door. He wondered if a guest had been inadvertently left behind after everyone else had gone, so he got up to check and met a woman in a long grey dress who disappeared in front of him. Had he witnessed the ghost of Dorothy Osborne? There were those, like one time Town Clerk Betty Entwhistle, who thought so. The City Hall stood on land once graced by Dorothy's large gardens, which surrounded her old home, the Grange. These gardens had their own courtyard entrance and were much admired during her lifetime.

In the late 1970s Paul Rolfe lived in a flat above the St Albans Antique Centre and he was bothered by the sound of running water, which used to wake him up at night. He would get up to find that his kitchen taps had turned themselves on. On one occasion he returned home at one o'clock in the morning, after a night out with friends, to see, 'the lime-coloured, translucent apparition of a woman in a lace dress'. She seemed to float a couple of feet above the floor as she glided away from him down the corridor before disappearing through the end wall.

The Gables, which became a branch of Laura Ashley, is one of the oldest buildings in the city, but before Laura Ashley took over it was home to a branch of Boots the Chemists. Even during the Second World War the place had a sinister reputation, particularly the top floor. Stock in the shop was sometimes found all jumbled up and in one storeroom the ghost of an elderly lady was seen. In the top floor stock room a 'Saturday girl' was frightened by the apparition of an 'evil looking man' who stood by the fireplace.

The three-storey building that occupies 17 High Street, which became the 'retro' shop, is associated with the ghostly 'corset maker'. The building dates back to 1665 and stands on part of the site of what used to be an enormous department store called Fisk's. Fisk's was demolished over thirty years ago, during the construction of Heritage Close. The tragic figure of 'the corset maker' (presumably that was her trade) is said to be the spirit of a former manager's daughter. She was kept locked in her room by her father after she fell in love with one of the young storemen. She ended up committing suicide. She was seen by some of the shopgirls and appeared in the Abbey churchyard. She also haunted Fisk's basement, to the consternation of the caretaker. Goods were reputedly still being thrown around during fairly recent times in the shops which presently occupy the site.

Stories of hauntings continue to be uncovered in St Albans, like the case which appeared in the October 2003 issue of *Hertfordshire Countryside*. David Flatau was a Londoner who, in 1965, moved to Pilgrim Close in St Albans. One of his hobbies was photography and another was looking at old houses. During a stroll around his neighbourhood he took some photographs of an interesting 200-year-old property, Park Cottage, in Park Street Lane. It was an attractive building, of half-timbered construction with a leaning chimneystack and it had an acre of gardens at the back of it. When he received his developed photographs Mr Flatau was surprised to find a mysterious figure standing in an upper window of Park Cottage because he knew that the owners were away on an extended holiday! He checked and found out that no one else was residing at the old cottage at the time the photograph was taken. Mr Flatau carefully checked and the figure could be clearly seen on the negative as well. He showed me the photograph and the 'person' at the window seems to have a bandage around their head and to be standing sideways on; to the right of the figure some ties hanging up are clearly visible. The photographer remembered seeing the ties but there was certainly no figure in the window when he took his photograph.

David Flatau mentioned the strange incident to a man who was walking his dog and this passer-by told the photographer that late at night he had occasionally heard laughter coming from the back gardens of Park Cottage, when he knew it to be empty. He further admitted that his dog refused to walk on that side of the road and it was rumoured that a murder had been committed at Park Cottage in the past. Yet one more strange St Albans story.

CHAPTER SIX

VILLAGES OF THE UNEXPLAINED

HERTFORDSHIRE'S MOST HAUNTED VILLAGE… DATCHWORTH

Datchworth is an impressive village, a completely different world to the bustling town of Knebworth, which lies just a mile away to the north. Winding country lanes, ponds, bluebell woods, ancient greens, acres and acres of open farmland and beautiful houses tucked away down sweeping drives typify this rural retreat. It is not surprising that boxing promoter Frank Warren and film critic Barry Norman have chosen to live here. Datchworth is also an ancient village; in 969 it was known as Decewrthe, which later became Daceuuorde (meaning enclosure of a man called Daecca) by the time of the Domesday Book in 1086. Datchworth is a scattered community of 'Greens' – Datchworth Green, Bulls Green and Burnham Green (as well as Mardleybury) which indicates the clearance and cultivation of woodland after the Domesday were compiled. It is also acknowledged to be Hertfordshire's most haunted village. Their final journey was made by cart, along Rectory Lane to the churchyard where their emaciated bodies were buried in a mass grave.

There are at least three well-known haunted lanes around Datchworth. One is Hollybush Lane where a red-headed woman, wearing bright clothing, is said to haunt a family home here, and her appearance is accompanied by the sound of tinkling bells. Hawkins Hall Lane is frequented by the ghost of a little old lady who happens to be headless! She has been seen on a number of occasions in the evening, shuffling along in what has been described as a purposeful way. If seen from behind she merely seems stooped with age but if met head on (sorry, I couldn't resist it!) it is plain that she has no head. Legend has it that in the nineteenth century an old woman hanged herself with a piece of wire in her Knebworth cottage following the sudden death of her husband. What has not been forthcoming is what her connection was with Hollybush Lane. Bury Lane, close by, has a haunted house too, where the family have reported a dark shape seen flitting past the back window. The man of the house once had a clear sighting of an old man peering through this same window and hurried out to confront him but found no trace of anyone outside.

The White Horse at Burnham Green is only one of two pubs in the county to be named after a ghost (the other being The Wicked Lady at Wheathampstead). During the English Civil War Cromwell's troops caught and beheaded one of the king's men at his farm in the Burnham Green area. They then tried to take away his fine white horse as a prize but the magnificent animal put up such a struggle that they beheaded it too. Afterwards there were sightings of a headless white horse galloping down the lane from Burnham Green. Villagers say that animals are wary of Whitehorse Lane to this day.

I decided to do my own investigations to see if the title of 'most haunted village' was really deserved. A contact was able to confirm that the hauntings continued in Datchworth as one of his closest friends had a brush with the unexplained in the village. It was around 1990 and the friend, Graham Young, a Hertfordshire man in his early twenties, was driving through Burnham Green late one night. Not far from The White Horse pub a horse and rider came galloping up behind him. Graham pulled over into the bank of the narrow lane, to let the horseman pass by. Horse and rider continued on their way, galloping past the now stationary car. The driver glanced at his dashboard to discover that it was now 11.45pm, strangely late for someone to be out riding these dark and narrow lanes. He looked up again to see that both horse and rider had completely disappeared. Only then did he realise that what he had actually seen was a ghost. Sightings of the ghostly horseman are extremely rare, and over a twenty-year period there have been only three or four recorded.

One of the strangest incidents that I investigated in Datchworth occurred in the 1980s on the Bramfield Road between Bramfield and Bulls Green. A young man by the name of Archer was driving along here when suddenly a woman in white, wearing Victorian clothes, stepped out into the road. Archer braked hard, but a collision was unavoidable. He brought the car to a shuddering halt a little further down the road, near the site of a Roman villa. He turned around to see a man emerge from the woods, pick up the fallen woman and carry her back off the road. Archer raced back to the spot, about a hundred yards from Clibbon's Post, opposite some woodland known as 'The Block', but there was no trace whatsoever of either the woman or the man. I discussed the case with gamekeeper Barry Davies, whose mother lived at Burnham Green. Barry knew the witness well and was able to confirm that Archer hadn't been drinking when he saw the apparitions, was certainly not the type to invent such a story and had never been able to understand his unwanted unearthly experience.

Datchworth Green has always been popular for both cricket games and the June Fête but at the east end stands a grim reminder of harsher times, a whipping post. Vagrants who didn't want to work in the parish would receive a whipping and this post was last used in 1665 for the public flogging of two vagrants. Nearby stood both stocks and a cage, but no trace of them remains now. Datchworth Green is also associated with several different hauntings. A ghostly old woman has been seen pushing a barrow and collecting firewood at this spot. Another female phantom wears an old fashioned dress and appears to float above ground level; she is also sometimes seen standing by the swings. A woman walking beside the Green one evening heard what sounded like a coach and horses racing along behind her. She turned around but could see nothing to account for the noise, which continued to get louder. Instinctively she backed into the hedge to experience a rushing wind, galloping hoofbeats, rattling coachwork and jingling harnesses – without the physical presence of a coach...

'Pettits' is a house on the Green that is also haunted by odd sounds; footsteps have been heard on the stairs and pacing from room to room when there is nobody about to account for them.

The Plough public house, beside the Green, was the scene of a strange story from more recent times. The landlady was plagued by the ghost of a man seen in her mirror, so she went to a clairvoyant for advice. She was informed that she had a ghostly admirer named 'Jacques', who had lived in the 1700s. Presumably the clairvoyant helped this lost soul to move on. Mirrors are thought by some people to reflect electromagnetic energy, which may be what spirits use to manifest themselves. Theoretically, if two mirrors faced each other they might magnify this energy to create some kind of 'energy portal' that ghosts can use both for travel and for manifestation.

A Roman road, edged with ash and oak trees, skirts the south side of Datchworth Green and at one corner it approaches a quaint thatched cottage, 'Hopkyns Hoo', built as a farmhouse in 1570. Sited where three old green lanes meet, it boasts a duck pond in the garden which is the remnant of a moat that surrounded the farmhouse and its outbuildings. This charming period dwelling has survived the threat of demolition, which was considered after the First World War as the property had been left empty and had fallen into disrepair. The main internal timbers were found to be in passable condition, so the place was reprieved. Residents at 'Hopkyns Hoo' have had some strange incidents which suggest poltergeist activity. The house's burglar alarm has gone off quite regularly even after being turned off and household items have completely disappeared from time to time.

Descendants of the Datchworth villagers who allowed the Eaves family to starve to death in abject poverty 240 years ago are to right a great wrong by putting up a memorial plaque in their Garden of Remembrance in 2009. Parish officers had tried to cover up the deaths but Philip Thicknesse, a former soldier, discovered villagers attempting to bury the bodies before an inquest could take place. Thicknesse began a campaign to highlight the plight of the family but no memorial was ever built. Thicknesse described the deaths in a pamphlet: 'These four unhappy persons died a more miserable and cruel death than the felons who we broke on the wheel or those who are tortured to death by the Inquisition in Spain or Portugal.' He ended the account by saying that the story was 'so shocking to humanity and so alarming in this Christian country'. His pamphlet was rediscovered recently at the British Library by the Royal Society of Chemistry, which was conducting research into the relationship between chemistry and food. The society contacted the Reverend Coralie McClusky at Datchworth, who agreed to give a sermon on the Eaves' story and to record the family's names and the date of their deaths on a plaque to show the village's respect. I wouldn't be at all surprised if the appearances of the ghostly cart with its load of dead bodies ceased after the unveiling of that plaque.

MARDLEYBURY

Mardleybury and Mardley Heath are part of Datchworth's scattered community. They have roads with names redolent of the highwayman, like Turpin's Ride, Hangman's Lane and the viewpoint Robbery Bottom Lane; not far away is Hanging Hill Wood. In Bramfield Wood there lived the legendary witch with the colourful name of Sally Rainbow, but her intentions were decidedly dark. She made a comfortable living by taking money from local farmers in return for not putting the 'evil eye' on their cattle, an early form of the protection racket!

Overlooking Mardleybury Pond is ancient Mardleybury Manor House, scene of a medley of manifestations. Clothes get thrown around, objects get moved, pictures drop off walls, the smell of incense wafts about, crunching, bangs and heavy breathing sounds echo through the property. On one occasion some very heavy flooring was moved about, yet the owners continued to assert that 'it was a friendly presence'. Mardleybury Pond is reputedly haunted by a long-haired woman wearing a flowing gown or cloak, usually seen by lone travellers. The British Psychic and Occult Society organised a much publicised night vigil here in 1984. A misty white figure was seen at 4.15am, hovering briefly above the water at the far end of the pond. A photograph was taken but no figure showed up in the developed print. On the sharp bend leading to the pond motorists have been forced to brake hard on seeing 'the pond lady' suddenly appear in front of them. A Welwyn man encountered the spook as he approached the turning for Woolmer Green. Anxious to avoid hitting what he perceived to be a woman in his path he swerved off the road and collided with a tree. I would dearly have loved to see the insurance report form, wouldn't you?

In calm, cold weather, with the chill of early morning, ghostly wisps of 'steam' can often be seen hovering over ponds. They rise slowly upwards before vanishing into thin air as mysteriously as they first appeared. This phenomenon is called 'steam fog'. In autumn, calm waters are still relatively warm. They give off heat and moisture into the cold air above. Just a few inches above the water's surface the warm air cools off and the moisture contained within it condenses into tiny droplets of water, which is what we see as fog. As the fog slowly climbs upwards it mixes with drier air, the water droplets evaporate and the fog vanishes. Is this, perhaps, the solution to the Mardleybury Pond ghost?

CURIOUS CROP CIRCLES

Wiltshire is the county most associated with crop circle phenomena in Great Britain, but 2006 was an exceptional year for Hertfordshire, when three different crop circle sites were reported in the county. One of these was seen at Datchworth, on 9 July. It consisted of ten circles of increasing size which formed a 'T' shaped design. Those who make a study of crop circles are known as 'croppies', or more formally, as Cereologists (from Ceres, goddess of cereal crops). Cereologists will tell you that the history of crop circles in this country began in Hertfordshire. The earliest crop circle, known as the 'Mowing Devil', was described in a pamphlet of 1678. It tells of spiralling circles that appeared in a field one night and which were said to be the work of the devil. Rather than being flattened, however, the stalks were cut and arranged. There is a woodcut illustration of the field being mowed by a devil with a scythe, accompanied by a text relating how it happened. When a farmer asked a neighbour to mow the oats in his 3½ acre field, the poor man 'endeavour'd to sell the sweat of his brows and the marrow of his bones at as dear a rate as reasonably he might... some sharp words had passed. The irritated farmer with a stern look... told the poor man, "That the Devil should mow his oats before he should have anything to do with them".' That night, locals saw the farmer's field 'to be all of a flame, and so continued for some space, to the great consternation of those that beheld it'. Cereologists noted that the event is recorded as having taken place in August, which tallies with the timing of most modern crop circles and many of them are discovered in oat fields. Since then thousands of crop circles have appeared in Britain. As well as the 2006 Datchworth formation there was another one at Aston, near Shephall, also in Hertfordshire, in early July of that same year. This was a series of seven circles increasing in size, arranged in a line. The previous month a mysterious set of circles connected by narrow pathways appeared in the Knebworth area of Hertfordshire, but what did it all mean, how was it created?

Dr Terence Meadon's studies of crop circles have led him to postulate what has come to be described as the Plasma Vortex Theory. This states that crop circles are formed by a spiralling vortex of wind which produces atmospheric electricity. This flattens the crop into the familiar configuration of a circle, which has been confirmed by some eyewitnesses. These witnesses have also reported hearing a high pitched noise and experiencing localised static electricity, which made their hair stand on end. This could explain some crop circles but it is unlikely to fit in with contemporary developments. Since 1991 crop circle patterns have become far too intricate and complex to fit in with the 'spiralling vortex of wind' hypothesis. Croppies' videos have shown strange balls of light flying about recently formed crop circles in daylight and this phenomenon is also not adequately explained by the Plasma Vortex Theory. These balls of light are just one or two metres in diameter.

An earlier crop circle appeared in 2004, on the Hertfordshire/Bedfordshire border, at Hexton in Hertfordshire. This was close to both the Icknield Way and the Iron Age hillfort of Ravensburgh Castle. The formation was seen in a cornfield during the summer months. It was of the geometric circular type with six triangular points, some 43 metres in diameter, situated in a cornfield. The whole area is laden with ancient burial grounds. Was this man-made, another hoax corn circle? Researcher Colin Andrews conducted a two-year investigation into crop circle hoaxing. His conclusion was that 80% of all circles studied showed 'unassailable' signs of having been man-made but he could not account for the other 20%. Crop circles and their accompanying balls of light remain an enigma.

SARRATT

Sarratt village lies to the north of Rickmansworth and it is a village of curiosities. Its place name is certainly curious, over the centuries it has changed probably more times than any other in the whole of Hertfordshire. Originally known as Syret, it later became Syreth in the eleventh to the thirteenth centuries. It did not rate a mention in the Domesday Book, which implies that the land did not produce any profit for the king. A clue may be derived from the Old English word 'steret', meaning 'dry or barren place'. By the sixteenth century, after three more variations to the name, it became Sarrett, only to change again in the seventeenth century when it finally became Sarratt. It is believed that Sarratt lay on a drovers' route where they could rest their sheep; their animals could feed on the grass and drink from the ponds on the village green. Gradually Sarratt embraced the modern world, and in the early 1920s a water supply was laid on and in 1932 electricity replaced candle power. The twelfth-century parish church is another curiosity, standing a mile south of the village, at Church End, rather than at its heart. It is situated on a former Roman cemetery, amidst a veritable maze of field paths, close to the border of Buckinghamshire. In the centre of the village was a pub, The Cock Inn, a manor house and a row of early nineteenth-century Gothic style almshouses. Legend has it that the twelfth-century church builders found it impossible to construct the place of worship near the village green because each morning, after work had begun, the stones and other building materials were found moved down the long hill to a different site, a mile away. Eventually these superstitious folk took it as a sign that 'a higher authority' was trying to make a point, so the church was finally erected in its present position.

The attractiveness of Sarratt has been recognised in more recent times with the award of Best Kept Village, in 1982. It retains its long-wide village green with houses surrounding it. Cottages, council houses, flats and bungalows blend together in a fusion of old and new properties. There is still a pond, a dell and an old water pump that have all been here for many generations. The May Day Fair is another strong link with the past as it continues, as it has done for hundreds of years, to fill the village with visitors, music and a cheerful hubbub.

Sarratt's Rosehall case deserves a special mention because it was the very first haunted place to come to the attention of Britain's 'King of the Ghost Hunters', Peter Underwood, who lived in Hertfordshire for the first twenty-eight years of his long life. The author of forty-six books on ghosts and other subjects, Peter heard his first true ghost story as a child, about his maternal grandparents' home, Rosehall, a famously haunted seventeenth-century farmhouse which stood on the site of a twelfth century manor house. Peter Underwood wrote about it in his autobiography, *No Common Task*. The story begins in November 1897 when a traveller was taken in by his friends. He had braved a horse-ride of several hours' duration, undertaken in the teeth of a particularly bad storm, all the way from London. After his cold, wet, exhausting journey he quickly fell asleep but was soon awakened by the barking of dogs. He overheard his host opening the window in his adjoining bedroom and calling out to calm his animals. The traveller fell asleep once more but was awakened again, this time by heavy pressure on his feet. The dying embers of the fireplace illuminated the smartly dressed figure of a man in a blue coat with shiny gilt buttons. The man was stooping and supporting himself on the bedstead. The traveller couldn't see the man's head as it was obscured by the four poster bed's curtains. It occurred to him that it might be his host come to visit him, although it seemed unlikely. He raised himself up and was just about to address this nocturnal visitor when the figure passed on and disappeared. He got out of bed and searched the room; his door was still locked so he went back to bed. It was now after two in the morning and sleep would not come to him for the remainder of the night. The next morning the guest was asked how he had slept, so he told his story to his hosts. They then admitted that the bedroom was allegedly haunted by the spirit of a headless man, although they themselves had never seen the ghost. They were sorry that their guest's sleep had been disturbed but there had been no other room available. A short time later the traveller was dining with some ladies and he related his strange tale to them. He was interrupted by another lady who had stayed at the same farmhouse and she corroborated his story, having had exactly the same experience. It was her belief that many people had seen this same ghost, said to be the spirit of a man, murdered and decapitated in that very bedroom some years in the past.

Peter Underwood's enquiries revealed that in the nineteenth century a prayer meeting had been held at Rosehall to 'lay' the ghost as it had been particularly active at that time. An unusual feature of this case was that the apparition was never ever seen by the owners of the house but only by strangers who were visiting. When he was the Ghost Club's President, Peter Underwood revisited Rosehall, in 1962. Other members of the society accompanied him and three of them, without prior knowledge of which room it was reputed to be, correctly identified the haunted bedroom. The headless phantom stopped appearing many years ago but recent occupants of Rosehall have declared that vestiges of the haunting linger on, with 'uncomfortable feelings' about the place and the disinclination of animals to venture upstairs.

ALDBURY

On the road from Aldbury village to nearby Tring the sounds of horses hooves and the jingle of harness bells have been heard on occasion and at least one motorist, during a late night journey, claimed to have seen a phantom coach 'in a blaze of light' beside the road at Two Waters. It is believed to be the coach and horses that was owned by Simon Harcourt, the long dead Lord of Aldbury. More often the ghostly conveyance has been heard rather than seen by local people. Signalmen used to report the Harcourt coach, complete with a huge dog running alongside it, crossing the railway tracks between the signal box and the railway line to Tring Station. A late night traveller returning home from Tring Station encountered an extremely large dog, of a breed that was unfamiliar to him. He attempted to pat the animal but his hand went straight through the hound. This may have been Lord Harcourt's ghostly Talbot, an extinct breed of dog. It was a big, strong beast, used for hunting and tracking. They were popular in coaching times when their role was to deter highwaymen. Talbots would happily trot alongside their masters' coaches, which they would loyally guard with their lives. On at least three separate occasions a man on a fine white horse has been seen by different witnesses. An older woman, a young woman and a man have all reported seeing this imposing figure on the road near Tring Station. It is thought that these were all manifestations of the well-travelled spirit of Simon Harcourt.

WILLIAN

Willian was a village before the arrival of Letchworth Garden City, which has now swallowed up its tiny neighbour. The post office at Willian is an extremely old building. Sheila and Bob Leverett moved in around 1991 and made considerable alterations to the layout as well as having a major clearout. Late one evening, after a hard day's work, as they sat relaxing in their lounge, they saw the figure of a smartly dressed little boy, wearing a bow tie. The 'child' disappeared as swiftly as he had appeared. Then objects went missing around the house only to reappear in different locations. Georgina and Jessica, two of the Leveretts' daughters were frightened by the phenomena they experienced at the old post office. Doors that had stood open would suddenly close behind their backs and sounds of ghostly talking and giggling were heard. They saw everything moved off a shelf and a picture flew off the wall with such force that shards of glass landed on the nearby mattress, yet the picture's hook was still in place on the wall. The Leveretts decided to go for a late night walk around the village one time and were mystified to hear the sounds of excited children playing at one in the morning. The noises were clearly heard and they came from the grounds of a private residence, which had once been the village school. The couple were even more startled by the sight of a little girl standing behind the hedge in what had formerly been the school playground.

Next door is the Fox pub, which is believed to date from the sixteenth century and at one time it was a private residence. I spoke with Lorraine Russell in 2005, when she was the manager, and she had been there for three years at that time. She told me that after eighteen months at the pub she had encountered a ghostly visitor. Lorraine was cleaning some pictures in the hallway when the ghost of a woman appeared, the vision continued down the hallway and passed right through the startled landlady. I asked her what it was like when a ghost passed through you, never having had this experience myself. She replied that it was 'a warm feeling' rather than the cold chill that is usually reported in similar circumstances. Lorraine went on to say that at least three other people had sightings of this ghost, in the kitchen, the passageway and coming down the stairs. Everyone agreed that this was a 'calm presence' and a tidy one; it moved ashtrays which had been left on the bar into neat stacks. Andy Thompson, who later told me about his paranormal experiences at a flat in Hitchin, had also, at one time, worked in the Fox. He related his brushes with the ghost at this pub. He saw beer mats which had been piled up by some unknown hand and he recalled the bad feelings felt by other bar staff when they had to go down into the cellar, an 'awareness' that they were not alone down there. He had seen for himself the ghostly lady walking down the stairs. He had also heard about the light bulbs which were known to fly out of the chandelier for no obvious reason. Steve Banks had managed the pub with Lorraine and he had caught the ghost's reflection in the mirror as he combed his hair. In a 2004 sighting of the ghost it was described as 'small and misty, about 5ft tall.'

Letchworth Hall Hotel is not far from Willian and it is another establishment with its own ghost. In this case it is, reputedly, the late Reverend William Alington, who died in the 1860s. I was informed that his ghost has been seen in the ballroom and the landing by a number of witnesses. Allegedly the churchman was suspended from office for heavy drinking and for 'behaving inappropriately' with some of his parishioners.

LILLEY

Four miles west of Hitchin on the A505 is the 'village of mysteries', Lilley, which is situated on the edge of the Chiltern Hills. It lies just inside north Hertfordshire but it is hard by the Bedfordshire border, a few miles from Luton. It was home to the famed alchemist Johann Kellerman, who lived here in the nineteenth century. Accounts of him

The Lilley Arms, Lilley. Former landlord Tom Connisbee's ghost is still felt in the bar. The attic and the barn are also haunted.

vary greatly; on the one hand he has been described as the secretive recluse, rarely seen outside his own home and it was rumoured that he lived in squalor in one room. He spoke with a strong foreign accent and it was claimed that he guarded the privacy of his large house with mantraps and barricades, while he toiled away at the furnace in his cellar. His ceaseless quest was to turn base metals into gold. Other accounts described him as a kind man, willing to help his fellow villagers in distress. On one occasion he heard of a party of gypsies who missed their way in the snow and ended up in a dell near the turning to Lilley Hoo, Kellerman had them dug out. He boasted that he could turn mercury into gold, but he was eventually chased out of the village and it is said that he died in poverty in Paris.

Lilley's air of mystery was enhanced by tale of the haunting of Fanny Ebbs, around 1895. Fanny ran a sweetshop and one night she saw the ghost of a man appear through her bedroom wall, he then turned and walked down the stairs. Fanny followed the apparition through the shop and into her kitchen. She watched, dumbfounded, as it went to the brick fireplace, knelt down and took up the hearth bricks to reveal a hidden large black kettle. From this kettle the ghost counted out scores of gold sovereigns and then counted them back again before revealing a second pot, which was similarly checked before both pots were replaced. After the spirit had disappeared through the bedroom wall the sweetshop owner searched the hearth. Fanny found the miser's hoard, which she took, but put everything else back as it had been before. The ghost returned the following night but finding all its treasure gone it never returned. Fanny Ebbs continued to run her sweetshop, but when she died the remains of her fortune were left to the people of the parish.

By far the biggest mystery in Lilley is its haunted pub, The Lilley Arms, which was originally called the Sugar Loaf before the name was changed to The Sowerby Arms in 1852 out of respect for the lord of the manor. It wasn't until the Great War that it became The Lilley Arms. It deserves its reputation as one of the most haunted pubs in north Hertfordshire. My investigation group, APIS, held our 2004 Christmas Dinner here, in the atmospheric old Crooked Barn, which we had all to ourselves. It was the ideal opportunity to talk to Sylvia Brown, who, together with her husband Peter, has been a licensee at the pub for over twenty years. She had a fund of stories to tell me about the hauntings and so did her staff. Sylvia had been cleaning her attic one day when she knocked over a bowl of walnuts, which she picked up and returned to the shelf before resuming her cleaning. When her back was turned to the shelf she heard some taps and clicks behind her. She turned around to see that the walnuts had been carefully placed in a straight line on the attic floor! I told her that this 'placement' was typical of poltergeist behaviour.

In 2001 a team of paranormal investigators stayed for three nights at The Lilley Arms. There were six investigators including two psychic mediums and they catalogued a considerable collection of phenomena. A cold draught constantly played around the saloon bar as well as the upstairs living room. Continuous paranormal activity caused Sylvia difficulty in sleeping for the three nights of the research. The psychic mediums saw orbs of light in both the bar downstairs and upstairs as well. It was their belief that these were the first stages of ghost manifestations. In the dining room, the investigators witnessed a Christmas decoration which was pinned above the bar begin to twist before falling down as if pulled by invisible hands. The Browns explained that there had always been difficulty in putting up, and keeping up, Christmas decorations in the saloon bar, which later became the dining room. A photograph was taken which showed an orb near to some other decorations. Everyone felt a chill in the air that was so strong that their breath could clearly be seen. Immediately after the photograph was taken three people witnessed the decorations snapping in the exact spot where the orb had appeared.

A séance was also held during the extended vigil and Sylvia went into a semi-trance, seemingly channelling the spirit of Tom Connisbee, landlord of the inn some 200 years previously. One of the mediums told 'Tom' that he was in the wrong century. Sylvia replied, in a masculine voice, 'No, you are in the wrong century!'

Some frightening events occurred in the Crooked Barn, behind the pub. A medium asked if anyone had committed suicide in there, with that the video cameraman felt 'his whole face being stretched back'. He tried to describe his weird experience later and said that it was as if something was all over him, making him taller. It scared him so much that he had to stop filming as the temperature plummeted and the mediums saw a tall, gaunt figure lying on the floor.

So who are the ghosts that haunt the Lilley Arms? They are many and they are varied. The Sugar Loaf (as it was originally called) was built in 1705 as a coaching inn. One of the earliest landlords has already been mentioned, Tom Connisbee, who was here from 1780 onwards and he may be here still, as he is believed to be one of the ghosts of The Lilley Arms! He even has his own seat, 'Tom's Chair', in the bar/restaurant, not only has a ghost been seen here but candles have been found inexplicably alight. 'Tom's ghost' is blamed for poking people in the back. Another ghost is said to be that of Frances Mitchell, she ran a millinery business at Stotfold in 1786. She often arrived by coach from Hitchin to see Tom Connisbee. Other ghosts that allegedly haunt the inn include John, a handyman when he was alive, a small deaf and dumb girl, an eighteenth-century postman, a former kitchen hand and 'Rose Anne', a small girl who plays in the orchard. In recent years a six-year-old boy who visited the pub one summer reportedly saw a shepherd standing in the yard, complete with 'see-through dog'. Sylvia wondered if Johann Kellerman is amongst the motley crew of Lilley Arms phantoms. My researches suggest that he was either chased out of the village or that he was murdered (given that he claimed to turn base metal into gold this would not be too unlikely). It has been said that he disappeared from his home without a trace. His laboratory was just across the road from the pub and it has been surmised that there may have been a tunnel from his house to the cellars of the Lilley Arms. It is just one more mystery that may never be solved in this village of mysteries.

WHEATHAMPSTEAD

Wheathampstead, near Harpenden, is believed by historians to be the likely former capital of the Catuvellauni (Celtic for 'expert warrior') tribe. An unsolved murder may be the cause behind a well-known local haunting at Marshall's Heath Lane. Murder victims quite often seem to return as ghosts. In December 1957 seventeen-year-old Ann Noblett disappeared after getting off a bus in Lower Luton Road. Her frozen body was found the following month in a wood at Whitwell. Detectives established that she had been strangled and stripped then redressed in the same clothes before being hidden inside an industrial freezer for about a month. She was discovered with her hands across her chest, still wearing her glasses and with no money missing from her purse. No motive for the killing was ever found. Seventeen years later, in 1974, what may have been Anne's ghost was making its presence felt at a plant hire business situated on the former pig farm, which was close to where the young woman had lived. Workers at the plant hire firm were plagued by odd incidents – locked doors would somehow open themselves and one man saw a young girl playing at the end of the sheds. He approached her to have a talk but when he reached the shed she had simply disappeared. He was certain that there had been nowhere for the girl to have gone but past him. Another worker reported that something unseen had touched his head while he was feeding the cat. This pet was noted at the plant hire farm for sometimes arching its back and hissing at some presence that was not visible to humans.

HINXWORTH

Situated some 3 miles to the north of Baldock, Hinxworth is the most northerly village in Hertfordshire. It is an out of the way sort of place yet the roaring traffic on the teeming A1 is only about a mile away. It was the rural aspect of the place which attracted the writer Monica Dickens, who lived here from 1947 to 1951. Hinxworth Place is similarly tucked away from the village with which it shares its name, as I can attest, having accessed it by cycling across the fields on my mountain bike one summer's day. I saw an old manor house with a cobbled courtyard and some large pieces of statuary in the gardens. The statues were the work of John W. Mills, who still lives in the greater part of the house. It seemed like a good location for a haunted house, in a rather isolated spot which, on one side, was surrounded by open fields as far as the eye could see. It has been much altered since the first building was erected here in 1390 but its ghostly inhabitants still make their presence felt, I was told as much by Mrs Mills about five years ago. On autumn nights screams and thuds have been heard, coming from the direction of the stairs, and a baby's crying as well as the sound of water gushing from a squeaky pump in the yard – these unexplained sounds were reported in 1968. It is thought that these noises are the replay of a tragedy that happened in the 1800s. One evening the owners of Hinxworth Place went out to the church and left their children in the care of a nursemaid. The young son thought it would be fun to dress up in a sheet and to make weird noises in order to frighten his sister. He succeeded only too well, with tragic consequences. The nursemaid attacked 'the ghost' with a poker, causing the brother to fall downstairs screaming. The cook tried to help the lad by putting his head under the pump and using the water to revive him, but he died. The sound of heavy footfall was also reported in the 1960s when Hinxworth Place was divided up and sold. They were heard in an upper corridor and seemed to continue moving along outside the existing house. Old plans of the property were consulted and they confirmed that there used to be a wing with a staircase at the point where the footsteps were heard descending the non-existent stairs. Hinxworth House is also well known for its mysterious monks. On several occasions a procession of monks has been seen, walking through the walls of the house, and a single monk has been observed in the porchway leading to the garden. I looked into the history of this medieval site and learned that Cistercian monks, from Pipewell Monastery in Northamptonshire, once lived here.

CHAPTER SEVEN

'LOCAL' HAUNTS

BALDOCK

For a small town Baldock has always been big on pubs, at one time there were as many as a dozen inns in what was regarded as something of a rural backwater. Over the years many have closed their doors to the public and have been turned into desirable residences for the upwardly mobile. In my lifetime the Eagle, the Bull's Head and the Chequers are three such lost locals. A pub that survives and that I know well, having enjoyed a few real ales here, is The Cock, at the end of the High Street. I talked with John and Lone (who is Danish) the couple who manage this attractive old inn. The couple's suspicions were aroused by their dogs, which were usually well behaved but would bark loudly and excitedly at a cupboard in an upstairs room that remains cold whatever the weather may be. Downstairs in the bar bottles left at the front of the shelves will, overnight, end up right at the back. A picture at one end of the bar was seen to fly off the wall at right angles and smash on the floor.

The George and Dragon has ceased trading as a pub but it is a still a local landmark, situated on the corner of Church Street (recently pedestrianised as part of the town enhancements) and Hitchin Street. It was about fourteen years ago, when Green King had the pub up for sale and it was empty apart from one of the brewery's travelling managers. His job was to act as a caretaker when one of the company's pubs became empty. We got talking in the nearby Rose and Crown and I happened to mention that I had heard that it was haunted. He then went on to tell me that the George and Dragon was also haunted, as he had discovered for himself. While he was alone there at night he regularly heard noises from the upstairs rooms. He knew that the building was secure and that he was the only occupant but he still had to check out the source of the noises. He never found a trace of any earthly visitors. I asked him if he ever got scared, he shook his head and said that it never bothered him, he was used to all manner of strange happenings in his line of work. There is a much older story associated with the George and Dragon and it concerns a notorious highwayman, 'Shock Oliver'. In the sixteenth century he terrorised the neighbourhood, one of his crimes was to hold up two men returning from the Baldock October Fair (still held annually, but without any highwaymen). Eventually this criminal's luck ran out, he was caught and hanged at St Albans *c.* 1790. He had lived in St Neots, so his body was returned there, via Baldock, where his wife worked. She was a cook at the George and Dragon so this was where 'Shock Oliver' lay in his coffin overnight, on his final journey northward. Disturbances reported in the

George and Dragon, Baldock. Does the wraith of highwayman 'Shock' Oliver still stalk this former alehouse?

kitchen and cellar have been attributed to this highwayman's haunting. The ghost of a man has also been seen in the bar and I was interested to learn that staff referred to the ghost as 'Ollie'.

I returned to the Rose and Crown in August 2004 and met the landlord, Roger Nicholls, to find out for myself if the rumours I'd heard were true. He confirmed that the place was still very much haunted. Roger had heard his name being called when the building was empty. He also heard ghostly footsteps and the sounds of things being moved about. He told me that the Rose and Crown's ghost goes by the name of Elizabeth and she haunts room 10. Children who have stayed at the pub have confirmed this, they have even told of having played with her! Many years previously the landlord and landlady at the time had also told me that one of their bedrooms was haunted. The story was that, about a hundred years ago, a housemaid committed suicide at the inn after discovering that she was pregnant by the butcher's boy. Perhaps this was the same Elizabeth, the child-friendly ghost? Another ghost has been seen in the corridor by guests staying at the Rose and Crown; she is a white-haired old lady, wearing a long cardigan, who is there one second then gone the next. At least one landlord has felt 'eerie' in the cellar, perhaps unsurprisingly given that, some thirty years ago, a regular requested that his ashes be scattered about down here and his dying wish was complied with!

Bell House Gallery, Buntingford. Murderess Hannah Bedwell's restless spirit made its presence known here.

BUNTINGFORD

In December 2004 I was in Buntingford, looking at the medieval and Georgian houses whilst researching the town's haunted locations. I began with the Bell House Gallery in the High Street, which is one of the better-known haunted houses in this small town. The building dates back to 1450 when it was the Bell Inn, where Queen Elizabeth I stayed while travelling by coach to Cambridge. The property was divided up into three flats at one time but nowadays it is a gift shop. During the 1940s there were three flats here and all three families living in them reported unexplained events at various times of the day and night. Door handles would turn on their own, footsteps echoed in empty rooms, a baby's crying was heard and a woman's heavy sobbing too. One tenant, Tom Parker, awoke to feel an unseen heavy weight pressing down on him, rendering him incapable of movement. He described his experience, 'I struggled to get free but couldn't. At last I had the idea of trying to roll from under the weight and after what seemed hours I managed to do it.' Another tenant awoke with the sensation that he was being strangled.

After two years of suffering with these paranormal phenomena the tenants spoke to the local press and two journalists from the *Hertfordshire Mercury* persuaded them to hold a séance. The traditional upturned glass in the middle of a circle of letters of the alphabet was employed. An entity calling itself Hannah Bedwell contacted the group. She explained that she had worked at the Bell Inn and was searching for the baby she had murdered (by laying on her). She had done it because she was frightened of losing her job and being turned out. Hannah told her questioners that she was just fifteen years old and the child's father, John Price, a porter at the inn, had been killed. Hannah was arrested, imprisoned in Bedford Jail and later hanged at Newgate for infanticide. It seems that 'Hannah' was responsible for most of the paranormal activity experienced in the flats. A second spirit was contacted, this was the one said to haunt the stairs. His name was Hugh but no more information about him seems to have been recorded.

In the early 1960s Max and Beryl Hodges were tenants in one of the Bell House apartments, which were owned by Jocelyn Chapman. Max recalled that there had been a nursery in Bell House, run by Zoe Ryder, and that the children here often saw a coachman on the stairs, wearing tricorn hat, long coat and boots. Could this have been Hugh? Mrs Chapman also admitted to seeing a ghost. On one occasion she heard a door close, footsteps and then she saw the silhouette of a woman 'dressed in Gainsborough clothing' who walked into a cubby-hole that had been a staircase at one time. According to Max an exorcism was later carried out, but was it successful?

In the 1930s three local Buntingford lads had an encounter with 'ghost lights', which led them on a journey to the Crown Public House. Charles Edwards of Greenways and Samuel Clark of Bridgefoot often played out in the evenings together with their friend Fred Lee. Around 7pm one November evening the boys were strolling along Chapel End when they saw something extremely strange. In the nearby river moving lights suddenly appeared under the water in the middle of the stream. The three pals were enchanted by this wondrous sight as the bright lights rose to the surface, then moved to the river's edge and climbed the banking. The youngsters followed the progress of the lights as they crossed the road and moved towards an area known as 'Tottie's Ditch' before forming up together at the rear of the Crown Public House in a rotating circle. At this point the boys took to their heels and pelted down the lane, their wonderment suddenly turned to fear. Charles, Samuel and Fred told their strange tale to friends and family and soon a crowd had formed to investigate this phenomenon. Nothing was found but the story spread far and wide, the police were informed and gas and electricity companies checked pipes and cables in the area. There were no faults discovered to explain away the weird light show experienced by the three lads. Journalists picked up the news and carried out their own investigation but admitted that they were completely baffled.

'Ghost lights' have been reported from all over the country and are thought by some ghost hunters to be the first stage of a ghost's manifestation. This particular story is interesting for several reasons. A number of paranormal researchers hold the theory that ghosts can manifest by using the energy of the living. Children have strong bio-electrical energy fields. We don't know the ages of the three boys when they saw the 'ghost lights' but I would guess that they were probably under the age of ten. Children aged up to ten most frequently see ghosts in comparisons drawn with people across all age ranges. Here were 'three strong energy sources' available for ghosts to draw on. Water also seems to be strongly associated with ghostly activity, as first postulated by the academic, author and paranormal researcher T.C. Lethbridge back in the 1960s. My dowser friends tell me that when they locate hidden, underground water sources they also receive 'tingling sensations'. This may suggest that water contains some sort of force-field similar to that which surrounds an electrical wire. The boys described the lights as 'moving sparks'. Is it possible that these were first stage manifestations which drew their energy from the river's 'force-field' as well as the boys own bio-electric energy? Their sighting is also reminiscent of 'corpse candles' sometimes seen in rural areas. These 'dancing lights' followed the route used by coffin-bearers of times past. Another possibility suggests itself – did the boys see the spirit forms of some people who drowned in the river and whose bodies were laid out at the Crown Public House? This was the custom in the days before there were any hospitals.

In more recent years, a house in Buntingford High Street, which must remain anonymous, was the centre of paranormal activity. The incidents coincided with renovation work which was being carried out. One evening a strange young girl in a nightdress walked into the dining room and then disappeared from view while the daughter of the house was fast asleep in her bedroom. The parents searched the dining room area thoroughly but there was no trace of the uninvited guest. Their daughter's bedroom was checked; she was still sleeping soundly. The strange young girl's apparition was never seen upstairs, but it was heard. Mysterious footsteps sounded on the landing, latches lifted and doors would swing open and closed, always when the couple's own children were sleeping. Their daughter was most affected by the entity. On one occasion she climbed sleepily to the open window (with quite a drop below) but fortunately was seen in time by her mother before an accident could occur. When asked what she had been doing the child replied that 'the lady in white' had told her to get out of bed. On another occasion the daughter was pushed aside just in time to avoid being hit on the head by a heavy wall-mounted clock, which unaccountably fell from its mounting. The clock caught the girl on the shoulder, giving her a nasty scare. The kitchen was also a focus for ghostly activity, whenever the spirit's presence was felt the Rayburn's temperature would drop low and then pick up again. The kitchen door was difficult to open some mornings and the reason was because it was blocked by a child's wooden rocking horse, which had been moved there in the middle of the night. It would have been quite impossible for any member of the household to have obstructed the door and then got back upstairs again undetected and unheard. Several months later the building work was finished and the hauntings seemed to cease, everything calmed down. Then some new owners moved in and they reported that the Rayburn was up to its old tricks again during the initial months of their occupation. The adults didn't see or hear anything out of the ordinary but their small son did. On a few occasions, soon after they moved in, he came into his parents' bedroom and asked to sleep with them because 'the lady in my room won't let me go to sleep'.

STANDON

Standon lies roughly midway between Buntingford and Bishop's Stortford on the A120. This village is home to the Star Inn, a delightful little pub by the green, opposite the church. It dates back to 1550 and in the 1700s was known as the Maypole, when it provided accommodation for coach travellers. When I visited the Star in November 2004 it was being run by David and Isobel Underwood who had been here for four years. They pointed out the article about the Star that made the pages of *the Mail on Sunday* on 31 December 1989, a copy of which could be seen by visitors. Back then the landlord was Frank Spelling and his strange experience

The Star, Standon. Home of party-loving spooks from a bygone age.

dated from a night in 1972 when he was awoken at 3am by noises downstairs. When he got to the bar he was amazed to find a crowd of people in old-fashioned dress, laughing and drinking there. The men wore tricorn hats and amidst them was a strikingly attractive Latin-looking woman. In the background flute-like music could be heard. As Frank went through the door to investigate further the room reverted to silence, emptiness and normality. He turned around to go back to bed, then changed his mind. Something made him take another look as he could not believe what he had seen seconds earlier. He peered through the small window above the bar door. 'My heart almost leapt out of my body,' the landlord was quoted, 'not only were they all back again, but this time they were joined by a buxom looking wench.' He opened the door and instantly the scene changed back to an empty bar. Frank kept his uncanny encounter quiet until one day, several months later, he met a visitor who claimed to have grown up in the Star. The old lady enquired if anyone had seen the pub's ghosts lately. She then shared her own story, vividly recalling a time long ago when she had arrived back at the inn late one night, after attending a party. As she crept through the back door she was taken completely unawares by the sight of a dozen or more people in the bar. She proceeded to corroborate Frank's encounter in exact detail, down to seeing both the buxom lady and the Latin lady. This was a great relief to Frank, who at last was able to admit to someone else his unexplained experience.

I spoke with David and Isobel's staff during my November visit and they confirmed, in their own words, that the Star was 'spook central'. When the very last customer of a session is engaged in conversation at the bar it is often noticed that 'someone else' gets up and goes out, 'someone' who wasn't there before. Footsteps are frequently heard running about on the landing at various times of the day and night. These sounds are noticed by both staff and customers alike, when there is obviously nobody upstairs. This can happen when the bar is full of people and it has even been known for the spook to visit the upstairs toilet. The workers in this charming old pub are quite sanguine about their other-worldly guests and are sure that they mean no harm. Staff members have a saying, 'They have been here a lot longer than we have and they'll probably be around for a lot longer too!'

BISHOP'S STORTFORD

Bishop's Stortford came by its curious name after the manor of Esterteferd was sold by Eddeva Pulchrima, a Saxon noblewoman, in 1060. It was purchased by the Bishop of London and it became known as Bishop's Stortford. The town's most famous son was Cecil Rhodes, the founder of Rhodesia, now called Zimbabwe. Hauntings in Bishop's Stortford are concentrated into a compact area centred on the road that runs from east to west through the town. This road starts as Wind Hill, which then becomes High Street and ends as Bridge Street. The ubiquitous 'grey lady' is the ghost that haunts various sites, including several pubs along this route. I paid a visit to Bishop's Stortford in November 2004 to find out for myself. I started my investigations at the Boar's Head on Wind Hill, opposite St Michael's church. I talked with Penny Haynes, who told me that the latest odd incident had occurred eight months prior to my visit. It was late at night and Penny's brother, Patrick, had been in the bar when the PDQ machine, for processing credit card payments, went off on its own accord, printing out streams of paper. Then there were several loud bangs at the front door but when it was opened there was no trace of anyone to be seen. Next the optics above the bar began shaking very violently. I wondered if the exorcism, which had been carried out thirty years ago, had been entirely effective!

I also visited the George Inn in the High Street, the town's oldest recorded pub, and the third oldest such establishment in Hertfordshire. The present exterior appearance is the result of a Victorian renovation, but the original foundations to the building were laid in the late fourteenth century. Charles II was a frequent visitor here on his journeys to and from Newmarket. I learned that the most haunted room was room 27, where a hotel guest was said to have been murdered. When this was a coaching inn a woman had stepped out of her room onto the balcony, where she was surprised by a burglar who then stabbed her. She fell back into the room and died. The old door that allowed access to the balcony was later permanently sealed up. Guests and staff have reported a 'watchful presence', doors opening by themselves and odd noises in room 27. In 1970 a guest saw the ghost as a 'swirling grey mist around the bed' and demanded to be moved. A few years later another guest staying in room 27 looked up to see a woman in a grey gown bending over the bed with her arms raised – possibly in an attitude of pain. The guest yelled out and the figure vanished.

George Inn, Bishop's Stortford. Room 27 is haunted by a murdered woman's ghost.

Tissmans is a contender with the George Inn for the town's oldest building and the 'grey lady' has been seen both here and in the Black Lion as well as at Coopers department store, made up of three inter-linked buildings, in Bridge Street. At the time of my visit the store had very recently been taken over by Coopers. From the mid-1980s till 2004 it had been known as Maslows and it had been a Bishop's Stortford landmark. I was told that Peter Maslow had once invited two paranormal investigators down from Cambridge University to investigate paranormal phenomena at his department store. The investigators' report claimed that two ghosts haunted the premises, a 'harmless man' and a 'woman of a violent nature' – the grey lady yet again? What prompted the investigation was that staff heard footsteps when there was nobody about to account for them, experienced items mysteriously falling from shelves and felt a 'terrifying presence'. Before it was owned by Maslow the store traded under the name of Hansdcomb's from the early 1900s onwards. Reports of hauntings were prevalent during that era too. A 'figure in grey' was sighted in an upstairs room and it would disappear into the wall at the same place every time. Alterations made to this room revealed a plastered-up doorway at the spot where this 'grey figure' was seen to vanish.

The landlord's wife at the sixteenth century Cock Inn at Hockerill also reported seeing ghosts at her pub during the 1980s. She described them as a 'serving wench' and a 'man in Civil War clothing'. When the place was renovated things turned nasty. An icy chill was felt in the air, tables were hurled about and some lamps were smashed. Responding to suggestions that the restless spirits were possibly unhappy about the alterations to their former home, the landlady decked out the whole pub with displays of flowers. An unusual form of exorcism but the landlady later claimed that the hauntings had stopped as mysteriously as they had started.

TEWIN

Tewin village, east of Welwyn Garden City, off the A1000 Hertford Road is known locally as the home of pop star Marty Wilde, father of Kim Wilde, who also found fame in the music business before turning to garden designing. In the world of the paranormal Tewin is known as the home of one of Hertfordshire's most haunted pubs – the Plume of Feathers, in Upper Green Road. This is a Grade II listed building, dating from 1596 and it was once a hunting lodge for Elizabeth I. A writer called Gerry Gingell wrote about the hauntings here in the January 2004 edition of *Hertfordshire Life* magazine. Paul Sims was the manager of the Plume of Feathers at the time of the interview and he had been there for over three years. During his management he had gradually become convinced that his pub was haunted. One morning, around 9am when alone at the bar, Paul saw two butterfly corkscrews, kept on a hook in an upright post suddenly start 'swinging violently, for no good reason'. The manager had already heard numerous stories from his 'regulars' and the catalogue of phenomena was extensive. Anyone who is psychically sensitive is likely to pick up 'something' in the area of the ladies' toilet, where many people have admitted to a 'creepy feeling'. Before it was a toilet this used to be a quiet reading room, a small, out of the way nook, with books and newspapers available for customers to peruse. Close by the toilet is the entrance door to the cellar. In 1999 a female member of staff found herself trapped in the cellar, unable to open the swing door, which eventually 'just opened'. A mysterious occurrence given that the door had no handle which could have been held against the lady's attempts to open it. Long ago the cellar was used as the servants' quarters, but these rooms have been bricked up now. The ghost of a little girl has been seen at the top of the cellar stairs but her origin remains unknown.

In the seventeenth century, during alterations to the Plume of Feathers, a woman's body was discovered behind a bricked-up fireplace. It was said that she had been murdered by her husband; he had been away at sea for two years and returned to find his wife pregnant. After despatching his unfaithful spouse he disposed of her body behind the fireplace, which was then bricked up. Table 8 in the dining area is close to the fireplace and the phantom of an old man has been seen sitting here. Mark Thomas, a former manager, was working alone one day when he heard a noise near table 8. He turned around to discover that the candle on this table had relit itself. Another apparition has been seen and heard at a long table behind table 8; an old lady with long grey hair and a see-through dress who cackles at observers. An ex-member of staff told me that sometimes, when he was laying the tables, the cutlery would be swept onto the floor so that he would have to relay it. Bar staff have seen an old man leaning on the bar, 'facing the wrong way' but at one time the bar faced the other way. Much has been altered over the centuries at the Plume of Feathers; this is evident from the quirky floor layout. Certain members of staff feel that the ghosts influence them in some subtle way, making them awkward and clumsy, prone to dropping things.

The kitchen is not immune from the attentions of the spooks, the oven regularly switches itself on and when the chef's back is turned the gas is turned up so that quite a lot of soup has been burnt as a result. Lights have a habit of switching themselves on too and electrical items, generally, can be troublesome. Beer taps are opened and closed by some invisible force and shadows are seen flitting about the place, just a regular part of life in the haunted Plume of Feathers.

ST ALBANS

In keeping with its reputation as the fifth most haunted town in the country, St Albans is famous for its haunted pubs (and ex-pubs), most of them extremely old, characterful and with interesting histories. Ye Olde Fighting Cocks claims to be the oldest inhabited public house in England. It has a strange, octagonal shape and its cellar stands where the abbey used to be. A manager, who was alone in the building, was puzzled when he returned from the cellar to find the pub's keys swinging violently from a key hook, as they had been missing altogether before his visit to the cellar. One member of staff was found in a state of fear but would not discuss any of the details of his ghost sighting. Another worker was more forthcoming about his experience in 2001. He saw a number of men dressed in brown monks' habits. They were only visible as far down as their knees, when they emerged from the cellar, crossed the bar and sat down at the fireside table before dematerialising.

A building on the corner of George Street was known as the Swan Inn over 600 years ago, later it was purchased by a rich merchant and transformed into the Abbey Guest House, later still it became a hardware store before changing use again, to an antiques centre, Mayle's Corner. Eventually the premises reverted to their original use and in 1963 it was renamed the Tudor Tavern. After closing time the bar staff reported a shadow following them around and it was said that somebody was actually chased out of the pub by a ghost. There were various theories about the identity of this spectre. Some said that it was a former landlord, others said it was a former guest and yet a third opinion stated that it was a soldier who had been brought here to die during the first battle of St Albans in the War of the Roses. A manageress claimed to have seen the manifestation of a man. She described him as having, 'dark, curly hair and a beard, wearing a black tunic with a neck ruff and buttons on his sleeves'. He was seen seated at a table, leaning on one elbow and with a glass in his hand.

The Goat Inn at Sopwell Lane is another hostelry with history; in 1500 it was built as a private home with wings connected by a hall, producing an H-shaped structure. In 1578 it became an inn, providing accommodation and refreshment for the stagecoach passengers who travelled up from London. It was within sight of the gallows where many prisoners were brought for execution. One room in particular, at the back of the pub, is pervaded by an unpleasant atmosphere and unaccountable noises. From 1978 to 1986 the Goat Inn was managed by Peter Ransom, who awoke one night to see, at the bottom of his bed, 'a ghastly face, scowling and staring' in a room that had become icy cold. This room was always considered unnaturally cold and many people had sensed a presence there. On numerous occasions Ransom's guitar was moved from where he had left it by some invisible agency. A door at the pub opened and closed of its own accord and has even been known to lock itself. When the Goat Inn was renovated an ancient cellar was discovered. A director of the company that ran the pub commented that he had found it difficult to open and to close a door which led to the yard yet on his return journey he discovered that the door had swung open by itself.

A more modern pub is the King William; it is situated on the edge of St Albans and was built in 1937. Two years after it was built a ghost was seen in the bar and glasses were hurled about by invisible forces. Later sightings were more detailed, 'A tall soldier with a moustache, wearing a greenish uniform with buttons on the tunic'. As late as August 1987 the chef saw a soldier's ghost and yelled for the manager, who hurried downstairs just in time to see the manifestation before it faded away (as old soldiers are wont to do). During the Second World War this hostelry was popular with the Home Guard and the haunting was believed to be connected with one of their number.

The Blue Boar Inn at Market Place became an optician's shop but it seems that the site continues to be haunted by the ghost of a little boy. A child is said to have been crushed to death under the wheels of a coach after running out of the inn. 'Charlie, the crying boy,' so it seems, is still searching for his mother. The Blue Boar was renamed the Wellington, but still the haunting continued. A barmaid claimed that an unseen presence had stroked her hair and kissed her forehead. A room over the saloon bar reverberated with the sounds of moving furniture, although it was empty and footsteps were heard on the landing. The pumping gas for the beer has been unaccountably turned off, a favourite trick for pub ghosts. Lights would turn on and off and sleeping was made difficult by 'something' which jumped up and down on the beds (as little boys are wont to do). A sceptical customer changed his views after seeing a soda siphon rise up in front of him. 'Charlie' was not alone. One landlord's children asked him about a man that they had seen in their bedrooms, and they told their father, 'Please ask that man to go away'. Sylvia, one of the barmaids, was singled out for special attention, maybe she reminded 'Charlie' of his mother? She was tidying up one day and had placed a clean ashtray on each table before cleaning the bar, when she turned around a packet of crisps had been placed in every ashtray. The little boy's ghost was also blamed for clutching at women's skirts as well as breaking glassware. The local press picked up on the story in 1971 when new licensees were greeted with 'bottles, jugs and glasses flying from shelves and smashing on the floor'. September 1975 heralded the extensive alterations of the old Wellington to become Matthews the butcher's shop. The phenomena were undiminished, female staff complained that 'something' touched their faces. Tills were interfered with, doors slammed shut and the manager blamed the spirit for the mysterious punctures which kept occurring to his car when it was parked at the shop. A butcher claimed that he saw a small, misty figure in the cellar, which was behind the shop, and another worker reported seeing the shadowy figure of a man. Female shoppers felt a classic haunted house impression – cobwebs brushing across their faces. Some were even subjected to ghostly, chilly kisses.

One winter's morning at 5.30am a butcher called Kevin turned up for work to see a man standing, with arms folded, in the yard. This had once been the stabling area for the old pub where 'Charlie' had played centuries before. As the butcher got out of his car the man's figure simply disappeared. On another occasion a young assistant went out to the dustbins in this same yard, late one afternoon. As he passed a pile of boxes he saw a hand appear above them before they tumbled down on top of him. He was startled to find nobody about to account for pushing the boxes over and he was certain that all the other members of staff had been in the shop at the time.

With the Christopher Place development both cellar and yard were swallowed up under new shops. In the area that later became an optician's shop women felt their hair or faces being stroked by invisible hands and at least one woman said that her shirt had been pulled. In more recent times CCTV cameras have recorded cleaning staff switching off lights only for them to come on again at 4am in the empty building. Subsequent electrical checks revealed no faults of any kind.

Another of St Albans' vanished pubs was the Crown and Anchor, an inn which dated back to Tudor times but which ceased to be a pub in the 1950s and changed to an estate agents' offices, Strutt and Parker. Leo Hickish arrived at these offices early one morning to be confronted by an agitated colleague. The colleague pointed to some fresh wet footprints on the flagstone flooring at the base of the staircase. The building was empty apart from the two workmates and neither of them had wet feet or were, indeed, bare-footed. It was later surmised that these could have been the ghostly footprints of a long dead pilgrim who had visited the nearby Abbey.

In the 1990s a member of staff working upstairs was packing up, prior to leaving, when he suddenly spotted the gaunt face of a woman peering at him between two filing cabinets. The frightened man rushed downstairs to tell his friends. On further investigation it transpired that the face had appeared where there had been a window to the gallery in the original Crown and Anchor. Staff who worked on the weekend in this same upstairs office felt uncomfortable, as if someone unseen was watching them. During filming at the building a camera battery pack mysteriously drained down and lights which had been turned off suddenly turned themselves back on. Some people have reported the smell of tobacco smoke and downstairs a Cavalier's ghost has been encountered, smoking his clay pipe.

Next door to the estate agents' offices was a private residence (this, too, had formerly been part of the Crown and Anchor) where the family became used to seeing the ghost of a monk standing by their fireplace.

The Hare and Hounds, in Sopwell Lane, proved to be a terrifying place for one unfortunate barmaid in recent years. Marion Powell arrived early one summer's morning to help with the cleaning and went down to the cleaning cupboard in the cellar. About half way down the steps she experienced an intense cold and became aware of a strong presence nearby. She described an 'overwhelming blackness' which rushed up to envelop her in an aura of what she felt was pure evil. Marion went on to say that it was 'as if something was opening up to swallow her completely'. Then she heard a voice screaming at her to get out, at which point she fled back up to the bar. On occasion the pub's sewage system got blocked up and the landlord would find a foul substance oozing through the cellar wall. In times past, next door had been the site of the city gallows. The bodies of executed criminals were pushed into a trough which now forms part of the pub cellar.

BENINGTON

Between Stevenage and Puckeridge lies the quintessential Hollywood vision of the traditional English village, Benington. It has a village green, tree-screened church, timbered cottages, Georgian stately home (The Lordship) a folly, duck pond and ye olde English pub, the Bell. This pub has overhanging gables, black timbers, white pargeting

– and a ghost story. One of the area managers at Greene King Brewery related this intriguing tale to me. Some work was being carried out at the Bell and it necessitated taking off the front door of the pub. This was when the trouble started. It began with a horrendous, putrid smell that lingered near the doorway; it was so bad you could almost taste it. No one could detect the cause, so the work was done as speedily as possible and the front door was re-hung. During the course of that hectic and memorable day the landlady was kept so busy that she didn't have time to go upstairs and visit her private sitting room. When she did finally get up there that evening she discovered every picture and mirror askew. It was as though someone had run around the room in a rage, hitting everything that hung on the wall. The landlady, at the end of her tether after the day she had endured, shouted 'You can stop it now, the work is done and we've put the door back!' Then she put everything back as it had should have been. It is sometimes a good idea to talk to your ghosts, especially when they've been trying to attract your attention by being naughty. This landlady had realised that the disturbances were connected with the removal of the front door. Perhaps 'something' had been let in which had been shut out while the door was in place. In times gone by 'witch bottles' were buried under thresholds to stop evil presences from entering the home. This practice continued up to the turn of the last century in remote corners of the countryside. It may be that the pub's threshold had been protected in the past by a charm against a local witch. When the door was removed it temporarily 'broke the spell'. What we do know for sure is that when the front door was replaced nothing more happened to disturb the tranquillity of the old Bell at Benington. This one-day haunting is probably the shortest on record!

AYOT ST LAWRENCE

The village of Ayot St Lawrence lies to the north west of Welwyn and its pub, the Brocket Arms, dates back to 1378. At that time it was the monastic quarters for the local church and in the twentieth century it became part of the Brocket Estate and remains part of that estate. Toby Wingfield-Danby became the proprietor in 1980 and stayed in that position until fairly recently. He was quite open about the hauntings at his pub. There have been problems with the alarms going off in the early hours of the morning when nobody was around. The alarms have then been checked but no faults have been found. Other noises have been heard from the first floor, including unexplained mutterings, thumps and footsteps. Toby himself has experienced unaccountable feelings of panic and claustrophobia in parts of his inn. The first report of an apparition was documented in 1969, as recounted by Betty Puttick in her book, *Ghosts of Hertfordshire*. Teresa Sweeney, a part-time barmaid, witnessed the appearance and swift disappearance of a monk, 'a little man with his head bent,' while she was on her way to the dining room one evening. She saw him again, this time in the morning, in the dining room. She described his appearance, 'a thin, old face, rather hazy' and he was wearing monk's robes. One night Teresa heard little tapping feet following her downstairs, which quite unnerved her. Guests have also encountered this frightening friar. One visitor reported seeing a monk staring at him, while, apparently, the friar was on fire! Another guest awoke to discover mysterious burn marks on her feet.

During the Reformation of the Monasteries a monk was allegedly hanged on this very site. The story is that Henry VIII's men visited the village while escorting Henry's wife to London. Catherine Parr was the king's sixth wife and she lived in Ayot St Lawrence. The soldiers guarding the queen happened on an unfortunate monk and decided to hang him on the spot. He was duly dispatched, from a beam alongside the bar, which can be seen to this day in the Brocket Arms. Visitors may read the poem, written in 1940 about history from the Spanish Civil War to the Second World War. The ghost has a mention:

> A monk had ridden as he fled from the mob of howling villains who feared no god.
> They slung him up from a beam in the bar declaring he should not have ridden so far.'

Following the monk's murder it was said that the villagers of Ayot St Lawrence wouldn't go back in the bar for three weeks afterwards. It is nearly 500 years on and the monk apparently continues his haunting. The most incredible story concerning this famous phantom friar was recorded in the December 2003 issue of *Hertfordshire Life*. Toby Wingfield-Danby was interviewed by a journalist by the name of Gerry Gingell. 'I've had one guest staying overnight, the only person staying upstairs that particular night, who told me in the morning that he had met this chap in a brown robe or dressing gown, and how this person was so interesting because he knew so much about the village, and how they chatted away. I thought, as he was telling me his story, that I couldn't possibly tell him that he was the only one staying that night, as it would have frightened the living daylights out of him. But there was no question about it: this guy had a conversation with the monk! (How was this achieved, by telepathy? A monk from the sixteenth century speaking perfect modern English? I consider this a pretty tall tale Toby.)

CHAPTER EIGHT

THE STATELY GHOSTS OF HERTFORDSHIRE

SALISBURY HALL

Sir William Beech Thomas in 1950 called Salisbury Hall 'quaintly isolated' and it was this feature that suited Charles II, who kept his lover, Mistress Eleanor Gwynne, here, away from the prying eyes of his courtiers. Like many others before me I was captivated by the place when I first saw it on a guided tour some twenty years ago. This was prior to the incursion of the M25 motorway, when the area still had a rural feel. The hall is an attractive, brick-built house surrounded by a moat, it remains in private hands but it is not open to the public any more.

Salisbury Hall is some 4 miles south-east of St Albans Cathedral and the land that the hall stands on once belonged, in 800 AD, to Agnar the Staller, an Anglo-Saxon dignitary. After the Norman Conquest King William gave the estate to a wealthy and powerful ally, Geoffrey de Mandeville. By 1380 it came into the hands of Sir John Montague, Knight of the Garter and Earl of Salisbury, hence the property became known as Salisbury Hall. Later the house was to have an even more illustrious and powerful owner, the most successful member of the Nevill family, who became famous as Warwick the Kingmaker. He was to die later during the War of the Roses, at the Battle of Barnet (1471) not far from his home. Salisbury Hall fell into obscurity for a time until Sir John Cutte, Henry VIII's Treasurer, discovered it and rebuilt it in 1507. It was to remain in his family for 250 years. During the English Civil War Charles I used the hall as a Royalist headquarters and armoury. It was extensively modernised and boasted secret tunnels most useful for concealing Royalists. After the king's execution his son, Charles II, spent many happy hours here with his mistress. Legend has it that Nell Gwynne threatened to drop their son into the moat because he had no royal title. The king's reply was, 'No, spare the first Duke of St Albans'. This story helps to illustrate that not only was Nell one of the greatest beauties of her age but she was also shrewd, manipulative and acquisitive.

Another dynastic family became associated with Salisbury Hall in 1905, when the widow Lady Jenny Churchill, mother of Winston, bought the house, together with her second husband, George Cornwallis-West. Winston Churchill would sometimes stay at the hall with his mother and stepfather. George Cornwallis-West wrote of his sighting of the ghost of Nell Gwynne in his autobiography, *Edwardian Hey-Days*, published in 1930: 'One evening at Salisbury Hall just as it was getting dusk, I came down the staircase which leads into the old panelled room that we used as a dining-room, and there, standing in a corner, I saw the figure of a youngish and beautiful woman with a

Salisbury Hall, near St Albans. Nell Gwynne's shade has been seen here.

blue fichu (a small triangular shawl, worn around a lady's shoulders and neck) round her shoulders. She looked intently at me, and then turned and disappeared through the door into the passage. I followed and found nothing.' A medium was consulted and confirmed that Cornwallis-West had indeed seen the ghost of Nell Gwynne, who had come to warn him of impending danger. Within six months of the sighting a solicitor absconded with over £10,000, money entrusted to him by Cornwallis-West, to pay off some mortgages.

From 1934 to 1939 Salisbury Hall belonged to Sir Nigel Gresley, designer of the record-breaking Pacific steam locomotives. Guests who were accommodated in the Red Bedroom were often troubled by unexplained footsteps in the night. With the outbreak of the Second World War, the hall was taken over by aircraft designer Sir Geoffrey de Havilland and it became a top secret establishment. In late 1940 the reason for all the security was revealed in the shape of the 'Wooden Wonder', the revolutionary, ultra fast and manoeuvrable fighter-bomber named the Mosquito. This most versatile aircraft helped the Allies to win the war. When fitted with cameras it was ideal for photo-reconnaissance work, it proved its worth as a night fighter too, successfully intercepting German bombers. It excelled, too, as a light bomber for small, precision bombing raids.

Once the war was over and Sir Geoffrey de Havilland had moved out, the hall suffered many years of neglect, until 1956 when it was rescued by Walter Goldsmith, a painter and art dealer. Goldsmith bought a near derelict property together with gardens that were badly overgrown with brambles, but after many years of renovation he transformed it all back to its former glory. During the course of this massive project the new owners discovered secret rooms, passageways, tunnels and cellars. Three years after the Goldsmiths acquired their new home they received a letter from Mrs Rosamund Stutzel, who had lived in the house when she was a child, in the 1920s. Mrs Stutzel remembered a 'something' that had stood by the bed in the room that was situated over the entrance porch. This unknown, unnamed horror was also experienced by her brother and sister; they were often awakened by the scary entity as small children. A governess who spent the night in this same bedroom refused to sleep another night in the property after saying that, 'Something terrifying came out of the wall near the fireplace and stood by the bed'.

A Mosquito Aircraft Museum was established in the grounds of Salisbury Hall with the help of the Goldsmith family. My correspondent Martin Oliver was a member of the museum and he recalled going past the causeway one evening on the way to the museum with some friends. 'We spotted that the staircase light was on in the hall and that there was a shadow visible. We paid no attention to this until someone said 'It's a pity we can't get into the house'. I was told that Walter Goldsmith and family were on holiday and all the staff were away.'

One of the 1960s most famous British clairvoyants was Tom Corbett and, in the company of writer Diana Norman (wife of film critic Barry), he visited Salisbury Hall to investigate the ghosts for himself. Their researches together are described in Diana's interesting and informative book, *The Stately Ghosts of England*. Without any previous knowledge about the house or its history Tom quickly identified the ghost of 'a very beautiful woman' in the Green Bedroom and he correctly claimed, 'Somewhere in the house you have a portrait of her', and it turned out to be Nell Gwynne. The Goldsmiths admitted to a number of ghostly encounters themselves. Walter felt 'A warm and friendly supernatural presence' in his top floor studio where a bloodstain had been reputed to appear and re-appear on the wall in times past. Audrey, his wife, heard ghostly footsteps in the passage outside her bedroom door in the night. Tom Corbett believed that these footsteps were made by a second ghost, a man, who walked a passage in the old Tudor Wing (most of the passage didn't exist any more as the Tudor Wing had been destroyed in 1818).

In more recent times author Betty Puttick visited the Goldsmith family when Walter and Audrey's son Robin lived in the Tudor cottage with his wife Maria. This cottage had long been known as 'Nell Gwynne's Cottage' with many stories of unexplained happenings attached to it. Betty Puttick interviewed the Goldsmiths for her book, *Ghosts of Hertfordshire*. Maria gave a good account of her own sighting, made one night by the coach house, of the ghostly Cavalier that has been linked with Salisbury Hall. He was dressed in frilly white shirt and knee breeches, his shoes were adorned with large shiny buckles. He was tall with long fair hair tied back in a pony tail and his face was young and serious although he seemed to be smiling when he looked directly at her until his image slowly dissolved in front of her eyes. The Cavalier was believed to be a messenger carrying secret dispatches during the English Civil War. It was said that he was cornered by a force of Roundheads but rather than be captured he committed suicide.

Another occasion that Maria recalled was a time when she slept in the room over the porch in the hall as there was no other bedroom available then. There was a chiming clock in this room which Robin stopped in case it woke her up. Maria had a bad feeling about this bedroom, although she was unaware of its haunted reputation in those days.

She didn't want to be in here and went to sleep feeling rather depressed. At 2am she awoke to the sound of the ticking clock, which seemed to have restarted itself. Next thing her bed started rocking very violently, back and forth for several minutes. Maria huddled under the bedclothes in terror and left her bed early that morning. Eventually she shared her scary experience with her mother-in-law, who remembered the governess's ghostly encounter in the same room, *c.* 1919, which had caused her to refuse to sleep in the house ever again. Maria also spoke about the haunted gardens, where people heard ghostly laughter... could this be echoes from the days of the 'Merry Monarch' and his beautiful 'Mistress Nell'?

Batchwood Hall

Earlier, in the story about St Albans Abbey, I mentioned Lord Grimthorpe as the philanthropist who made possible the restoration of the Abbey with his generous £130,000 donation. He was an eccentric lawyer who designed his own home, Batchwood Hall, situated just the other side of Watling Street from Gorhambury. When Lord Grimthorpe died in 1905 his fortune was estimated at several million pounds, a colossal amount then. His grand old house is now a nightclub and sports centre, which suffered a fire in 1995. People escaping the fire told of a ghostly woman scattering burning coals over the floor with a shovel! There had been another fire here, about a hundred years earlier, and a man named John Beckett had run into the hall to save his wife. In recent times John was said to still search for his wife's body, which was never found. After the fire in 1995 it was speculated that the ghostly woman may have been the spirit of John's wife and it might have been her that started the original inferno. In 1989 Batchwood Hall was being refurbished when various supernatural activities in the hallway and cellar were reported. Objects mysteriously seemed to move themselves from their original positions, lights turned themselves on and off and padlocks that had been locked were found inexplicably opened. These strange events began soon after a Victorian fireplace was removed.

Ashridge Manor House

Little Gaddesdon village lies a few miles to the east of Berkhamsted and Ashridge Manor House is a well-known landmark in the village. It dates back to Elizabethan times and is haunted by the ghost of churchwarden William Jarman, who died in the eighteenth century. Locals refer to the structure on top of the chimneystack at the manor as 'Jarman's coffin'. The unfortunate Jarman lived in a house close to the manor house. Jarman's house was destroyed by fire some time around 1870. The churchwarden was in love with the heiress to the Earls of Bridgewater's Ashridge Estate. It was an unrequited love and Jarman committed suicide, it is thought that he hanged himself from an oak tree. The latter is considered to be the most likely version of events. His ghost has never actually been seen in the house but it has been glimpsed by the pond. Jarman's spirit, however, was felt around the house, as candles would dip and expire and later on electric lights would be similarly affected. On one occasion two people who were talking in the drawing room remarked on the fact that

Ashridge Manor House, Little Gaddesdon. William Jarman's unhappy, unfulfilled spirit lives on at this house.

all the lights, one after another, went out. This report echoes the story of the seven parsons who came to exorcise Jarman's ghost in times past. The seven candles they carried were extinguished one after the other until just one remained. It stubbornly refused to be snuffed out by the ghost, which was subdued after the exorcism but still occasionally made its presence felt. In the 1960s Miss Dorothy Earhart lived at Ashridge Manor House and she said that her standard lamp used to be switched off by something unseen. She regarded Jarman's shade as benevolent and friendly. In 1963 there was a Ministry of Housing enquiry which mentioned the building of a new house near the Elizabethan house as a possible influence on the resumption of the haunting at the manor. A monastery used to stand on the site of the Ashridge Estate and an old manuscript was discovered there. It was entitled 'Johannes de Rupesscissa' and it concerned occult rituals, with advice about burning incense in order to rid a haunted house of evil spirits!

Former Rolling Stones' lead guitarist Mick Taylor used Ashbridge Manor House as both a home and a recording studio in 1977. Valerie Jarvis, Taylor's partner, confirmed that the lights were still being interfered with at this time. They would be flicked on and off and unexplained noises would, on occasion, interrupt recording sessions. Valerie was interviewed by the *Observer* newspaper, and admitted that 'none of the guitars and recording equipment have been touched, but the ghost has made recording a struggle'. Mick Taylor also spoke with the newspaper's reporter, 'I did hear voices in the kitchen the other day and when I went in no one was there, but it didn't really worry me. We've been told a spectral churchwarden called

Jarman, who committed suicide over an unrequited love, haunts the house. None of us think he is malevolent though.'

CAMFIELD PLACE

Essendon village lies a couple of miles due east of Hatfield and it is home to Camfield Place. I will never forget my first sighting of Camfield Place, an impressive, bright, whitewashed grand old house in the Italianate style surrounded by 500 acres of parkland. It stood alone on a hill amidst green fields, overlooking a valley and the rise beyond. It is so picturesque that it could have come straight from the pages of a fairy tale. It has certainly proved inspirational for two famous writers who once lived here at different times, Beatrix Potter and Barbara Cartland. This estate existed in Tudor times, but the original building was demolished in 1867 by Beatrix Potter's grandfather, to make way for the present rambling Victorian mansion. Beatrix wrote that Camfield Place was the place that she loved best. Her classic *Tales of Peter Rabbit* was written in the garden potting shed. She admitted that her home was haunted and described an evening when she was sitting in the lounge and suddenly felt very cold. One by one the candles were unaccountably snuffed out, as if by invisible fingers. The ghosts were also said to haunt the hall and the stairs. When best-selling author Barbara Cartland (Mrs Hugh McCorquodale) moved here in 1950 she took no chances. As a strong believer in the supernatural one of her first actions, before she even moved in, was to have the house blessed. This was in order to save any trouble with ghosts and it seemed to work well until 1955. That was the year she had to put down her younger son's Cocker Spaniel called Jimmy. The dog had developed a serious problem with its throat. Soon after this she noticed her other dogs were getting jumpy at feeding time. They seemed to be responding to something unseen, watching it and barking at it. One dog, Murray, was particularly badly affected. He would back away from his food as if threatened by an invisible aggressor. Sometimes he would jump in the air and yelp as if under attack. As time wore on Jimmy the ghost dog began to appear around the house. Barbara herself saw him as did her maid, Miss Rose Purcell, lying around in his favourite places. For some time afterwards the other spaniels did occasional battle with the spirit-dog that was Jimmy.

MARKYATE CELL

Markyate is situated a few miles to the west of Harpenden, in the northwest corner of Hertfordshire, in close proximity to the Bedfordshire border. The name Markyate is derived from the Old English *mearc* and *gate* meaning gate at the (county) boundary. It is an area steeped in history and the most interesting legend concerns Katherine Ferrers, 'the Wicked Lady'. She was the lady of the manor by day and a highwayman by night. In Hertfordshire there was a saying about the area of Markyate, Harpenden, Wheathampstead and Kimpton. When the west wind blew up these valleys in December (season of storms and ghosts) hard enough to rattle the window panes, it was the Wicked Lady galloping by.

The manor of Markyate is known as Markyate Cell and it was built on the site of the former twelfth-century nunnery, the Priory of St-Trinity-in-the-wood. By the seventeenth century Markyate Cell had been the seat of the ancient Ferrers family for several generations and now there was only one son, Sir Knighton Ferrers, to carry on the line. He married a beautiful heiress, Lady Katherine Walters of Hertingford, but within a year Knighton was dead. As no male heir had been produced the line was now dead but the couple did have a daughter together, who was also called Katherine. Her mother was now a rich widow and prey to fortune hunters during that most perilous of times, the English Civil War. The elder Katherine was persuaded to marry Sir Simon Fanshawe of Ware Park. He was an ardent Royalist and his estate was eventually overrun by Parliamentary forces so that his new wife and step-daughter were forced to flee to Huntingdonshire for their own safety. As soon as the girl reached the legal age to marry (twelve years old) Sir Simon had her married off to his own sixteen-year-old son, Thomas. This was so that he could gain control of Markyate Cell. Some years later the elder Katherine died and her daughter Katherine Fanshawe found herself much neglected by her husband Thomas and the rest of the Fanshawe family (now that they had the estates that they had coveted for so long). The lonely eighteen-year-old took herself off to a place where she had once known happiness, her natural father's rambling old brick-faced mansion, Markyate Cell.

Another chapter in Katherine's troubled life began when she met farmer Ralph Chaplin, whose land overlooked Watling Street, to the south of Markyate. The farmer had a dark secret – by night he was a 'moonraker' and it is believed that he introduced the impressionable, teenaged Katherine to the thrilling adventures of highway robbery. On one of his ventures further afield he was caught and shot while in the process of robbing a baggage wagon on Finchley Common. His heartbroken partner began her dreadful campaign of revenge, for she certainly didn't need the money. Now no traveller in the vicinity of Markyate was safe. Stagecoaches travelling along Watling Street were under constant threat, houses were set ablaze, cattle were slaughtered and the parish constable was murdered on his own doorstep. This trail of wanton destruction could not last forever and during her final attempted robbery Lady Katherine received mortal wounds after an exchange of gunfire with one traveller who was prepared to shoot back. She was still young, only in her mid-twenties at the time. Her swansong came at Nomansland Common when she tried to rob a man travelling from St Albans with supplies for an inn at Gustard Wood, a village near Wheathampstead. He had given a lift to two travellers, who settled themselves into the well of his waggon amongst the baggage. At dusk the trio were rolling across Nomansland Common when out of the gathering gloom a masked rider galloped up and rapidly closed in on the lumbering vehicle. Without any warning the unfortunate driver was shot from his seat, dead before he hit the ground, but one of the men travelling under cover in the back had armed himself with a gun. He rose up and blasted the masked rider who sheared away and raced for home. Somehow the mortally-wounded Katherine Ferrers managed the ride back to Markyate Cell and, pouring with blood, she staggered over the threshold to collapse and die in her own home.

Unsurprisingly Lady Ferrers has no grave in Markyate; she is thought to have been buried in secret at St Mary's church at Ware, but certainly not in the Fanshawe's vault. It wasn't long after her internment that the hauntings began; it seemed that the Wicked Lady's thirst for revenge was reaching out from beyond the grave. The phantom of a galloping highwayman was reported to travel the lanes as far north as Kimpton and along Watling Street. Markyate Cell was haunted too as succeeding owners confirmed sightings of the late highwayman's ghost.

Markyate Cell. Former home of the legendary Lady Katherine Ferrers. Her soubriquet, 'The Wicked Lady', was quite undeserved.

More than 300 years after her death the Wicked Lady was still making news. Douglas Payne, the landlord of the pub that bears her name was out walking his dog late one night in 1970 on Nomansland Common. He heard the thunder of horse's hooves rapidly approaching him then passing by, there was no visible evidence of a horse or rider yet the dog was plainly terrified. The Wicked Lady is one of only two pubs in Hertfordshire to be named after a ghost (the other is the White Horse at Datchworth). It is thought that Katherine Ferrers met her partners in crime at this inn; however the woman who haunts the place is not thought to be the highwayman. A number of customers have reported hearing the sounds of sobbing coming from an empty upstairs room. Another pub, the Tin Pot, was also associated with the Wicked Lady, it is where she is alleged to have changed into her highwayman's garb before her forays and a few people have felt a strange 'presence' in the room that was supposedly her changing room. One of these experients was moved to write some poetry and the lines were hung up in the bar.

The legend of the female highwayman is one that has captured the public imagination and spawned the romantic film, *The Wicked Lady*, starring Margaret Lockwood and James Mason. There is also a famous rhyme about the outlaw's supposed hidden booty:

Near the Cell there is a well
Near the well there is a tree,
And 'neath the tree the treasure be.

If so it still remains to be discovered...

So much for the legend, what about the facts? There is not a shred of evidence to back up the claims that Lady Katherine Ferrers was ever a highwayman! Fact: Lady Ferrers was born into wealth and married into another wealthy family. Fact: Katherine was probably living with her in-laws in Ware at the time when she was allegedly holding up coaches since Markyate Cell was sold to a man from Kent, Thomas Coppin, in 1657. Fact: Katherine was buried on 13 June 1660. The cause of death is unknown, but at the tender age of twenty-six and being childless, there is a strong possibility that she died after suffering a miscarriage. Unfortunately in Oliver Cromwell's time, archive material was not always well maintained, particularly around 1643-1660, around the time of the English Civil War. Katherine was the last of the Ferrers line. Fact: Ralph Chaplin, her so-called 'partner in crime' only exists in legend. Hertfordshire Archive Library has no mention of Ralph Chaplin of Markyate. The Parish Registers contain no mention of such a person; ergo he is fictitious.

How do such legends become so deeply entrenched in the public consciousness? In the mid-seventeenth century highway robbery was practised by a number of 'gentlemen of the road', men of property and influence who were former Royalists. They found themselves without property or income after supporting the losing side in the Civil War. Such men became desperate and desperation sometimes breeds crime. The notion that the same 'romantic' occupation might be conducted by a woman held a tremendous appeal, and still does today. There is a nineteenth-century ballad that concerns a lady, Maude of Allingham. She was courted by numerous eligible bachelors but rejected them in favour of highway robbery. She held up one young lord, who later became Mayor of Redbourne, and he had her hunted down. Maude was chased and shot but reached home, where she died. Sound familiar? 'Savay' is an English folk song which tells how a young girl disguises herself as a highwayman in order to test her lover. The twin themes of highwaymen and ladies who disguise themselves occur again and again in English folklore. It is a matter of historical fact that in 1760 Laurence Shirley, 4th Earl of Ferrers, was hanged at Tyburn. He had murdered an old and faithful servant. Ever after he was known as 'Wicked Lord Ferrers' – it's easy to see how Lord Ferrers, in the course of the retelling of tales, may have become the 'Wicked Lady Ferrers'... If one myth has been exploded we are still left with another intriguing mystery. Assuming that Lady Ferrers wasn't at all wicked, much less a highwayman then who or what was seen on a black steed with white blazes, haunting the lanes of Markyate? Who or what was seen swinging from the old sycamore tree in the grounds of the old manor house? Whose entity was encountered on the secret staircase in Markyate Cell?

James Snooks was another notorious Hertfordshire highwayman and some four or five years ago a strange encounter was recorded from his old stamping ground, Boxmoor, near Hemel Hempstead. A lady who wishes to remain anonymous gave the following account. 'I was out till after midnight with a friend. We were walking back along Boxmoor past the twenty-four-hour garage on the opposite side of the road near the fields. I spotted a strange figure of which I'm most sure was a body hanging from a tree. Also there was thick white fog across the moor and the horses looked frozen stiff as they did not move. I knew something strange was happening and didn't really know what to do apart from go home. Next day nothing about somebody hanging themselves was on the news or anything. That's when it really hit me.' Could this sighting have been the ghost of highwayman James Snooks, who was, long ago, executed by hanging on this moor, the scene of his crimes?

WALL HALL

Wall Hall, at Aldenham, is a building with a chequered history dating back to the thirteenth century; it has been owned by Admiral Sir Morice Pole and the fabulously wealthy Pierpoint Morgan family, American bankers and steel mill owners. Then, in 1945 it became one of the campuses of Hertfordshire University. A woman's ghost was seen in the Philosophy Block on more than one occasion. She was thought to be a former housekeeper from the time when the mansion was in private hands. There was a confirmed sighting as recently as 2001, by the housekeeping manager, Lynne Bright. She gave a detailed description of 'a woman with grey hair, wearing a long grey dress, nipped in at the waist with a bodice that had a white collar and long sleeves.' So real did the apparition appear that Lynne had a conversation with the ghost, though as is usual in genuine hauntings, it was a one-way conversation. The ghost made no reply but her body language said it all. She merely frowned hard, put her hands on her hips and then folded her arms. The ghostly housekeeper clearly disapproved of the modern cleaning regime. When Lynne told one of her cleaners about talking with a woman in grey the other woman hurriedly left the room. The grey lady had obviously not been visible to this cleaner – it was then that the realisation hit Lynne – she must have been talking with a ghost! Children's laughter is another phenomenon that was regularly reported by security staff at Wall Hall. One room, lecture room M7, was singled out as a particularly creepy room. It had an odd atmosphere and was always cold, even on the sunniest of days. Various staff members attested to other paranormal phenomena – lights were switched on and off by an invisible agency and the swishing sound of a long skirt was heard. Wall Hall is yet another property that ended up in the hands of property developers; a company called Octagon converted the mansion and campuses into executive homes in 2005.

HATFIELD HOUSE

Hatfield derives from Old English, *haeth* and *feld* or 'heathy open land' and the town can be traced back to Saxon times when King Edgar gave 5,000 acres of land to the monastery at Ely. Hatfield House was formerly Hatfield Palace, built around 1485 and during Henry VIII's reign the monarch exchanged other lands for Hatfield with the Bishops of Ely. It was convenient as a home for the king's offspring; the younger ones were educated at Hatfield. On Henry's death in 1547, his nine-year-old son Edward was taken from Hatfield to London for his coronation. The sickly boy was only to live another six years before his half-sister Mary took the throne. During her brief, five-year reign, 'Bloody' Mary kept her younger half-sister a virtual prisoner at Hatfield. Eventually the highly unpopular Mary died and the learned and wise Elizabeth is said to have received the news of her accession to the throne under the Hatfield Oak. Queen Elizabeth I's childhood things can be seen at Hatfield House when it is open to the public. Her yellow silk stockings, her garden hat and many of her letters are kept here, along with two famous portraits of the monarch. Hatfield was to be swapped once more, by Elizabeth's successor, James I. The King wanted Theobalds, a Hertfordshire country house of legendary beauty, where he was destined to die in 1625. The new owner of Hatfield was Robert Cecil, first Earl of Salisbury, the King's Chief Minister. In

1611 Lord Salisbury had three sides of the medieval palace of Hatfield pulled down and he had the present Hatfield House built. The cost of rebuilding was £38,000, a vast sum in those times, but its Jacobean architectural style was then the most modern style. The house was built in the shape of an 'E' to commemorate Queen Elizabeth's popular reign. Hatfield House was both extravagantly decorated and elegantly furnished; it boasted the most luxuriant of gardens. The Great Park of Hatfield House has been restored to its former glory and is best visited in June if the roses are to be fully appreciated. The grand old house is now the country seat of Robert Gascoyne-Cecil, the 7th Marquess of Salisbury, Conservative politician and Chancellor of the University of Hertfordshire. Lord Salisbury is probably the wealthiest man in Hertfordshire. He owns land in America, property in London, two stately homes and an extensive art collection.

The old palace part of Hatfield House has a haunted passageway. It is known for the sounds of unexplained footsteps; followed by noises of a door opening then slow, steady footsteps as of a careful descent, down the stairs. On moonlit nights a shadowy woman's form has been seen, passing through the old palace gateway, crossing Fore Street then entering the church. In the central part of Hatfield House Queen Elizabeth I is rumoured to return in spirit form. The first Marchioness is also said to haunt this stately home. The dowager Marchioness was burnt to death in 1835, when she was eighty-five, after she knocked over a candle in her bedroom. This started a blaze which destroyed the majority of the house's west wing. A certain twenty-three-year-old reporter, Charles Dickens by name (later to find international fame and fortune as a novelist) was sent to Hatfield to cover the story for the *Morning Chronicle*. During her long and eventful life the Marchioness was renowned for her hobbies of gambling and hunting. She was a frequent traveller to London in her coach, which is the most famous and impressive apparition associated with Hatfield House. According to various reports, the phantom coach has appeared at the gate with four black horses, then travelled at breakneck speed down the long drive and thundered on through the front doors before it continued upstairs where it dematerialised.

KNEBWORTH HOUSE

Knebworth is derived from *Chenepeword* meaning 'the house on the hill', as mentioned in the Domesday Book of 1086. In Norman times it was a small manor house, built like a minor fortress, and surrounded by hundreds of acres of land. It was given to one of William the Conqueror's stewards, a knight called Eudo Dapifer. The house changed ownership many times over the next 400 years until 1492 and the arrival of the first Lytton, and it has remained in that family ever since. It is a rarity for an English family seat to continue to be in the same hands for over 500 years. Sir Robert Lytton, known as Sir Robert of the Peak, began the dynasty at Knebworth. He came down from Derbyshire and became the Keeper of the Wardrobe to Henry VII. Sir Robert set about tearing down the original manor house and he replaced it with a huge mansion of Tudor red brick. The four sides were built around a central courtyard with a gatehouse and remained this way for some 400 years. Due to long term neglect three sides had to be demolished and stucco was added to the remaining wing in the nineteenth century.

Knebworth House. A terrifying family ghost – the 'Yellow Boy' and a benign guardian, Sir Edward Bulwer-Lytton are said to haunt this grand house.

Knebworth's 'family ghost' was known as the 'Yellow Boy' or the 'Radiant Boy' and if a member of the Lytton family was due to die a violent death the childish spectre would appear and by his gestures he would indicate the manner of their passing. Unsurprisingly the room that he was said to haunt was carefully avoided by the family but they had no qualms about offering it to their guests. One of these guests was politician Lord Castlereagh who stayed here one night during his time as Foreign Secretary. The following morning he complained about a night-time visitation by the apparently solid figure of a young boy with yellow hair. The boy had held Castlereagh's gaze whilst slowly drawing his finger across his throat several times before vanishing. In 1822 Lord Castlereagh did indeed die a violent death, by cutting his throat with a penknife. 'Radiant Boys' are a worldwide phenomenon with several well-documented cases around Great Britain. Knebworth's 'Yellow Boy' is typical of these manifestations, which appear as beautiful male children, tightly surrounded by an unearthly bright light of various colours, most often white or blue. No one knows the identity of these otherworldly visitors or the exact purpose of their appearances. The commonly held opinion is that they are the spirits of children who were murdered by their parents. More often than not they are the harbingers of ill fortune for the spectator...

There is an earlier alleged haunting, from the eighteenth century, of 'Jenny Spinner', a young girl who worked on the estate and who fell pregnant either by one of the Lytton family or by a local of low birth. She was locked away in the east wing, which is no longer standing and she had nothing to do but spin yarn for cloth. She eventually went mad and died in this room. After her death the sound of a spinning wheel could sometimes be heard in the halls of Knebworth House. In her 1987 book – *Albion: Guide to Legendary Britain* – Jennifer Westwood explodes this myth. The tale was invented by a Miss James, a guest at a Christmas party held at Knebworth in 1800.

Sir Edward Bulwer-Lytton (1803–73) succeeded to the Knebworth estate in 1843 and he established himself as a famous and successful novelist, the male equivalent of today's J.K. Rowling. It was said of him, 'Everything he wrote, sold as though it were bread displayed to a hungry crowd.' Over a career that spanned forty-five years he wrote twenty-four novels which included various genres – historical romances, tales of magic, spiritualism and science, novels of high society, light novels of middle-class domestic life and philosophical novels. He also found time to write ten plays, eleven volumes of poetry, two collections of essays, numerous short stories, a pioneering sociological study, a history of Athens and translations of Horace and Schiller. This gifted individual managed to combine both a writing career and a political career; he was a member of Parliament for over sixteen years. He was a lifelong friend of Charles Dickens, whom he greatly influenced and Dickens was a frequent visitor to Knebworth House. Sir Edward was a man of many interests, among them was an enthusiasm for the occult. Two of his most chilling stories are *The House and the Brain* and *The Haunted and the Haunters.* In the mid-nineteenth century he was widely regarded as England's leading man of letters. He will forever be remembered as the author who first penned those immortal opening lines, 'It was a dark and stormy night'. These are the ideal conditions for a haunting and not just because of the dramatic atmosphere. The static electricity which builds up in the air during thunderstorms is believed to provide the energy that spirits require to produce their manifestations.

Sir Edward completely changed the character of his Tudor mansion by modernising it with copper domes, gargoyles and more castellations which were the fashion in Victorian times. He created his own Gothic fantasy and his great house now had the status of a palace. The author/politician delighted in presiding over his palace, he would greet his guests clad in rich velvet suits and his hospitality was extended to a wide circle of friends. There were politicians, writers, artists and fellow students of the occult. He was responsible for making the idea of occultism fashionable in England and many mediums visited Knebworth. The most eminent of these was Daniel Dunglas Home, a remarkably gifted Scottish spiritualist and medium for whom the word 'psychic' was coined. Home achieved worldwide celebrity and he attained it by personal demonstrations of his powers to members of European high society. There has been nobody since Home to have equalled his many paranormal feats. He was said to be able to move solid objects by the power of his thoughts alone and he was credited with the ability to change the dimensions of his body. It was also claimed that he was impervious to fire when in a trance. Observers saw him materialise ghostly forms and most astonishingly of all – he was able to levitate at will! Hundreds of witnesses, in various parts of the world, over a forty-year period, attested to his unique powers. It is most regrettable that all of this took place just before the era of the Society for Psychical Research, which was founded in 1882. The SPR would have found, in Home, a most worthy subject for research and investigation. The astonishing claims made about him might then have been scientifically validated.

Daniel Dunglas Home moved with his family from Edinburgh to Connecticut when he was nine years old. He was a sickly child who became an adult plagued by ill health. By the age of nineteen he had experienced his first spontaneous levitation; eventually he was able to control it to such an extent that observers claimed that he seemed able to fly. Home left America to come to England in the summer of 1855 and was welcomed into society by Sir Edward Bulwer-Lytton, who invited the medium to visit his residence in Park Lane, London. Later on Home was a guest at the baronet's country home, Knebworth House, where a number of séances were held. These events provided thought-provoking material for Sir Edward's novel *The Haunted and the Haunters*.

Home's most famous phenomenon was produced at Lord Adare's house in London. The medium was in a trance when he was seen, by several prominent witnesses, to float out of a third floor window and then float back in again via a different window. That same year attendees at another trance session attested to Home putting his head into a fire and handling red-hot coals without so much as a blister! Home never knew how or why he was chosen to be the recipient of such awesome psychic gifts. He explained that he was just a medium for the spirits, over which he had no control. These spirits included his main guide, who was called Bryan. Daniel Dunglas Home was a fascinating and tragic individual, the 'original psychic' who died young (he was aged just forty-four) and who is largely forgotten today.

Sir Edward Bulwer-Lytton was raised to the peerage in 1868 and thereafter was known as Lord Lytton, his son, Robert, was the first Earl of Lytton who succeeded to the title in 1873. In modern times Knebworth House is recognisable as the backdrop for many films (it was Wayne Manor in *Batman*, the first in this series of movies) and it also plays host to pop concerts as well as vintage car rallies, fairs, pageants and other events. Its 260 acres of parkland have been the setting for concerts by musical megastars such as Robbie Williams, Pink Floyd, Led Zeppelin and the Rolling Stones. The house still retains its ghosts. In recent times an American guest staying in the Queen Elizabeth Room was startled one morning when she found a strange young girl, with long blonde hair, leaning over the four-poster bed staring at her. The unearthly visitor then faded from view. The Picture Gallery is also reputedly visited by a female spirit from time to time. The strongest presence, however, is felt but never seen, that of Sir Edward Bulwer-Lytton. He has been sensed by family, members of staff and visitors alike, in both the old study and the adjoining drawing room. This seems to be an example of an earthbound spirit bound to a particular location by love and affection for this most special place.

Chapter Nine

Hertford and Ware Wraiths

Hertford

Fore Street

Hertford is named after two Old English words *heorot* and *ford*, meaning 'ford frequented by harts or stags'. It is Hertfordshire's county town and a 2006 survey commissioned by Channel 4 Television ranked it within the top ten places to live in the UK. It is also one of the paranormal 'hot spots' of Hertfordshire, probably second only to St Albans, and in this most haunted town the most haunted street is undoubtedly Fore Street. I was well placed to conduct my research into the paranormal aspect of Hertford because I worked in the allegedly haunted Red House at 119 Fore Street during 2003/2004. I didn't see the ghost myself but a number of people have seen 'the matron', carrying her tray, at the top of the stairs. The Red House is some 400 years old and it was originally a part of Christ's Hospital, for the orphaned children of London.

Albany Radio is located at 63-65 Fore Street; this shop was once a private house called Cupboard Hall. When Susan Brown occupied Cupboard Hall she reported seeing a ghostly woman wearing fine Georgian clothing, leaning over her bed at night.

Threshers wine store, opposite the post office, is another Fore Street property with a history. It has been home to various wine merchants since 1933. Nobody likes to go down to the cellar here; the atmosphere has been described as 'chilling'. Staff have quite often opened up the shop first thing in the morning to find taps turned on fully or bottles placed neatly on the floor. The bottles have been arranged in a star shape, with the necks of the bottles all facing inward. How this happens in a locked and empty shop overnight remains a mystery. On one occasion, when the staff were present, a crash was heard from the bottle store and everyone rushed out to find six bottles neatly laid out in the by now familiar star shape.

On the other side of Fore Street is Marshall's Furnishings, where you might still pick up a copy of the video, made some years ago, about many of the Hertford hauntings. In 1996 Marshall's had its own strange episode to add to the growing file of unexplained incidents in Fore Street. A major fire at the back of the premises had left the shop vulnerable to looters. A woman police constable maintained a constant presence throughout the night of the 30 September. During her solitary vigil she looked up at one of the windows to see a man with long curly black hair and a moustache looking back down at her. The WPC later described the figure as Cromwellian. She called for back-up, but when some colleagues arrived and searched the place they could find no sign of anyone in the ruined building.

Another active spirit was abroad in 1996, at Sheffield's the Chemists. It started in May that year when the pharmacist heard a knocking in the floor, wherever he moved to in the room the knocking followed him. Pat Blake, who worked here, was most helpful in providing details of this case. A bottle of Paracol D, a preparation for diabetes sufferers, was seen to travel along the passage and smash on the ground in front of startled witnesses. Then a shelf noisily hit the floor too. On another day there was an apport (a physical object that appears from nowhere, without any normal explanation) – a bottle of strychnine. It 'came out of thin air and dropped to the floor without smashing' according to Pat. Often, as in this instance, an apport will be relevant to the spirit that delivers it and may give a clue as to its identity. Interestingly strychnine is classed as poison today but in times past it was used as a medicine. As well as an apport there was an asport (a physical object that suddenly, completely and inexplicably vanishes). One of the 200-year-old prescription books was discovered on a toilet seat, opened at a particular page but the next day it disappeared. Pat asked out loud, 'Can we have our book back?' About an hour later it literally appeared through the wall and dropped to the floor with a bang. Even stranger, it was still opened at the same page as before. 'It was like it was trying to tell us something.' By now Pat had established a system of communication with the spirit; it would rap once for 'yes' and twice for 'no'. This was a case worthy of investigation by the Society for Psychical Research but when Pat tried to contact them all the postage stamps mysteriously disappeared and the phone line suddenly went dead. She tried the direct approach again with the entity. 'One day I asked if it had a story to tell and it tapped out "yes".' A code of letters and knocks was worked out and eventually a message was deciphered. 'It [the spirit] had been killed by its brother in order to inherit the business.' With the successful delivery of this message the paranormal activity at Sheffield's ceased completely.

Further up Fore Street, at the junction with Bell Lane, stands the Salisbury Arms Hotel, Hertford's oldest hostelry. Keith Marshall, of Marshall's Furnishings, who sells the Hertford hauntings videos, used to organise ghost walks in the town. In his opinion the two most haunted locations in Hertford are the Salisbury Arms Hotel and Café Uno. It has been said that the ghost of no less a person than Oliver Cromwell has been seen in the Salisbury Arms. It is also claimed that bedroom No. 6 is haunted and the corridor is reputedly visited by a Cromwellian figure. On the first floor a cleaner saw a middle-aged man in black who entered a small room but didn't come out again. The cleaner checked the room but there was no trace of the man in black and no other exit that he could have used.

It is my opinion that the Café Uno (now renamed Brasserie Gerard) is the most haunted location in Hertford's most haunted street. Trouble first started when the building was altered by shop fitters who converted a musty old charity shop into the new and trendy café. It was as if something unseen objected to the radical changes taking place and soon the builders became spooked. Pieces of timber were seen to move, unaided, across the room by the shop fitters. Wires which had been clipped to the ceiling were discovered ripped out of their fastenings and left dangling. Bricks were moved around overnight. A weird mist was seen rising up out of the basement by some of the workmen. The café staff bore the brunt of the haunting though the women refused point blank to use the ladies' loos. They preferred to walk to the public toilets in the Gascoyne Way car park; such was the intense feeling of 'something evil' surrounding the area of the café's toilets. Café staff who were cashing up one day were disconcerted when they saw weird 'marching shadows' on the walls. A terrified cleaner heard a thunderous crash when working on his own. He rushed downstairs but could find no explanation

Brasserie Gérard, Hertford. Impressions of 'something evil' have frequently been felt and reported at these Hertford premises.

for the sudden loud noise. Reports continue to come through regularly from people who have been affected by either feeling or seeing 'a presence' in the toilets upstairs at the Café Uno.

Before they removed to new offices at Ware Road, staff at the *Hertfordshire Mercury* recounted some strange experiences at their old premises, which were not far from Fore Street. Hard-headed journalists like Gary Matthews were persuaded about the reality of the paranormal after experiencing it first-hand. Late one Christmas night Gary was working alone. 'I suddenly became aware of the lights in the building switching on and off. I checked my computer screen and that was OK so I knew it wasn't a power cut. Then I heard the door handle moving and when I looked over at the door the handle was indeed moving up and down.' He went to check the building to make sure no one was playing a prank, but the whole place was empty. As he returned to his seat the lights went out completely then came on once more and the door handle started moving again so Gary made a rather hasty exit.

Mike Poultney was another newspaperman who had a weird encounter when working on his own at the *Hertfordshire Mercury*. He was locking up one Sunday when he heard a door slam on the floor above him. He contacted the police as he thought that there might be an intruder in the premises. A policeman arrived, together with a large alsatian and the pair of them thoroughly searched the building. The dog was sent to the cellar to make certain that nobody was hiding there. After a matter of minutes the badly frightened animal was frantically scratching at the door to be let out. When the cellar door was opened the dog tore out of the place with all its hair standing on end. The search was continued; the cellar proved to be empty but in an upstairs office there was a bunch of keys, one of them was inserted in the door lock. The rest of the keys were swinging wildly, as if someone had just closed the door. The police officer rushed into the room, only to find it empty. Soon afterwards he left with his dog, none the wiser as to the 'intruder'. Mike subsequently learned that the cellar had a reputation for being haunted. Two stories were in circulation as to the ghost's identity. Before the newspaper had offices on this site there had been another business based here and a machine operator from that company had died while at work. It was thought that it might be his restless spirit that haunted his old workplace. Further back in time the property had been used as a private house, complete with servants. The butler allegedly murdered a kitchen maid and it was rumoured that it was this former maid's spirit that haunted the cellar.

Maidenhead Street

Residents of Hertford who know about the town's history always point to the busy shopping area around Maidenhead Street as a centre of paranormal activity. There was, before the 2008-2009 credit crunch, a branch of Woolworths (built in 1931) in Maidenhead Street. Staff here talked about poltergeist activity in the storeroom behind the audio section in this sadly-missed retail outlet. A heavy two-metre clothes rail was thrown across the store room and clothes and other items were found scattered about the place. Originally a seventeenth century inn called the Maiden Head existed on this site; it was demolished in 1930 to accommodate the Woolworths store. Market Place is also in this shopping area and in January 2005 a reporter from the *Guardian* visited Hertford and interviewed Gemma, who was the manageress of the Monsoon Accessorize shop at the time. They were talking about the legendary tunnel supposed to exist under the building. Gemma was quite insistent that there was no tunnel beneath the shop; 'Just the store room – but it's definitely haunted. When we have our sales meetings there you can hear someone walking over our heads, or doing the vacuuming. But upstairs the shop's closed and empty.'

Saint Andrew's Street

Wigginton's toy shop is a Hertford institution, the building it occupies can boast over 500 years of history and it is also one of the most haunted properties in town. Many customers have sensed a presence in the upstairs room, formerly a bedroom where manager Roy Roberts's daughter, Jane Holt, used to sleep until she was eighteen. The young girl frequently saw the ghost of a Victorian lady at night in this back room. The lady would stroke the child's brow and a feeling of love pervaded the room, so this ghost was not at all scary. Sometimes a white-haired, bearded man, who wore a morning suit, also stood at the end of the bed. The late psychic investigator, Graham Wylie, visited Wigginton's. He said, 'Immediately I entered the haunted room I went cold. This indicates there is a presence here. There is a feeling of grief in the room. A young lady nursed her dying father here, hence Jane's experience of the hand across the brow.' Graham had the impression of a benevolent spirit but in the attic store room there was something entirely different. Dogs will not venture up the stairs to the attic, they growl and whine at some unseen intruder. Jane Holt refused to go up there and Graham

Wigginton's, Hertford. A caring female spirit and the male spirit of a murderer/suicide have been encountered at this Hertford landmark.

Wylie sensed negative energy, saying, 'There is something nasty and evil in this room, I can't wait to get out. I got a choking feeling in my throat as soon as I entered. I feel it was about 1750 and a young man, on the run for murder and feeling the net closing in around him, came up here to hang himself from one of the beams, thus cheating the gallows. It is the evilness of this man's actions for taking another's life that remains in this room.'

Wallace House was once the home of a famous Welshman, Alfred Russell Wallace, who died in 1914. He was a naturalist who travelled extensively in South America and Malaya collecting plant samples and he propounded a theory of evolution by natural selection independently and at the same time as Darwin. His former home is haunted by three different male apparitions. Staff working in the building have seen one of these figures in the corridor, another looking out of a window and a third standing in a corner. Wallace House is currently occupied by a doctor's surgery.

Bull Plain

Lombard House is an attractive old place situated near the river, in Bull Plain, it was built in the sixteenth century and the façade was added to in the eighteenth century. Lombard House is the former home of Sir Henry Chauncy, Recorder of Hertford and he wrote most of his County History of Hertford here in 1700. It is now known as the Hertford Club and it is haunted. The snooker room is the most affected area; a barman reported the sounds of male conversation and laughter when he opened up the club early one evening, but when he checked, the snooker room was quite empty. Snooker balls were scattered across the table as though a ghostly game had been interrupted. Unsurprisingly the ghost is known as 'Old Henry' and his footsteps are heard when the house is supposedly empty. Perhaps the former historian is still visiting his old home.

Not far from the Hertford Club is Hertford Museum, housed in a seventeenth-century building. If you visit the museum and experience a chill in the air you will be sharing something that has been felt by many visitors. Near the staircase an 'uncomfortable feeling' has been expressed by some people along with the impression of a distinct drop in temperature.

Railway Street

Loftcat Limited, in Railway Street, was formerly Pearce's, the baker's shop, until recent times. I visited it a number of times whilst working in Hertford and was surprised to learn that this friendly little shop had a ghostly reputation. Pictures would fall off the counter for no reason and items also mysteriously fell off the shelves quite regularly. One staff member who was prepared to discuss it was Sheila Woodford, 'We're not allowed to smoke down there (the cellar) yet there's the distinct smell of cigars sometimes. I get a cold shiver when I have to go down there, it gives me the creeps.'

Another property in Railway Street, No. 12, was in the news in the 1960s. At that time Wally's Butchers occupied the site (until 2002). The flat over the butcher's shop became notorious because the couple who lived here heard ghostly noises. Every night at the same time – 10pm, they heard a baby crying, when their own children were fast asleep. One night they heard what sounded to them like a child's tricycle riding over the bare floorboards in the attic. It got louder and louder until the couple got to the attic door to open it, whereupon it stopped abruptly. No explanation was ever forthcoming about these unearthly noises. What is known is that the site was formerly home to the Black Horse Inn from 1857 to 1919.

Ware Road

The Value Centre, opposite the police station, in Ware Road, used to be occupied by a post office. Some thirty-five years ago Mike Sage lived here for a period of three years and he told me all about his unusual experiences during that time. One room in the house always seemed to be damp and cold, at all times of the year. This was the main bedroom, directly above the shops. Mike's cat was obviously terrified by this room; its fur would stand on end when near to it and it would run away rather than go inside. Although it was the biggest bedroom the oppressive atmosphere experienced there made Mike avoid it too. He much preferred to get a good night's sleep in the smaller bedroom, so never used the more spacious room. He still heard odd thumps and bumps emanating from this bedroom when settling down to sleep. Later on he learned that a former postmaster who lived in the flat during the late 1960s had been a very heavy drinker. The postmaster got into terrible debt and one day he put a shotgun to his wife's head, dismembered their cat and used a revolver to shoot himself.

Church Street

The Old Vicarage is well known in Hertford for two reasons, it has a garden path made out of old gravestones and it is haunted by the ghost of a woman wearing Victorian clothes. This apparition is only seen from the knees upwards indicating that floor levels have changed considerably since her time. She has been seen strolling around the waiting room and across the entrance hall. There was also a claim made by a lady some years ago; she allegedly saw two Roman soldiers guarding the front gate of the house.

Peg's Lane

Leahoe House in Peg's Lane was originally built in the nineteenth century for a medical man, Dr George Elin; it was acquired by Hertfordshire County Council in 1935 and was initially used as a recreation and leisure centre. Now the charity, The Hertfordshire Society for the Blind, trades union Unison and the Hertfordshire Probation Service all lease offices from the council. During the 1980s a volunteer worker called Tony Joshua was locking up Leahoe House. As he walked through the snooker room he felt an unaccustomed and unaccountable fear stealing over him. He continued on into the corridor and found that his eyes were drawn to the top of the stairs. He saw a woman standing there wearing a long skirt and a nun's habit. Tony's fear was replaced by a feeling of great calm and he stared in fascination for some time before finally switching off the lights and as he turned to leave he saw that the nun was still there. On subsequent occasions Tony felt the nun's presence but never again did he see her.

Balls Park

A huge development of new homes is being constructed in over 60 acres of grounds at Balls Park. The site was purchased by the developers from former owners the University of Hertfordshire. Originally Balls Park Mansion belonged to Hitchin Priory and then, following the Dissolution of the Monasteries it passed into the possession of the Wills family. The mansion dates from the seventeenth century and it is a listed building. When it was part of the University of Hertfordshire several staff members laid claim to a sighting of the 'anniversary ghost'. These ghosts are so-called because they always appear at the same time of year and in this case it was during the month of October. There have been a number of sightings in the vestibule and the upstairs corridors, always in October. The most recently documented manifestation was in the early evening of October 2001. A member of the University staff was working late and as she went to leave the mansion she discovered that the security staff had locked the front door. She turned around to seek an alternative exit and was startled to see a grey figure standing under the balcony. After this incident a security guard who was on patrol one evening claimed that an unseen force suddenly 'threw him backwards several feet'. Legend has it that a woman committed suicide when she jumped from the balcony into the vestibule one day in October. It will be interesting to see if the haunting tradition is maintained when the new residents have settled in at Balls Park Manor!

WARE

Amwell House

Amwell House was formerly the home of John Scott, the eighteenth-century poet whose family made their fortune in the malting business; it had extensive grounds which contained an interesting grotto. John's daughter Maria inherited the property on her father's death in 1783. Maria died in 1863, the estate was sold to a property development company and Scotts Road was built. Scotts Grotto was preserved and renovated and is a Grade I Listed Building. The garden, including the summerhouse, is Grade II Listed. Scotts Grotto is open to the public from April to September and it is well worth a visit. Amwell House is now used as the administrative headquarters building for Herts Regional College. It is haunted, particularly the attics, which at one time were used as a caretaker's flat. I have been told about a number of reports of unearthly footsteps being heard, the sounds are said to emanate from the unoccupied attics. There have also been occasional sightings of a 'grey lady' seen in Amwell House, is this the spirit of Maria Scott?

The Haunting of Steve Webster

A friend of mine, Steve Webster, is an intelligent and careful person, who is also extremely rational and one of the most methodical witnesses to a haunting it has been my pleasure to interview. He currently works for the Probation Service but in the 1970s he left his native Widnes to study at the London School of Economics and Political Science. After graduation he was offered a one-year temporary contract to work in Hertfordshire. The employment prospects back in Widnes looked decidedly unpromising so it wasn't a difficult decision to make. He accepted the temporary post and set about finding lodgings. Young Steve considered himself fortunate when he discovered a room to rent with a family in Ware as it was not too far from his workplace. He was later to regret ever moving to this particular house. I will let Steve tell the story in his own words. 'The house was a Victorian one, in Watton Road. The father and mother both worked and there were three children. The eldest was in his teens, the middle child was an eleven-year-old girl and the youngest was a boy of seven. The couple, who we will call the Smiths, had their own bedroom, the sons shared another room, the daughter had her own room and I was given the fourth bedroom. The family hadn't had lodgers before and as far as I know they didn't ever have any again after I left. The geography of the bedrooms was such that there was a flight of stairs up to a right-angle landing of about a yard square, up a few more steps and my bedroom was on the left, off another mini landing (itself another right-angle turn). There were a few more steps and then entrances to the other three bedrooms and a bathroom. My bedroom was on its own and overlooked the rough ground at the back of the house, which was being worked as a quarry, with much earth being moved on a regular basis. Since those days a housing estate has appeared. I lived in the house between late September 1974 and late January 1975 and it was particularly dark there at night. I should say at this point that I am not given to remembering dreams, to sleepwalking or flights of imagination. I have no history of mental illness, was not on any medication, didn't use illegal drugs and drank alcohol rarely and in small amounts. Even after more than thirty years since the events I am about to describe I cannot recall any dream I have ever had.

I didn't question why the youngest boy preferred to share his brother's room rather than sleep in his own room. The Smiths told me that he'd slept for a short time in the room I was now renting, but preferred to share with his older brother; the room was standing empty so they decided to take in a lodger. It was the cold which started to wake me up. Again, let me say that I'm not prone to this either. At night in bed I tend to roast. It always occurred about 5.15am to 6am. I began waking up shaking with cold which went right through to my bones. It would last until 6am at the latest and then revert to normal temperature. This was the first sign. It wasn't every night but it was very regular. Then another detail was added. The room was a rectangular one and from the bed I would look down at the door, which was kept closed at night as were all the doors. I'd see light under the door as well as shadows and hear the footsteps of someone walking to left and right on the landing behind the door. At this point, after it had happened a few times I queried it in my head. The landing was too small for more than one or two steps at most and it didn't lead anywhere else, so why would someone be walking it and why was the light on? I couldn't find any answers so I determined to open the door the next time it happened and get a rational explanation. I duly did this – but there was no light on and nobody there. Once I looked out the footsteps stopped. Back in the room it didn't start again. I looked out on several occasions and got the same result each time but the intense cold would still be felt until 6am and then it would dissipate. Soon, yet another detail was added. The steps would come into the room (without the door opening) and walk up the room on my right hand side. I'd hear the footsteps come up and down but there was nobody there, or at least, no one that I could see. Much as I tried in the hard light of day, I could never make my footsteps make any sound on the fully carpeted bedroom floor. The cold now seemed more intense than ever.

I began applying scientific methods. I needed to prove that I was awake when the manifestations occurred, so I began to put my wristwatch and the alarm clock together on the bedside cabinet. Then, when strange things started to happen I would wind one of them forward or backward in random fashion by two hours, five hours, twenty-three minutes. After 6am I'd go back to sleep for an hour and then wake up and be able to confirm to myself that I'd been awake and done this. I added something else. I began putting the alarm clock underneath an upturned metal waste paper bin on the floor. No one else could touch it without my hearing it. I proved to myself that it was really happening but that left the big question – what exactly was happening? I did ask several times if there was anybody there and what they wanted from me. That didn't stop the footsteps coming and going – they didn't even pause. All this time I never mentioned it to the family – that is until my mysterious visitor added another effect. One morning, at the same time as always, the cold was even more intense than usual. I was shivering and shaking and my teeth were chattering. I put my head below the duvet cover seeking any spot of warmth I could find. Some moments later my unwanted visitor grabbed my left upper arm in first one and then two places and shook me vigorously. He, she, or it said nothing. In any other circumstance wouldn't someone address the person in bed by their name or say, 'it's 5.45am, it's work today?' My visitor remained silent and to my regret I dived down into the bed and stayed there. In due course I heard the footsteps going away from me and then out of the room, but without the door opening and closing. I stayed under cover until the temperature returned to normal and then I looked out. With hindsight I should have responded, perhaps my visitor wanted my help with something. Maybe he or she had manifested but I didn't even ask a question or take a look, just automatically went into 'scared mode'. I should have made a positive response, however my visitor didn't try to contact me subsequently. The light, moving shadow, intense cold, visits to my room and the footsteps happened a few more times, rather less regularly, but they didn't stop altogether.

In an as matter-of-fact a fashion as possible I asked the Smiths if there was anything odd about the room. I gave them no detail of my experiences and on the first couple of occasions they laughed away my query. When I persisted and they could sense there was a reason for my asking I gathered a few more details. They had travelled a long way to this neighbourhood in their search for work and then they had started house hunting. The couple viewed several properties but for one reason or another turned them down. Then an estate agent told them about this house, which was 'a bit unusual' as it had stood empty for two years and remained in exactly the same condition in which the previous occupants had left it. There had even been a half-eaten meal on the table and a tomato sauce bottle with its cap off was also left behind. It was as if the residents had suddenly fled the place in terror. The owners subsequently instructed their agents that the property should be sold. They refused point-blank to return to the house to give any instructions for the sale or to make any arrangements for it to be cleaned up and left all this detail in the hands of the estate agents. A few days after the Smiths bought the place they were all downstairs when they heard a loud crash from upstairs, as though a chandelier had fallen from the ceiling and smashed to pieces. They went upstairs to investigate; there was no chandelier and no sign of anything lying broken on the floor. The youngest boy had originally slept in the back bedroom but said that he didn't like it and moved into the front bedroom with his brother.

I went on from these lodgings to stay in a caravan in Bayford Wood for a few months. I would hear scurrying inside my new home at night, which later proved to be the sounds made by some mice. I also heard a thud and scratching noises on the roof, but that turned out to be an owl. At no point did I ever think that the caravan might be haunted. I never experienced here, nor anywhere else that I subsequently stayed, any periods of that ephemeral yet intense cold that always heralded my unwelcome experiences at that house in Ware.'

CHAPTER TEN

SPECTRES OF STAGE AND SCREEN

BRITAIN'S 'HOLLYWOOD'

Borehamwood is Britain's answer to Hollywood. For Los Angeles, California, read Borehamwood, Hertfordshire, where our mainstream, homegrown, movie making industry is based, with enormous studios located at nearby Elstree and at Leavesden, just outside Watford. A cluster of studios, permanent production bases and film locations are all located in this south-west corner of Hertfordshire. Some 85% of the industry's skilled workforce lives within a 25 mile radius of these 'dream factories'. Filming in Elstree dates back some ninety-five years, to when the first studio was built. It was rapidly followed by five more studios, thereby establishing the largest production capacity outside Hollywood and just two of these original studios remain. Elstree Film Studios, owned by Hertsmere Borough Council, is where the *Star Wars* trilogies and the *Indiana Jones* trilogies (six of the top grossing films of all time) were all made during the 1970s and 1980s. *Who Wants To Be a Millionaire?* and *Big Brother* are also produced here. Some years ago these studios were extensively renovated and they now offer outstanding on-site facilities. They provided pre-production facilities for the film *Saving Private Ryan* and the development of special effects for *Tomorrow Never Dies*.

The BBC centre at Elstree was purchased by the BBC in 1980 and it is situated where Neptune Studios, the first film studio in the UK, was opened in 1914. The BBC centre is best known as the home of *East Enders* and *Holby City*. To this already impressive list may be added programmes such as *On the Buses* and *Inspector Morse*, which were also Elstree products. In the Tesco store at Elstree there is a large mural of *Moby Dick*, in tribute to the famous movie which starred Gregory Peck. It is a reminder to shoppers that they are standing on the site of the studios where that great film was shot.

Borehamwood's Gate Studio dates back to 1928, when it was originally called the Whitehall Studios, and was the smallest of the local studios. The Gate Studio was once described as 'a glorified aircraft hanger' and it was used for the making of silent films. With the advent of 'the talkies' its proximity to the railway station made it a less than ideal location for movie making. A man with a red flag and a loudhailer was employed to warn of the impending arrival of trains so that recording could be delayed till the train had gone again. The most famous film associated with the Gate was *Odette*, made in 1950, about the Second World War French Resistance heroine, Odette Churchill, who was awarded the George Cross. Starring Anna Neagle and Trevor Howard, it proved to be a very successful British movie. British film magnate J. Arthur Rank owned the Gate for a time and, as an active supporter of the Methodist Church, he made several religious films there. He made another fortune from photocopying machines when he joined forces with an American company to form Rank Xerox, which still has a presence in Welwyn Garden City to this day. From the 1950s to 2003 the Gate was home to Harkness Screens, manufacturers of cinema screens, and Aerofilms, Britain's leading supplier of aerial photography.

The Gate seems to have been haunted by several ghosts. The apparition of a former make-up artist who committed suicide in one of the offices was seen in recent times at Harkness Screens, before the building's closure in 2004. In the room where the cinema screens were made the ghost of a workman was also witnessed, he is believed to have died in a fall from one of the roof walkways. *The Borehamwood & Elstree Times* reported the Gate Studios hauntings in 2003 and interviewed Steve Oake, the maintenance man at the site, who had an encounter at the end of 2002. 'I was working on the floor looking up at the cinema screen and I saw someone, out of the corner of my eye, walk up the gangway and go behind some piles of foam. Usually the person comes out of the other side, but nobody came out. I went to look and there was nobody there.'

Simon Jones and his colleague Dave Blake were locking up the old studio building one night and knew that they were the last people to leave there so when they saw a figure move from a corner of the room and exit through a doorway they beat a hasty retreat.

The Edgware and Mill Hill Times picked up the story of the haunted former film studios in April 2003. They interviewed a personal assistant, Sue Carpenter, who had worked at the Gate Studio site. One day she noticed that the air had gone cold in her office. She described her experience as follows, 'I felt someone standing there and I looked around and there was this man. I did a double-take and he disappeared.' Sue gave a detailed description; the man was smartly dressed in a white shirt and black trousers. He was tall, bearded and in his forties or fifties. This was not her only sighting, as she had two more encounters whilst working late at night organising exhibitions. The heavily bearded man appeared in the corridor, this time he was wearing a long jacket. She said, 'When he went he faded. He did not make any movements, he just went.' On another occasion she did not get such a clear view of the ghost. 'I felt this rush of air. A plastic bag hanging on the door was swinging. This shadow, the form of this man, went whoosh past, outside the office door. It all happened in seconds. I walked out of the door and he had gone. There was a very distinctive wind. I had never felt that rush of wind before.' At the time of the interview Sue was looking forward to moving to smarter offices, with the imminent prospect of the Gate Studios being demolished (they were actually knocked down in 2006). She believed that there might have been a link between the uncertain future of the old studios and the apparitions, 'My mum always said if you are moving or changing things they get upset.' She mused about the fate of the ghost, 'I just feel sad. Where is he going to go?' Sue admitted that the apparition's identity remained unknown although she had heard about the accident in which a man was killed in a fall from some rigging. 'People have said that someone died here. There is definitely something.' Interestingly another female employee also met up with the very same apparition because her description tallied with Sue's, this was despite the fact that Sue had given her no details of her own visitation.

I made a journey to see the Gate Studio for myself in May 2005, at which time it had been acquired by Bryant Homes. It was an ugly old building, long neglected, with many broken windows. The Gate was separated from the railway station by a brick-built building which was directly in front of it. It struck me then that there is nothing remotely glamorous about film studios. 'Glorified aircraft hanger' was an apt description, as these places are freezing in winter and baking hot in the summer. Studios are merely 'factories for making movies' after all. I felt obliged to take a photograph, before it disappeared from the skyline forever, taking its ghosts with it no doubt.

A MOST HAUNTED LOCATION...

The Bushey and Bushey Heath area is located near Elstree Studios and so featured frequently as a backdrop for many film and TV shows including episodes of the *Avengers* and *Grange Hill*. One of Bushey's landmarks is the former International University in The Avenue. With its long, gated drive, huge clock tower, substantial buildings and extensive grounds this Grade II listed edifice has the most imposing of aspects. This attracted film and television production companies who used it for location shooting on feature films, television programmes and commercials. Many episode of *Judge John Deed* have been shot here and it has also featured in *Silent Witness*, *Midsomer Murders*, *Holby City*, *Little Britain* and *Monty Python's Flying Circus*, to name but a few. Sometimes a film crew have had to stay overnight in the residential area and they have been pleased to leave when the shoot was over, as some of the former students' quarters were quite creepy after dark. Electrical problems, particularly with the lighting, have plagued the site; this is often a sign that a place is haunted. There was an upstairs room that was said to be always cold and a little girl died at the school, allegedly after being thrown from her pony. I was determined to get to the bottom of this story. The little girl's ghost reputedly haunted the stairs of the old school, as the International University was formerly the Royal Masonic School and this tragedy dated from that era. When I first visited the site in 2000, it was empty and when I had a chat with the security guards I learned that some of them were uncomfortable when patrolling the corridors and grounds alone at night. I also found out about the underground tunnels beneath the school, which had to be checked out from time to time, were not an inviting place to be. One security man, who wished to remain anonymous, was certain that the Royal Masonic School was haunted. He was a bit reluctant to talk about it but I managed to prise out of him that he had heard unexplained noises here at night, like whistles being blown and also loud sobbing noises, as if someone was in great distress. He also said that some children had died in accidents at the school, but he couldn't or wouldn't go into any details. It also transpired that some of the 'television people' who worked here had been 'freaked out' by odd occurrences in the school. These included doors and windows opening of their own accord, strange noises being heard and objects which were mysteriously moved about when no one was around.

I renewed my acquaintance with the International University in May 2005, when I was fortunate enough to meet one of the custodians of the sprawling complex of buildings. Stephen was a young American ex-student at the university and he was able to tell me all about the ghost, whose name was Hillary. She had been the daughter of a former headmaster when this place had been the Royal Masonic School. There

The former International University, Bushey. The wandering ghost of a young girl (Hillary Sinclair) has been seen in what used to be chapel.

were various stories about her premature death; some said it was suicide, that she had thrown herself from one of the school towers, others maintained that her death was the result of a bad fall from a horse. Stephen related a strange personal incident that happened during his first week as a student at the university. He was studying alone in his room on campus when he distinctly heard the sound of galloping hooves passing by his window. When he looked up there was nothing to be seen and he got up and had a good look around. There was no trace of a horse and no horses were kept on the grounds. He didn't know it then but later on he learned that a headmaster had, many years ago, used a pony and trap as his regular means of transportation. At the time of our discussions the site was owned by some wealthy Irish property developers and was due to be redeveloped as luxury apartments.

My next contact was Gordon Metcalfe, a former art teacher at the RMS, who told me that there was an *Old Masonians* magazine which was circulated to 1,100 ex-members of staff and students. Gordon was a teacher at the RMS from 1960 until it closed (it was sold in 1977). He was able to confirm that a former headmaster, Norman Sinclair, had indeed lost his sixteen-year-old daughter, not to suicide or a riding accident but more prosaically as the result of an infection. This happened in 1947, some thirteen years before Gordon joined the staff. The former art teacher was aware that Hillary's ghost had been seen 'wandering in the chapel'; at least one security guard had refused to set foot in the place. Some years ago, when the chapel was being prepared for a film, electrician Steve Smith took a series of photographs of his handiwork with his new digital camera. Steve had taken about ten or so shots as he made his way up to the altar without noticing anything unusual. The final photograph, however, showed a strange, smoky figure, which could not be explained.

Gordon Metcalfe had also talked with a number of security guards and he discovered that they had seen young boys 'larking about' on the playing fields many years after the school had closed down. The lads were playing football and some were turning somersaults. Determined to catch the trespassers the guards formed a pincer movement to cut them off so that they wouldn't get away. The men quickly rounded the corner but there was no trace of any children, they had just vanished into thin air. The guards could only conclude that they had seen some of the ghosts that haunt the site at first hand.

I arranged to meet Gordon Metcalfe on Friday 20 May, 2005, exactly one hundred and five years to the very month since the foundation stone was laid at the school by the Duke of Connaught and Strathearn. I felt extremely privileged to be given a personal guided tour of the fascinating 60 acre site. It was a final opportunity to see the original RMS, as just three months hence Comer Homes were scheduled to redevelop the site into luxury apartments. We met in the grand entrance hall and made for the Chapel, a short walk past the headmaster's house. We entered the detached building and I was struck by the musty smell associated with disuse and damp. Building work on the Royal Masonic School had begun in 1900 with Charles Keyser as the chairman of the building committee and treasurer of the board of governors. It cost £396,950 and as the money began to run out the chapel was scaled down from the original ambitious grand design. It now seemed forlorn yet atmospheric and an overnight vigil might have produced some interesting results. Except for one day a week the school day began here. On one wall was a plaque to the memory of former headmaster, T.R.N. Crofts, MA, head from 1915–1938. Gordon mentioned that this head was the one who had travelled about in a pony and trap. As we made our way out of the chapel my guide pointed out some of the brass memorial plaques set into the wall, dedicated to the memory of former boys who had either died at school or during the school holidays. One tragic story was about a lad who died on the playing fields when a hockey ball hit him in the chest. It transpired that he had a heart defect and the sudden blow killed him. It was not so surprising then that the playing fields were subjected to the ghostly manifestations of children. Gordon, my guide, had devoted a large part of his life to these fatherless boys. I was touched to learn that every boy who attended the Royal Masonic School had lost his father and his education was paid for by his late father's fellow Freemasons. The Freemasons are indeed a most generous society; they are major league players in the realm of British charities. As a secret society the Freemasons have generally suffered a bad press due to uninformed and biased reporting. It may be said that the Brotherhood has a history of persecution, but here was a shining memorial to their charitable works. The Royal Masonic Hospital in north London, now also closed, existed due to the patronage of Freemasons as did various old people's homes across England and a girl's school in Rickmansworth. Moves have been afoot for some time to make the Masons' meeting places and their lodges less secretive and more open to the public. This should help to redress the balance in favour of a more positive image of Freemasonry.

We continued on to the 'big school' as it was known in RMS days, when school assemblies were held here. I peeped around a curtain to see actor Martin Shaw dressed in his robes, filming an episode of *Judge John Deed*. We hurried through the quadrangle and saw one of his co-stars, Jenny Seagrove, deep in thought, obviously mentally rehearsing her lines. I am not in the slightest bit star struck but it was still quite exciting to suddenly and unexpectedly come across two well-known stars of the small screen hard at work. Our tour led us through the dining hall where teachers and pupils used to eat their lunch together. We then made our way into the masters' dining hall; teachers would meet to have both their breakfast and their evening meal with colleagues in this room. The stained glass ceiling was most impressive – Gordon pointed out the symbols of Freemasonry set into it – the level, set square, square and compass and the mallet. The imposing fireplace had the words 'audi, vide, tace' carved into the stonework, which is Latin for 'I see, I hear, I take note'. I learned from my guide that a 'lewis' (a piece of lifting equipment) was the term used for the son of a Mason and the daughter of a Mason was known as an 'aslar' (a piece of masonry).

From the masters' dining hall we made our way outside again. Television vans were scattered around the buildings and there were generators, cabling, sound and lighting equipment everywhere. We passed the old tuck shop, Gordon's former art and craft block, the observatory and the swimming pool, now empty of water but with a set under construction inside it. We strolled on to 'Croft's Piece'; a large swathe of green-belt landscaping that was completed in 1938. It took eight years of toil by the school's pioneer corps. The boys had worked with hand-tools, picks and shovels, to create their own rugby pitch, and a huge earth bank had been made by them too, also using only manual labour. The resultant space this created had been turned into a cricket pitch, surrounded by a 400-metre running track. This was situated at the back of the school, bordering Finch Lane. Croft's Piece land will remain verdant, it is protected green-belt acreage and any new buildings would be built only on brown-field sites, where there are existing buildings. We passed more school landmarks – the laundry, sanatorium and infirmary. There had even been a mortuary at one time, which was later used as a store. Many Irish girls worked at the RMS, where they had been variously employed in the dining hall as domestic maids and as cleaners. In South Drive there once resided a number of tradesmen, carpenters, electricians and plumbers, as well as a chef. I discovered that there had been some famous Royal Masonic old boys, actor Anthony Andrews, Sir Stuart Hampson, former chairman of the John Lewis partnership (he had achieved considerable academic success at this school and, later on, at university) as well as Sir Dick Evans who went on to become chief executive of British Aerospace despite leaving the RMS with no 'O' levels.

After the guided tour we sat and chatted in the entrance hall, where I asked about the underground tunnels that I'd been told existed under the school. I was informed that there are subways which led under the cloisters to each house and to the laundry. The subways carried the hot water and gas services; they were big enough for a man to walk along standing upright. They had come in useful during the Blitz in the Second World War when they had served as temporary air raid shelters. Masters and boys took refuge here, they had eaten and slept and apparently it had 'got rather smelly' down there. As the school lies in a basin the fire-watchers on duty in the clock tower could see the huge fires of London reflected in the clouds at night. The RMS was deprived of its headmaster for part of the war when Norman Sinclair was reclaimed by the Army because he held a regular commission in the reserves. He served with the officer training corps and held the rank of Major. He served between 1938 and 1940 but a campaign to restore him to his beloved school was eventually successful and he continued as headmaster right up till 1957. I am extremely grateful to Gordon Metcalfe for a glimpse into a vanished world.

My next stop was to visit Steve Smith, the electrical contractor at the old school. He lived just a stone's throw from the grounds. When I met him I found a friendly, pragmatic tradesman with a keen interest in photography. The photograph that he had taken in the chapel was puzzling him, nobody had been able to offer an explanation and no fault could be found with his camera. He was certain that there had been no mist or vapour present when he took his photographs yet it was plainly visible on one of the shots. After careful scrutiny of the picture I explained that he might have captured what some paranormal investigators term a 'stage three manifestation'. This is the stage where a ghost has utilised enough energy to assume a sub-physical form with the aid of plasma. Plasma, sometimes called the fourth element, is not solid, nor is it a liquid or a gas – a good example of plasma is a candle flame. Sub-physical phenomena may be invisible to the naked eye but videotape or photographs can capture this ethereal presence. It may be seen as a swirling bright blue or dull grey indistinct shape, as illustrated by Steve's picture. Typically the outline or silhouette of an apparition is created but it may also resemble the shape of a figure or face. If Steve had been psychically sensitive he may have sensed the presence of a ghost particularly strongly at this stage. Stage three manifestations' movement is smoke-like and can occur at slow speed or in sudden brief and irregular bursts of great speed. At night-time torches and camera flashes have been known to highlight entities at this level so that they become visible to the human eye.

Over many years the Royal Masonic School has provided a backdrop for a multitude of cinematic and televisual productions. Between 2000 and 2005 it was estimated that well over 200 episodes from a variety of films, television series and commercials have been shot here. The entertainment industry is a hard taskmaster, a day's filming may sometimes be required to produce as little as five seconds of actual screen time. Many film crew members will have found Bushey's Royal Masonic School an eerie place, particularly after dark when a phantom school matron has been seen patrolling the buildings.

LEAVESDEN

Leavesden Aerodrome, just north of Watford, attracted the Millennium Group, which bought the site and established Leavesden Developments Ltd in 1995. The first movie to be filmed here, that same year, was *Goldeneye*, one of the most successful James Bond movies ever made, starring Pierce Brosnan. Since then the company has established world-class studios and film-making facilities, with over one million square feet of studio space and over a hundred acres of clear horizon backlot. Leavesden has drawn in top production firms including JAK Productions with the *Star Wars* prequels, directed by George Lucas. Leavesden was also home to *Sleepy Hollow*, starring Johnny Depp, which was made almost entirely here. All of the *Harry Potter* series were filmed here, as was *The Dark Knight*, one of the Batman movies, which was made in 2008.

There is a ghost story attached to this site, dating back to an accidental death during the Second World War, when Leavesden Aerodrome housed the Rolls-Royce factory. An RAF corporal tried to open the hanger door on hanger number two, using a ratchet which operated the chains to lift the door. Unfortunately gale force winds were blowing through the country at the time and a sudden gust caused the heavy door to come crashing down on the unfortunate airman and he died from his injuries. It was said that on windy nights the sound of rattling chains could still be heard, although both chains and hanger are history now. The ghost of an RAF corporal wearing Second World War uniform has been seen in the area where the hanger used to be.

PALACE PHENOMENA

The Palace Theatre, in Clarendon Road, Watford, was built in 1908 as a music hall and it is famous as the venue where Charlie Chaplin performed in the days before he achieved his tremendous Hollywood success. The Palace Theatre has also achieved notoriety as one of the many haunted theatres in Great Britain. One incident happened at 3am in the morning while workmen were busy erecting a new set, they were startled to see some curtains, covering one of the entrances, part as though someone had just walked through – but there was no one there. Immediately after this footsteps could be heard, they crossed to another door and then the curtains were once again moved aside, but still no presence could be seen. At another time an usherette was locking up the gallery when she saw a figure that walked down the aisle, leapt over the barriers and disappeared. Backstage staff have sensed an invisible presence and heard unexplained footsteps. One dressing room in particular has strong feelings of a presence, an icy-cold atmosphere sometimes prevails and ghostly footsteps, which stop at the door, are heard. Maintenance staff and two of the theatre's executives have heard the unearthly footsteps. For some reason which is lost in the mists of time the Palace Theatre ghost is known as 'Aggie', but it may well be a multiple haunting as at least three people have died here during the theatre's long history. A follow spotlight operator is known to have died when he fell from the gallery. A dresser was also killed in a fall and the third fatality was a stage hand.

THE PHANTOM PLAYWRIGHT

Hertfordshire's most famous literary luminary, Irish playwright George Bernard Shaw, chose Ayot St Lawrence as his adopted home. It is a small village which lies between Harpenden and Welwyn, in tranquil rural surroundings yet conveniently close to London. I was intrigued to learn why the great man had chosen this particular place to live out the rest of his days. GBS's choice of abode was made when he visited St Lawrence's churchyard and came across the grave of Mary Anne South, who died at the age of seventy. The inscription on her tombstone read 'Her time was short'. If longevity was associated with the village then this was the place for Shaw. It proved to be a wise choice as he lived to the ripe old age of ninety-four. He arrived with his wife Charlotte in 1906 and rented the rectory which had been built four years previously. The Shaws continued to rent for about twelve years before buying the property outright. They lived in the village from 1906 to 1950 and the Irishman wrote over forty plays and continued writing into his nineties. George Bernard Shaw achieved the unique distinction of winning both an Oscar and the Nobel Prize for Literature. When he first moved to Ayot

Shaw's Corner, Ayot St Lawrence. George Bernard Shaw's spirit returned to his former home to prove that there is life after death.

St Lawrence the playwright used a bicycle and a motorcycle to get around. With his increasing fame, success and wealth he upgraded to a huge Rolls Royce. GBS employed a chauffeur, Fred Day, but often drove the big car himself which led to some close shaves on the locality's twisting country roads. Ayot St Lawrence can only be approached by way of lanes so narrow that two cars cannot pass one another and even a moderate snowfall has been known to cut the village's connections with the outside world. The playwright's Edwardian rectory home was affectionately known as Shaw's Corner by the other villagers.

The eccentric, quixotic Shaw was convinced that there was an afterlife and he told his housekeeper, Alice Laden, that he would prove it to her. Shortly after the great man's death Alice heard a knock on the kitchen door and, without thinking, from force of habit, invited her employer in. Framed in the doorway stood Shaw, 'I heard a noise and thought you may have had an accident,' he said. As Alice started to explain that she was only sorting out her cupboards she realised that she was alone in the kitchen. The late playwright made one final visitation to his trusted housekeeper some days later. While she was standing at the bottom of the stairs she clearly heard his footsteps on the landing, then he called out 'Are you there, Mrs Laden?' before his footsteps faded away again. Questioned by a reporter from the *Herts Advertiser* in 1980 the housekeeper said, 'I was not afraid. I do not question these things, neither am I interested in the supernatural. I only know that Mr Shaw had appeared and that he had spoken to me.'

Shaw's Corner is now a National Trust property and various paranormal phenomena continue to manifest here. Custodian Paul Williamson has found doors open which he was certain that he had closed and a chord was played on the Bechstein in front of Williamson and two other witnesses when nobody was anywhere near the piano. Custodians have become acquainted with a ghostly tradition at Shaw's Corner. On their first night at the house the security alarm sounds off for no apparent reason.

It is clear that George and Charlotte were a devoted couple and extremely happy together in their Ayot St Lawrence home. Both had their ashes scattered in the garden near the little revolving summerhouse where GBS penned much of his work. Some of the National Trust staff and volunteers at Shaw's Corner are convinced that the place is haunted by its former residents. It may be their love for their old home that binds the Shaws to the former rectory. Lawrence of Arabia was a good friend of GBS and there are stories that his ghostly presence has been felt too. It has been said that the distinctive exhaust sounds of an old Brough Superior motorcycle, the particular model that Lawrence owned, has been heard around the lanes surrounding his former friends' house.

CHAPTER ELEVEN

UNINVITED GUESTS

EVIL AT BROXBOURNE

The following stories are taken from my extensive case notes made on APIS investigations over recent years. They involve people and places haunted by unwelcome presences. It is not always easy to get rid of these often quite terrifying, invisible assailants, as some of these incidents illustrate.

A few years ago Julie Salmon emailed me about some strange experiences at her flat in Cozens Lane East in the Silverfield area of Broxbourne. Her problems began in June 1989. It started with the minor annoyance of light bulbs constantly blowing. This was familiar as I come across the phenomenon frequently. One indicator of a haunted house is light bulbs which blow far more frequently than is normal. When spirits are trying to appear they may use an electricity source to manifest and it seems, often, to be drawn from light bulbs and batteries. Small, unaccountable noises were heard in the night. Then one morning Julie got up to find knives embedded in the kitchen walls as though a mad knife-thrower had been at work. The knives were kept in a magnetic knife-holder, well out of the way of the children and the kitchen door had been locked, so how had the knives come to have been hurled at the wall? More strange things happened during the night. In the mornings shampoo would be found spread all over the bathroom floor or cat food would be strewn around the kitchen. Then something weird happened in full daylight. One afternoon Julie's record deck, which had a cup standing on it, started up all of a sudden and the turntable spun around, sending tea flying everywhere. Dark shadows appeared on the walls in the daytime and the children's bedroom got so cold that icicles began to form. As Julie went to answer the front door the teddies that had been on top of the children's clothes cupboard were unexpectedly 'thrown off the top of the wardrobe in one sweep. I just ran into the living room and was panicking because I was very scared.' Julie's friend Clare tried to calm her down while the sound of bells could be heard in the bedroom. There was a walk-along toy in that room with bells which rang when it was pushed. Something unseen was pushing along the toy now and Julie noticed that her cat had made itself scarce.

In an effort to understand what was going on in her flat Julie visited the library to check the history of Cozens Lane East. All that she could find out was that greenhouses had once stood on the site, which wasn't much help. She continued her search with a visit to the vicar of St Augustine's church. At this stage Julie's eldest child was making strange noises in her throat and insisting that she saw a strange man on her bed. The vicar visited the flat one afternoon and blessed every room with holy water. Unfortunately, as is sometimes the case in haunted properties, things actually got a lot worse after this blessing. Julie's daughter said that 'the man' was in the corner and then he was in another corner, darting all around the room. Various household items were moved about the place too. Julie was becoming so scared that she now wanted to leave the flat as soon as possible. In desperation she called in a psychic from Enfield called Teresa. Teresa arrived, accompanied by her husband, and together they used a censor to spread incense smoke in every room while they recited prayers from their Bible. Before leaving the couple advised Julie to remain in the flat for twenty-four hours because they had 'put a seal on every door and window', figuratively speaking. Julie's boyfriend, Paul, came to stay, to lend his support and the couple were advised to only talk about happy things. The morning after the 'cleansing' strange things were still going on around Julie, odd little draughts and wall shadows were noticed. Paul said that he had seen some unexplained lights in the bedroom. Teresa returned the following night, she assured Julie that whatever 'it' was, had gone now. The psychic took Julie into the children's bedroom, which had always been cold before, and showed her how warm and calm it now felt. Teresa's husband carried out healing on Julie, placing his hands above her. 'A kind of warmth ran down my body to my toes, it made all my fears go and I felt calm and relaxed like never before, I felt I could have slept for a week.' Teresa explained that the lights which Paul had seen were from the tunnel that had been provided for the spirit to move back to the place he had come from. Julie's awful two months' ordeal was finally at an end.

Julie eventually came up with her own theory about her haunting. She remembered that her 'ex' had been seeing a Norfolk girl and Julie and her husband parted company at the same time as these weird events began to unfold. Her 'ex' later revealed that his Norfolk girlfriend was a follower of the 'Dark Arts'. Julie surmised that this strange girl might have sent something sinister to plague her home. Norfolk has sometimes been called a 'witch county' due to the historical prevalence of witches in this locality. Witchcraft certainly has been strongly associated with Norfolk, along with other parts of East Anglia.

CECIL HOUSE, CHESHUNT

In my books about the paranormal I have concentrated on ghost reports from within the previous thirty years but occasionally I come across an older story which intrigues me. Such was the case with the Cecil House haunting, which I came across whilst researching in the Waltham Cross and Cheshunt area. Cedars Park is the site of Theobalds Palace, built by William Cecil, Lord Burghley, between 1560 and the early 1570s. In 1607 Theobalds was exchanged for Hatfield House and it became one of King James's favourite homes. He had the buildings enlarged and the park extended. Theobalds remained in use till the establishment of the Commonwealth of 1649-54 which was a republic, following the execution of Charles I. During this interregnum Theobalds was almost totally destroyed on the orders of Parliament. Only fragments of the palace survive along with some small sections of the park wall. On several occasions I have enjoyed strolling in the sun at Cedars Park, a site that is steeped in history.

Cecil House once stood opposite the entrance to Cedars Park. In the days when fine houses had servants to ensure their smooth running, a well-known senior executive in the publishing industry was persuaded by the extremely low price to purchase the lease of Cecil House for seven years. He moved in with his family and lived there for some considerable time quite happily without anything mysterious happening. At dusk one evening the executive's wife entered the oak bedroom and was startled by the sight of a strange female, draped in white with shoulder-length hair standing looking out of the window. The stranger seemed to be watching and waiting for someone. As suddenly as it had appeared the figure disappeared. Soon after this one of the maids claimed to have seen an ugly old woman peering at her through a lobby window. In the light of her own experience the mistress of the house was inclined to accept her maid's story, particularly in view of her employee's distressed state. A thorough search of the house and grounds produced no trace of the uninvited guests. The family now became alarmed by anomalous phenomena like footsteps walking up and down the staircase and in the oak bedroom as well as loud knocking noises from the courtyard outside. Nerves were further stretched by footsteps at night which were heard following both family members and their staff who went upstairs or into the oak bedroom. All noticed that the footsteps stopped at the corner near the fireplace, but nothing and nobody was ever seen to account for these sounds. The family began to feel intimidated, when they were all sitting together the door latch would lift then the door would very slowly open, yet no one would enter the room.

Then one night a servant, who had seen the old woman's ghost, had a dream and awoke screaming. The family calmed her down and she was able to tell them that she had been dreaming that she was asleep in the oak bedroom. The voices of two women quarrelling woke her up. The maid saw a young woman in an old-fashioned dress standing by the fireside. In another part of the room was the old woman whose ghost she had seen previously. The two people were arguing over the disappearance of a child. The young woman turned to the maid and said, 'I have never spoken to mortal before but I will tell you all. My name is Black and the old woman there is a nurse who has been long in our family.' With that the old woman came over and put her hand on the maid's shoulder which caused such excruciating pain that she woke up from her dream still screaming.

The maid's bizarre story made the mistress resolve to find the answer to the mystery surrounding her uninvited guests. She made many enquiries in the village and eventually discovered that seventy or eighty years back a lady had lived at Cecil House together with her niece, a Miss Black. So, it seemed, the younger figure was the ghost of the niece. This same apparition continued to be seen in the oak bedroom wringing her hands and looking at the corner near the fireplace. The floorboards were taken up at this spot but nothing was found. After the family moved out they learned that several previous tenants had encountered the same ghostly visitations. The full story of Cecil House was never determined as it was partially demolished and rebuilt and after this the manifestations ceased.

UFOS OVER HEMEL HEMPSTEAD AND WELWYN GARDEN CITY

From an 'olden times' story about uninvited guests let us move on to consider an altogether more contemporary paranormal mystery. In November 2008 and January 2009 reports of UFOs were made in the Hemel Hempstead area of Hertfordshire. On

Saturday 15 November 2008, at about 10.50pm, Caroline Weller of Tattershall Drive in Hemel Hempstead was travelling on the M25. She was about one or two junctions away from her hometown when she saw seven or eight lights in the sky. They were very low, seemingly in formation and were too big, too low and too bright to be either stars or an aeroplane. Caroline was aware of many other motorists slowing down to get a good look at this spectacle. She got closer and was literally beside the lights on the other side of the carriageway. She focussed her attention on the slightly larger one; she said 'It was a shuttlecock shape with some lines like a wave on a graph just above it.' Caroline described her encounter in the *Hemel Hempstead Gazette*, 'I truly have never seen anything like it in my life and I doubt I will again. It was one of those moments that would have been wonderful had someone been there to share it.'

The day after this, Sunday 16 November at approximately 5.50pm, Tony Lowe of The Flags, at Adeyfield in Hemel Hempstead, was moving the rubbish bin from his back garden in preparation for the Monday-morning collection. When he returned to shut the back door a bright orange light appeared from beyond the house opposite and headed across the sky heading south-east. At first Tony thought that it was a helicopter but became intrigued when he heard no sound, even when the object was overhead. The orange glow gradually diminished and revealed, in the witness's statement, 'an arrow-head, triangular-shaped object, dark grey, which moved to the west and then into the low cloud.' A few minutes later a second orange glow appeared, coming from the same direction, moving at the same speed. This time Tony called his wife Lorraine, who went to the front of the house and took a photo with her mobile. Tony was able to get a good look at the object with his binoculars and saw that it was a double arrowhead shape. The glow stopped and the object disappeared. This was then followed by third orange glow, which followed the same path, after which nothing more was seen.

On Thursday 8 January 2009 at around 10.20pm Curtis Miall was watching television when he spotted an orange sparkling light through his French windows. He reported the incident to *Hemel Today* and told them, 'It was just around for about five minutes – then it just went. It was very strange – quite bizarre. There was a UFO sighting in Costa Rica that looks very similar.' He got a photograph of the mysterious moving light which was posted on the *Hemel Today* website along with a video of the sighting. Some people speculated that what Mr Miall actually saw was a Chinese lantern. This Hemel Hempstead report came days after an unexplained incident at Conisholme in Lincolnshire. In the early hours of Sunday 4 January a wind turbine had one blade broken off and another badly damaged. It sparked claims of a possible UFO collision.

The *Welwyn & Hatfield Times* was inundated with reported sightings of UFOs over the weekend of 8 August 2008. Readers saw a massed group of lights flying in formation on several separate occasions. On the Friday night 'eight orange-coloured, diamond-shaped objects' were seen at 11pm in the skies across the Welwyn and Hatfield area. Rachel Albuquerque, of High Grove, Welwyn Garden City was quoted, 'I heard one of the taxi drivers say what on earth is that in the sky?' She continued, 'I looked up to see a number of probably eight orange diamond-shaped objects. One of the objects travelled to a different position whilst the others appeared to be hovering. They were definitely not aeroplanes, my husband is a pilot and he would know; he would estimate they could have been 20 or 30 miles away if not further. We watched for a couple of minutes and as some cloud cleared there appeared to be more coming in from the west.

I felt panicked by the sighting and hurried home, thinking something awful might be about to happen. It did feel like being in a sci-fi film for a few minutes.'

The previous weekend, on Saturday 2 August, Emma Madgwick was at a house party in Valley Road, Welwyn Garden City. She looked up to see lights flying in formation across the evening sky. She was quite definite about her sighting saying, 'There is no way they were aeroplanes or anything like that. I was the first to see them and at first I thought they were just stars but they were glowing yellow, a really unusual colour. I then called out everyone and we were all out watching them for ages. My friend was so convinced that they were some kind of UFO that she turned on the news.'

SOUTH OXHEY 'GUARDIANS'

'Psychic consultant' Lynn lives in Oxhey and she told me about an interesting case that she investigated in South Oxhey. Lynn claims to be clairvoyant (from the French for 'clear seeing') clairaudient (from the French for 'clear hearing') and clairsentient (French for 'clear sensing'). In short, she claims the ability to see, hear and sense spirits. A lady from Oxhey contacted Lynn in March 2005 and needed her help quite urgently. One particular light in this lady's cottage would switch itself on; it was the type that you had to touch three times to bring it to its full intensity. No faults could be found with the wiring or the lights, which are frequently a favourite target for spirits' attention. On visiting the lady's home Lynn clearly saw a ghostly elderly couple, first a white-haired old woman appeared and then a man. The woman wore a pinafore dress and carried a duster. The couple looked shocked on realising that Lynne was able to see them. They seemed to be caretakers of the old cottage rather than previous owners and they were from the north of England. Lynn described them as 'a hard-working pair'. She asked them to stop playing with the lights as it was upsetting the present lady occupant and her child. The trouble ceased; the 'caretakers' are still about according to Lynn, but they no longer bother the current residents. From my own experience I have found that if you clearly and firmly tell ghosts not to bother you because they are frightening, inconvenient or otherwise being a nuisance to you, it is often enough to do the trick and get them to leave you in peace.

Over the years I have come across many, many claimants to advanced clairvoyant and mediumistic (communication with the dead) abilities. The overwhelming majority of these claims are vastly exaggerated. Many so-called psychics are self-deluded, attention seekers and/or money-grabbing charlatans intent on parting vulnerable, newly bereaved people from their cash. Happily there are a small minority like Lynn who have genuine psychic abilities and you can recognise them by certain character traits. They are usually giving rather than 'taking' people. They are down to earth, not showy or theatrical. They are matter of fact about their gifts like Chris Robinson, the 'Dream Detective', whom I wrote about in *Paranormal Bedfordshire*. Chris, along with other genuine psychics, is surprised that more of us aren't aware of our own latent psychic potential. Genuine psychics are also keen to develop others who are interested in the subject. They will volunteer their advice, training and encouragement without thought of financial gain. Above all they don't see themselves as something special, they aren't divas, indeed it is their very ordinariness which is so extraordinary! They don't charge inflated sums of money for their services. They are often reluctant about asking for any money at all in return for their help. If they do charge it is at a level that is easily affordable to everybody. As a general rule of thumb the less genuine the abilities the higher the charges that are demanded. The greedy, untalented majority, sadly, give all psychics a bad name. This is nothing new; during Victorian times along with a vast increase of interest in the supernatural there was an upsurge of unscrupulous and mercenary 'mediums'. Their aim was to fleece naïve, trusting, desperate and lonely victims but many charlatans were exposed by investigators like the magician Harry Houdini and the scientist William Crookes.

My own approach to paranormal investigation has always been that the spiritual and scientific approaches can and should be mutually compatible. We are all working to the same end, to try and make sense of the phenomena which we encounter on a regular basis. Psychic investigators with the right attitude may have as important a role to play in an investigation as our technical and scientifically-minded team members. It is gratifying when two psychically developed investigators corroborate each other's findings. The Chicksands Priory case is a good example, as documented in *Paranormal Bedfordshire*. Former self-confessed sceptic Roger Ward, the Priory's historian, was given many psychic impressions by medium Marion Goodfellow, during her 1999 visit. When he compared these statements with those made by Rose Gladden (the outstanding psychic healer and medium of her time) in 1976, the results were astonishing. 'It was as if the first clairvoyant had returned after twenty-three years,' he told me.

ASHWELL'S COTTAGE OF TERROR

Ashwell is a highly desirable north Hertfordshire village with a variety of timbered buildings and natural springs that feed the River Cam. The High Street is one of the most attractive of its kind in the whole county. It has its traditional pubs and, in a hollow beside the High Street, the little River Rhee rises clean and pure to form a pool in the chalk shaded by ash trees – hence the village's place name. Ashwell has managed to retain a post office, a butcher's shop and a bakery where other villages have not been so fortunate. House prices here reflect the added value that is attached to living in such a chic yet ancient village. Many residents commute to lucrative London jobs and are quite happy to pay the premium that is asked for village properties. Once a windmill stood on almost every hill surrounding Ashwell; now the only remnant is the well-restored example at Cromer village, which is well worth a visit. Ashwell is known as the village that used to be a town – at the time of the Norman invasion it was the sixth largest town in Hertfordshire. It lies about halfway between Royston and Baldock, where I live. My connection with Ashwell is my membership of the local writers' circle, the Morden and District Writers (MAD Writers, for short – rather appropriately). Our president is successful novelist Sarah Harrison who lives locally.

At the heart of the village is the iconic fourteenth-century church of St Mary the Virgin which dominates the skyline for miles around with its 'Hertfordshire spike' steeple. At weekends it is floodlit and especially impressive. Inside it is unexpectedly spacious with some remarkable Latin graffiti on its north wall. It translates as '1350 – miserable wild distracted the dregs of the people who alone survive to witness and tell the tale and in the end with a tempest Maurus this year thunders mightily in all the world 1361.' This is a reference to the storm on St Maur's Day, 15 January 1361,

Tower Cottage, Ashwell. Fan Anderson endured some truly terrifying paranormal phenomena when she lived here.

which may have cleared the air of any lingering infection from the Black Death. The Black Death, or bubonic plague, paralysed the country and Ashwell became infamous as Hertfordshire's 'plague village'. Part of the churchyard, opposite the Bushel and Strike pub, is occupied by a massive medieval plague pit. The deadliest pandemic in history was responsible for the death of seventy-five million people worldwide. On the first pillar near the south door there is another piece of a medieval message which translates as 'The corners are not pointed correctly I spit on them', a rebuke from the original architect. There have been several reports of strange happenings at St Mary's. One sighting in 1850 was particularly well-documented. Chorister Georgianna Covington saw a headless black figure glide silently through the churchyard from the rectory to the church door. She managed to rush through the chancel door before fainting and falling to the floor in front of the assembled choir.

Another haunted place in the village is Bear House, a local landmark, where the shade of an old man has been seen quite regularly, sitting quietly (and no doubt contentedly) drinking his beer. An altogether different and far more sinister haunting is associated with Swan Street's Tower Cottage, so called because there was a tunnel (since bricked up) between the cottage and the tower of St Mary the Virgin. I interviewed Fan Anderson, whose mother is my friend, the best-selling author Sarah Harrison. Fan had a remarkable story to tell. She moved out of Tower Cottage after only three months occupancy. In the summer of 1995 the twenty-one-year-old single mother moved into the Grade II listed sixteenth-century cottage by the church with her baby Ollie. She had joined a long list of tenants who have rented Tower Cottage over the years from absentee owners who live in Australia.

The cottage seemed perfect, conveniently located with plenty of character, but from the day that the young mum moved in she had an uneasy feeling as soon as she crossed the threshold. The place appeared small on the outside but surprisingly spacious inside. There was an attic and a large cellar; there was an outside toilet and various other outbuildings. Fan's best friend helped with the removals and with the unpacking but she, too, felt distinctly uneasy. They called out to each other for reassurance when they were in separate rooms, and neither one of them was comfortable when on their own. That night the real fear began as the young mum lay alone in her bed. 'I felt the fear of a child and I was terrified without knowing why,' she said. Her one-year-old son, who shared the same room, slept soundly. That first sleepover at the cottage was so bad that she was too scared to go downstairs, too frightened even to visit the toilet. She just lay in bed wishing that it was morning. It never got any better at Tower Cottage, Fan and Ollie spent many nights at her mum's house in Steeple Morden. Even during hot July days it was 'never welcoming' at the cottage, she always felt anxious when alone and there was often a bad smell in the main bedroom. She wondered if a mouse had died under the floorboards but each time she decided to do something about the nasty smell it would go away again. The young mother worried about her unexplained feelings, the unpleasant atmosphere, the fact that she never seemed able to relax here. Her son Ollie, however, seemed inexplicably content and able to sleep particularly well in his new home. Affairs reached a climax on the night of 31 July 1995, during that year's very hot summer. Fan awoke suddenly, at 3.45am, she was sure of the time because her bedroom overlooked the church clock. It was that special time of night, between night and dawn when the sky had 'gone from black to navy blue'. Her heart started thumping as, in the corner of her bedroom there appeared 'some fuzzy dots of light' which gradually joined together until they formed the image of a tall man who seemed to be looking intently at the young girl. She badly wanted to call out but felt unable to. The atmosphere in the room was heavily charged with anxiety and unhappiness, time seemed to stand still, and she could hear nothing. The tall, thin man looked unwell, distressed, in great need and the young woman also noticed that his skull looked badly deformed. 'As he held my gaze he seemed as real as you are. When he turned slightly the floorboards creaked.' She was never so frightened in her whole life; it was just as well that her little boy lay sound asleep. Somehow, despite her terror, she managed to reach down and grab the phone. She was about to call her father and as she looked up again the intruder had disappeared. Within ten minutes her father was at the front door and he searched the place thoroughly but there was no trace of the unwanted visitor. Unable to spend another minute in her bedroom Fan spent the rest of the night on the sofa downstairs. She was never to sleep in Tower Cottage again. For the next six weeks, before finally moving out altogether, she stayed with her mother at night-time. The morning after the haunting Sarah Harrison rang her daughter with the sad news that one of Fan's distant uncles, John, had died the previous evening. He had suffered with cancer of the head and neck. Some time later Fan saw a photograph of her uncle John, whom she hadn't seen since she was a child. Her reaction was to rush out to the toilet, where she was violently sick. The shock was too much, as he was the intruder that she had seen in her bedroom. She was unable to work out why an uncle that she hardly knew, who lived a long way off in the West Country, should choose her, of all people, to return to at the moment of his death. Her days of fear were, however, far from over.

The rector, the Reverend Patrick Bright, came in answer to his parishioner's appeal and he blessed Tower Cottage, but still Fan refused to spend her nights in her rented home. Even during the day the place was creepy, when she was in the sitting room with her friend Emma they heard movements on the bedroom floorboards, directly overhead. Fan described to me 'round lights, with streaks attached to them' that she had seen. They sounded like genuine orbs or 'alps' (anomalous light phenomena) to me. She took a photograph of the upstairs while she was in the garden. On the photograph, at one of the windows, were the head and shoulders of a woman.

One morning she returned to her cottage with one of her friends and they were mystified to find that every single door in the place, including the fridge door, had been thrown open. They went around systematically closing each door only to discover that every drawer, in every room, had also been yanked open, but nothing was missing, it had not been burglars.

Fan wondered if she might get some answers by researching the history of Tower Cottage and spent quite some time poring over books at the library. She learned about the tunnel which connected the church and cottage and she checked her cellar and found where the tunnel had been bricked up. Somewhere beneath her house or garden there was reputed to be a monks' hiding place. She traced former cottage occupants and talked to a number of Ashwell residents and a strange story began to emerge. Tower Cottage had the reputation for being a 'ghost magnet'; a variety of previous residents had reported a plethora of paranormal phenomena. There was a long history concerning the rapid turnover of tenants. I wondered out loud if the site itself may have been the focus for paranormal energies. Fan confirmed my supposition; she told me that several ley lines (earth energy lines) intersected at this point. Twenty years previously some tenants reported ghosts of 'ancient market traders' that were seen from the knees upwards. In order to reach Tower Cottage you have to go up several steps. My young friend's historical research indicated that before the cottage was built a street market existed on this site which would have been on a slightly lower level to the present site.

The late Marge Kite was a highly respected psychic medium who also lived in Ashwell, so I wasn't surprised to learn that she had visited the haunted cottage and that she had revealed a disturbing story. Marge wasn't there long before she picked up horrible impressions and didn't want to stay any longer than she had to. Marge found the whole atmosphere highly charged and she soon picked up the spirit of 'Ivy', who had lost a child. 'Ivy' had been made pregnant by a priest and had the clergyman's son in the cottage. As if being a single parent back in the sixteenth century wasn't bad enough, her neighbours thought that she was a witch. The child died in what was now Fan's bedroom and Marge asked if Ollie had been disturbed in his sleep. The young mum replied that while he was at the cottage her baby had slept particularly peacefully. Marge said that this was because Ivy was 'looking after him', which was just as well since Ivy definitely didn't like Fan. Marge then asked Fan if she had done something very bad to which the answer was no. Marge commented 'What comes around goes around'. I told my friend that this may have applied to a former life, as spiritualists believe in reincarnation and consequently that we have to atone for the sins committed in our former lives.

Christine Schofield lived in Swan Cottage, directly opposite Tower Cottage and one night she was awakened by a baby crying at her neighbour's home. It was so persistent that she got up and knocked at the door of Tower Cottage, but there was no reply and the place was in total darkness. There was no reply because the place was empty; it was one of the many times that Ollie and his mum were staying at Sarah Harrison's house. At nearby Church Path the end house is called Dove Cottage and next door a woman and two children died in a fire. Dove Cottage's windows overlook the village graveyard and footsteps have often been heard, hurrying past the cottage when there is nobody about. Fan wondered if these were Ivy's ghostly footsteps, making her way to the church for secret assignations with her priestly lover.

It was the week before she was finally moving out and Fan and her father wanted to check her cottage, they went inside and heard the sounds of running water – every tap in the place had been turned on. The daughter noticed that her normally sceptic father now seemed anxious. As she crossed the low-ceilinged corridor that separated the bedroom from the bathroom a fresh shock awaited her. In the bedroom doorway stood a strange woman. She was very tall and attractive; she wore her hair piled up, was in her late thirties or early forties and had on a long dress. Somehow the room appeared darker than usual but the woman seemed real enough, right down to the creak of the floorboards and the rustle of her dress when she moved. Was this Fan's first and last encounter with the ghost of Ivy? She yelled out for her father but the apparition vanished before he could reach the bedroom.

I was struck by the intensity of my young friend's experiences and fascinated by her narrative. I felt strongly sympathetic towards this pretty, personable and intelligent young woman. She had undoubtedly suffered a terrifying and traumatic few months in a badly haunted property ten years prior to our meeting. My strong intuition, that this case was absolutely genuine, was vindicated about a year or so after I first wrote about it. I received an email from some other former Ashwell residents who confirmed that they had also been haunted and badly scared and they, too, had been mightily relieved when they closed the door on Tower Cottage for the last time.

PHANTOM CATS OF TEWIN, BRAUGHIN AND CODICOTE

Alien Big Cats (ABCs) are a nationwide phenomenon that is more often associated with Yorkshire, Lincolnshire and Dorsetshire than Hertfordshire. Alien in this case means out of place rather than originating from another planet. An alternative name for them is phantom cats. The fact that they are (usually) black and extremely elusive may account for the 'phantom' tag. Researchers are known as cryptozoologists (from the Greek kryptos, 'hidden' + zoology, literally 'study of hidden animals'). The best authenticated sighting of an alien big cat in Hertfordshire happened in Tewin in 1998. Two police officers were on patrol in the neighbourhood one Monday night (August 3rd). It was at 11pm that they came face to face with a mystery big cat. PC Robin Juniper, a rural officer with East Hertfordshire Police later spoke to a reporter from the local newspaper, the *Herts and Essex Mercury*. 'We drove into the Bury Lane car park by Bramfield Park Woods and saw what we thought was a fox's eyes reflecting in the car's headlights. We turned the lights off and made the sound of a rabbit squeaking to entice it towards us. When it was about 120yds away we realised it was a big cat.' PC

Juniper was accompanied by PC Robin Ansell who described the cat as being the size of a labrador. The animal ran away before the officers could get a closer look to determine what breed it was.

This sighting followed a big cat encounter by a Braughing couple the previous night. On Sunday, David Dinwoodie and his girlfriend Ruth Fawcett were woken by the sound of an animal growling outside their bedroom window. 'In the middle of the night I was woken by our cat, Ellybon, who was sitting on our bedroom window sill,' said David. 'She was standing there frozen-looking. I woke Ruth up and we heard a very low growling sound, which was very frightening.' The couple found clumps of fur and claw marks in their garden the next morning.

In 2005 a Hertfordshire celebrity witnessed a big cat sighting. Ex-pop star Kim Wilde, who changed career to become a garden designer and author, saw an ABC in Codicote, Hertfordshire. Interestingly Codicote is home to the Cat Survival Trust, the rare leopard conservation society. Some members of this society are convinced that two panthers have visited this location. There have been several sightings and claw marks have been found too. Big cats will typically sharpen their claws on trees and leave scars on the bark about 4 to 5ft off the ground. Both Codicote and Tewin villages are close to Welwyn Garden City where a black leopard was reportedly seen on a golf course in May 2008. The vast majority of big cat sightings are of black animals, leopards that are black are known as panthers and they have always been both rare and valuable. Pumas are light brown in colour but this breed also features heavily in big cat encounters.

If anyone is in any doubt as to the existence of ABCs the facts speak for themselves. In 1987 a puma was shot by a police marksman near Greenwich Observatory in Greater London. In 1988 a farmer shot and killed a leopard at Widecombe-in-the-Moor at Dartmoor in Devon. In 1996 a caracal (also called Persian lynx or African lynx) was shot by an RUC marksman at Fintona, County Tyrone in Northern Ireland. On Friday 4 May 2001 a female Eurasian lynx was caught at Cricklewood in North London. She had been spotted sitting on a garden wall and when she was found she was injured. This lynx was rather more fortunate, as she was taken to London Zoo.

My own viewpoint is that ABCs should not be categorised as paranormal in any way. The fact that some have been killed or captured proves that they exist. Some people live near eagles, otters or badgers yet they have never seen these animals. The big cats have senses that are far sharper than humans and if they don't want to be seen then they won't be seen. There are several possible explanations as to how they came to be out of place, roaming the British countryside. They may have been accidentally released into the wild from zoos or travelling circuses or even deliberately released by private collectors. The Dangerous Wild Animals Act was passed in 1976. The Act required owners of big cats to be licensed. Many owners may have released their animals into the wild rather than comply with the terms of the Act. Did a number of these big cats adapt to their new conditions, manage to breed, learn how to hunt or scavenge? I would say that it is perfectly possible that this is what happened in some cases.

THE WESTON HAUNTING

Weston is another highly desirable rural location yet it is conveniently close to the towns of Letchworth and Baldock. The country idyll was destroyed for one couple, however, when they had to abandon their dream cottage after discovering that it was badly haunted. In 1995 Jill and Tom Brown found their perfect country location in Weston village. It was a seventeenth-century farm worker's cottage that had variously served both as the village post office and, at another time, as the village police station. One long-term resident of the village famously described it being 'as haunted as hell!' but Jill was unaware of this when she moved in. She said to me,

> When I mention the goings on to people they say to me 'how could you stay there?', but in reality there were long periods of calm. When freaky things occurred we just had to live with them. All in all we stayed there seven years, when we had just bought the cottage we didn't live in it straight away. I didn't ever really like the place but it was where we wanted to be and it was at the right price. I'm not sure when things started to happen but I'm sure it was after a couple of years of living there. I do remember that the cat would sit on a cupboard just staring at the wall in the lounge, which seemed very odd. One morning I came downstairs and the lounge furniture was about a foot away from the wall, it was very heavy to move it back again. The taps would be turned on at night – it became a regular occurrence and once, when there was a lot of unrest in the house, there was a loud bang as my son's wardrobe door flew open and his clothes emptied themselves out onto the floor. His wastepaper basket then launched itself across the room, scattering rubbish everywhere. He was in bed at the time but strangely he wasn't particularly upset by these events. I recall it being a Sunday night because I'd been ironing and was cross that the clothes I'd spent ages ironing were strewn around the floor. I tried to keep calm as I cleared up the mess, and my son, Jack, went back to sleep in his bedroom. Inside myself I felt anything but calm.
>
> After this event I thought that the house needed some help, although nobody had seen any ghosts there was definitely some unrest. I always felt that whatever it was went with the building and not necessarily with the occupants. I enquired about getting our home blessed by the local vicar, but didn't get a good reaction there. The new female vicar, when asked for help just laughed and admitted that she wouldn't know what to do. I 'phoned Sally, the previous owner and asked about her experiences in the place. She told me that she had always liked living there, but that there was a benevolent, mischievous presence about, whenever anything went missing she would just have to ask for it back. I felt much better about things after this conversation, but when I thought about all the things that had gone missing I would have a large pile! Around this time a colleague offered to visit, to use her dowsing rods. I was interested in this theory of energy channels causing unrest, as it seemed to make sense. When she came over she was very uneasy – didn't want to stay long or even sit down. She said she could instantly feel cold spots in the lounge, close to where the cat would sit looking at the wall. She found two energy channels running from a corner of the lounge to the back door. I thought it all very interesting but didn't know what to do with this information. A while later I also dowsed the lounge using a basic ring and thread. It freaked me when the thread would spin almost horizontally at a certain spot.

I learned from Jill that Tom Brown, her husband, had got very sick in the house; he had rheumatoid arthritis, diabetes, a thyroid defect and other auto-immune problems. Jill and Tom's son, Jack, was also adversely affected, he suffered with depression and was regularly subjected to scratching and banging noises in his bedroom, at one time all four walls were banged at once, which really spooked the boy.

Copper Cottage, Weston. Jill, Tom and Jack Brown's residency was marked by a catalogue of unnerving, unexplained and uncanny experiences.

Little did I know that something entirely different to my previous weird experiences in the house was due to happen to me. I was almost asleep in bed when I felt the most tender, loving kiss on my cheek. When I think about it now it still makes me feel emotional. After a while I turned the light on and was shocked to find an empty room, yet I could still feel that kiss on my cheek. Soon after this I went on holiday to France with the kids, but I think I took something extra in the car with us, because the same thing happened over there. I was kissed on the cheek again, just as I was falling asleep. It worried me greatly this time, because my theory about 'it' belonging to the house seemed to have gone out of the window. The kissing never happened again and the house was fairly quiet when we returned – now I wondered if I had left 'it' behind in France! The next big event in my life was meeting my present partner David, who instantly disliked the house. This was rather upsetting as the cottage was, after all, our home and supposedly in a most desirable location. For the first few nights Dave stayed there he felt a great pressure on his chest, as if someone was bearing down on him. He would often sleepwalk and seemed almost possessed, often we would have to rescue him in the night and point him in the right direction back to bed. His personal things would go missing so often that he didn't like to leave anything in the house. I thought that when we moved again (to Stevenage) they would turn up but sadly they never have been found. Taps were frequently turned on at night; thankfully the noise from the water tank in the loft would wake me. Although we were really anxious to move by this time it took a good year to sell the place. During this waiting time we spoke with a man who had

> spent his whole life in Weston and he said he wouldn't want to live in our house due to its spooky reputation. When Sally, the previous owner, had put an extension on the builders had refused to be alone in the place and their tools were always going missing.
>
> It was a great relief when we eventually found a buyer and a new house to move to. I was worried that 'it' would misbehave before we went, what with the disruption, boxes lying everywhere etc. We were treated to one more 'tap episode' the night before we left and, mercifully, that was all. Since moving to our new Stevenage home we can't help noticing that the cat never sits staring at the wall any more.

I also talked with Dave, Jill's new partner – he confirmed everything that she said. The house at Weston had always been cold, always difficult to get warmed up. In the year that they spent trying to sell the property there had been lots of viewings before it sold. Dave had got tired of things like video tapes, books and keys disappearing only to turn up in exactly the same spot months later. Sometimes things would disappear entirely, never to be seen again. He had seen taps turn themselves on; often they nearly flooded the house. One particularly weird experience, that had really bothered him, happened in the bathroom – he just could not locate the door to get out again. 'It was as if the room had changed altogether, the door had disappeared!'

After talking with the couple it became obvious that their former home had left a deep and unpleasant impression on the family, an impression that they were, unfortunately, unlikely to ever forget.

CHAPTER TWELVE

NORTH HERTFORDSHIRE NIGHTMARES

BALDOCK'S GHOSTLY RESIDENTS

When I moved to Baldock from Finchley, North London, over twenty years ago, I was intrigued by the lack of any mention about Baldock in books about the paranormal, so I decided to do my own research. Baldock is an ancient town which gets its name from a corruption of Baghdad, due to the influence of the Knights Templar, who owned the land that Baldock was built upon. The Templars were 'soldier monks' founded around 1118 AD to protect the pilgrims who visited Jerusalem and the Holy Land. Within fifty years of being established they owned some 7,000 manors across Europe as well as vast stores of treasure. The order was finally extinguished by Pope Clement in 1312. In my research I found a rich vein of paranormal phenomena experienced by the people of Baldock. Elsewhere I have mentioned some of the many haunted pubs associated with the town but they are only a small part of the ghost stories from my adopted hometown. Church Street residents have seen the figure of 'an old bent man' dressed in clothes 'not of this century', walk past their windows. The first house in this street is next to the churchyard and takes its name from the church, St Mary's House. A boy is said to haunt the kitchen, reputedly a boy was killed at this house when scaffolding fell on him. Many years ago, during renovations to some houses in Church Street, skeletons were discovered in the walls. At one time it was the custom for those too poor to afford a funeral to dispose of the remains of the recently deceased at home, by walling them up in the cottages. St Mary's church, the town's main landmark, has its own resident ghost – John Smith, who was rector here from 1832–1870. He is famous as the man who deciphered and transcribed the coded diary of Samuel Pepys. Smith did this when he was a student at St John's College, Cambridge. You can still see his grave in the churchyard, his shade, however, has often been seen sitting at the back of St Mary's.

In the highly haunted High Street we have a haunted restaurant, Il Fiorno, an Italian establishment once regularly patronised by Nigel Hawthorne. The late, great actor, former star of TV's *Yes Minister* and the movie, *The Madness of King George* lived at nearby Radwell village. The building that houses Il Fiorno is of seventeenth century origin with an eighteenth century façade. The earlier building would, therefore, fit in with the period of the English Civil War. I was interested to learn that it was haunted by the ghost of a Cavalier who appeared dressed in a large black hat, black cloak and black boots. Sightings date back to the time when the building was used as a baker's shop, called Hanscombes. When I first came to Baldock it was a sleepy little town and the former Hanscombes was then known as the Montmartre French restaurant. This was home to the 'Healing Chair', said to cure anyone who sat in it of their ailment. One diner put it to the test whilst out celebrating a wedding anniversary as he was suffering with an extremely heavy cold. He sat in the 'Healing Chair' for a while, next day his cold had completely gone. Was this a case of a psychosomatic cure, pure coincidence, or had the ghostly man in black been a physician, hence the 'Healing Chair'? Moving down the High Street on the same side of the road, there used to be a small shop called the Mayflower. It was run by Denis and I was accustomed to buying my Sunday newspaper there. It changed hands and became a combined sweetshop and gift shop called Truly Scrumptious and now it has changed yet again. When it was the Mayflower, about five years ago, I learned from the staff all about the odd goings on that occurred here from time to time. Various items frequently rearranged themselves; the contents of boxes on high shelves would frequently be disturbed. One incident I remember being told about was when little toy pistol cap boxes were found opened and all the reels of caps were left in a heap on the floor. On another occasion the Mayflower's owner was engaged in conversation with a female sales representative and the shop's sales assistant, who had been tidying up in the back, came forward to manage the sales counter. After a few minutes the representative left and the assistant returned to her tidying up but she was surprised and mystified to find two golden wedding glasses in the middle of the floor. They had been taken out of their boxes and placed on the ground where shop owner and representative had so recently been talking together. Denis was equally puzzled as to how they suddenly got there. Perhaps the ghost had a sense of humour and thought that the two people would have made a lovely couple. Denis was alone behind the counter another time when he heard the door open. The counter was directly opposite the cold drinks cabinet in the tiny shop, affording anyone behind the counter a reflection of anyone coming in, but there was no reflection of anybody this time. Shortly afterwards the door opened again and a woman came in – and she was nearly hit by a box of chocolates that launched itself off the shelf! The flat above the shop was also subject to the attentions of the unseen presence. Things were often moved around upstairs as well. A couple, who lived in this flat, told how they had watched, fascinated, one day as two coasters moved themselves down the length of a perfectly level table.

Next door to the old Mayflower was a property called The Gates. This place was known as the home of 'the electrical ghost' or 'the man in the cupboard', all things electrical were affected by it. Some examples were; a hairdryer which was seen to switch itself on and off as did a microwave oven, on countless occasions, and a cooking hob cooked a meal despite having been switched off. The ghost seems to have had a fascination for all things electrical – there was probably no electricity in this spirit's time! Across the other side of the High Street is Costcutters, reputedly haunted by a young boy and girl wearing Victorian clothes. One young witness described the pair so vividly it made her mother's flesh creep. There have also been reports of a violent ghost that has thrown people against the wall.

Just off of the High Street is a narrow lane called Bell Row and my suspicions about a house there were confirmed by a letter I received from Doug Elgood. He wrote,

> 'My wife and I moved into a property in Bell Row, Baldock, in July of 1973. It was a company property, owned by Sketchleys at that time. The house has a bay window overlooking the High Street right by the zebra crossing (which crossing was moved during the town enhancements). After we had been there for a couple of months we used to experience the most awful smells suddenly appearing in the flat that would disappear after a short while.

> This went on for some time until we called the environmental health people, who could find no source or explanation for the occurrence. We also had a cupboard door at the top of the stairs which could not be opened properly as it scraped along the floorboards. Many a time we would discover it wide open when no one had either been in it or even near it. After a while we began to spend quite a bit of time at my parents' home in Letchworth. We couldn't bear to be in the flat for too long a period as everything would just start happening over again. As we felt so uneasy in the flat I decided to 'borrow' my mother's dog for a while to keep us company, especially when one of us was home alone. On the first visit the dog wet herself all the way upstairs and subsequently cried all night on many occasions for no apparent reason. When you were alone there you would often feel someone in the same room, or behind your shoulder. While passing the old flat we have often looked up, to see if anyone was living there. Over the years we have come to the conclusion that while it may be occupied for a short time, it soon looks empty again. It leads us to believe that we may not have been the only ones to have had one visitor too many.'

I was unsurprised to hear about the dog's behaviour in this account as all dogs are psychically perceptive. Their reactions, crying or barking, as though at some unseen intruder, following something not visible to human eyes, or refusing to go upstairs or to enter certain rooms are all indications that a location is haunted.

In May 2008 I received an email from a reader of *Ghostly Hertfordshire*, an earlier book of mine. This lady had studied my piece about the Bell Row haunting with particular interest. Her name was Margaret McIntosh and her daughter, who was a nurse, had rented an apartment at 14b High Street, Baldock. The nurse's unexplained experiences included the following incidents. She heard footsteps when she was alone. Cups that had been left dirty would be found washed clean on her return home. The nurse would think about bills that she had to pay and then find them in a neat pile together with her coat. When she packed to go on holiday there would be a strong feeling of depression in the atmosphere. She described it as 'a feeling of walking through treacle'. A friend had refused to stay in the sitting room after seeing a man dressed in a purple gown standing in the corner. Margaret McIntosh visited in early October 1999 together with her younger daughter and grandson. As it was a one-bedroom apartment the three guests slept in the sitting room. At about 1am in the morning Margaret was woken by a man's voice which said, 'Twenty years ago my wife went out shopping and never came back'. A few minutes later Margaret went into the kitchen to make a drink and found her elder daughter there. She had been woken at 1am by the sound of the telephone ringing but the phone was in the sitting room and it had not made a sound. When the family discussed the night's events the following morning it transpired that both the younger daughter and the grandson had been unaware of anything untoward happening. On the final day of the nurse's tenancy she had sensed a powerful feeling of despair in the flat as she packed her possessions for the last time.

Pembroke Road, just off the High Street, has the reputation of being Baldock's most haunted street. Jean and Tom moved here some fifteen years ago as they wanted a central location. Before finding their present home they viewed a house nearby in The Orchard, a private road just off Pinnock's Lane. After showing them around the owner asked if they minded that the place was haunted. Every so often a Roman soldier would appear at the top of the stairs. Jean and Tom didn't buy the Orchard property but the one they did buy, in Pembroke Road, also turned out to be haunted. Their son's friend was staying over for a few weeks and when the couple heard footsteps bounding up the stairs one evening they assumed it was their young guest. They hadn't actually heard anyone come into the house, just the footfalls on the stairs. Next they heard the sounds of doors opening and closing above the living room. They thought it strange that their son's friend hadn't come in and said hello to them as he would usually have done. After a little while longer they went upstairs to offer him a drink, but there was no one up there. The unexplained footsteps and closing doors have subsequently been heard on several occasions and the smell of tobacco smoke has also been noticed, though none of the family smoke. Jean and Tom seem to have become accustomed to their ghost.

Several years ago a young couple who live in Pembroke Road saw a Roman soldier walking across the bedroom, but the floor was at the level of his knees. He walked on oblivious of his observers, and went through the bedroom wall.

George and Wendy's house in Pembroke Road is yet another affected by paranormal phenomena. It is an ordinary Victorian terraced cottage. Both George and Wendy were keen horse riders and one day George threw his jodhpurs onto the settee as he settled down to watch a boxing match. Out of the corner of his eye he saw some movement and he turned to witness his jodhpurs rising up of their own accord then moving a couple of feet along the settee before settling down again. Another time a teddy bear that sat on a seat, propped up by a cushion, suddenly lurched sideways while a dent appeared in the cushion as though some invisible entity had just sat down there. Wendy has also heard what she assumed to be George's footsteps behind her in the kitchen and moved aside to let him pass only to find herself quite alone. At night the couple have felt 'someone' sit on the end of their bed. Wendy was quite nervous of being on her own in the house at night but George was more philosophical. He had the distinct impression that their ghost was a benevolent one, possibly a previous long term resident who was happy here – too happy to leave, in fact.

Raban Court is a well-known landmark in Baldock that stands on the corner of Station Road with entrance gained through an archway in Royston Road. It is distinguished by one room which is supported by pillars on the pavement. Originally built in 1540, this building was originally the Talbot, a coaching inn. In 1959 Mr Raban, a local builder, bought the property and converted it into six houses. One resident of Raban Court shared her experiences with me some years ago. This lady had a problem with her arms and her doctor's treatment didn't seem to ease the aches and pains. Night after night she would lie awake unable to sleep. One night she led with her arms outside the blankets, hoping the pain would go away. As she lay there she sensed a presence which walked around the bed before stopping and standing by her side, whilst pulling some invisible covers over her arms. Soon she was asleep and enjoying the most restful sleep that she'd had in a long time. Other unusual things have been reported, like the smell of tobacco smoke in an apartment where nobody smoked, and the sighting of a jester where there used to be a gallery in the former Talbot Inn.

HITCHIN'S OLD TOWN ODDITIES

For centuries Hitchin has been a market town, it once enjoyed a thriving wool trade when sheep grazed on the hillsides and crops of wheat, barley and lavender were grown to provide a living for many agricultural workers. The Old Town, dominated by St Mary's church, has many haunted sites. Bridal gown suppliers, Jayne Boulton of Churchyard, was once a bookshop, during alterations to the premises a shoe was found and after that manifestations were seen. Just over the road at Charisma, staff have been pelted with beads by some invisible presence and at night the lights have come on by themselves in the empty shop. Not far away is Queen Street, once called Dead Street because not one person living there survived when the Great Plague struck in 1665. In the Market Square is Bar Amigo, haunted by an old man and a little girl, who, with arms linked, have been seen to walk through a solid wall. Across from the Square in the High Street stood Woolworth's, until the credit crunch struck. Many stories have been exchanged about 'the lavender lady' who haunted the place. Her shadowy form was seen, accompanied by the strong scent of lavender, so popular in Victorian times. One ex-manageress told me that she had been at a meeting in the town's Sun Hotel when her mobile phone rang but nobody spoke when she answered the call. She dialled 1471 and was given her own number back at the store. 'Someone' had called her at night from the locked and empty building – was it 'the lavender lady'? Sun Street, home to the haunted Sun Hotel has many other haunted premises. Numbers 10-11 Sun Street, a Queen Anne building, is home to house furnisher's Philpotts. This place has long had a scary reputation, since the time when the upstairs part was first used as a storeroom. Rumours tell of a gruesome event which took place up there; one account claims that a person was locked in and died behind the trapdoor. A family who used to live here heard heavy knocking sounds, when they opened the hatch they are alleged to have been assaulted and warned to leave by the ghost. There are also unconfirmed reports that a paranormal investigation conducted here went badly wrong, since then nobody has offered to 'lay the ghost'. I passed this way recently and noticed that the windows on the top floor were all still boarded up.

Bucklersbury runs parallel with Sun Street and two floors above Hawkins Department Store is a very haunted apartment. Footsteps echo across the empty landing, cold spots are experienced and two different apparitions have been reported. One is of a woman in a blue dress, and the other is a tall, thin man with straggly hair, described as 'vampiric' in appearance. A friend of mine, Andy Thompson, used to live in this same flat. He too, heard the footsteps, as well as odd scratching noises on his bedroom door at night. When he became fully awake the noises would stop. One particular night is etched in his memory, there was so much noise that he thought someone had broken in. He went to investigate and was confronted by an English Civil War soldier standing on the landing. Andy checked the mirror but saw that the figure was not reflected in it. He described it to me as follows, 'He wore a red tunic, he was a very big man (Andy himself is bigger than average), bearded, with a scar on his face. I was only about three or four steps below him on the stairs and I saw him quite plainly.' Another weird experience that Andy had in this flat took place during a party held there. Everyone had been sitting, talking, in a circle in the middle of the room, when somebody got up and left. The group assumed that this individual had gone to the toilet, but this 'person' didn't return. Everybody began to wonder who it could have been before realising that every guest was accounted for. Some of the group checked the rest of the flat but no one was found. So who was it? Everyone at that party remained convinced that 'another guest' (uninvited) had joined them that night. Andy decided to try and capture on tape the inexplicable sounds that were often heard around the apartment. One evening he played back the tape recording to a few friends and they were all startled to hear fearsomely loud snarling and growling animal sounds which the tape had captured on the landing area. Another witness who had lived in the same flat confirmed Andy's story about the tape recording, having heard it for himself. He recalled that everybody had been quite shaken on hearing the inhuman noises.

The most interesting and most haunted site in Hitchin is Hitchin Priory, which is currently used mainly as a conference and training centre but hosts other events including weddings, seminars and private dinners. In the fourteenth century a Carmelite (White Friars) Monastery was sited here, and in the Georgian era it was rebuilt as a private family home. Hitchin Priory was owned by the Delmay-Radcliffe family for over 400 years. There are many well authenticated stories about paranormal phenomena witnessed there and the following are some examples. It was December 1973 and Ivan Smith was on a school day trip with an overnight stay at Hitchin Priory. He was sharing a room on the second floor with his classmates and the room was reached by an old oak staircase. During the evening Ivan and his friend David walked up this staircase and then down a long corridor to their dormitory. About half way along the corridor both schoolboys stopped in their tracks as a 'Strange, mist-like figure appeared from the wall on the right, crossed

Hitchin Priory. Card-players, monks, a lady in grey and a Cavalier are just some of the apparitions that have been seen at Hitchin's most famously haunted site.

the corridor then floated back across and into the wall.' The boys looked at each other and fled back down the corridor and the stairs as fast as their legs would carry them.

The 19 acres of parkland which surround Hitchin Priory are also haunted. Night porters have reported seeing a phantom coach and horses at the back of the building. Roman soldiers have been seen (and heard) marching through the grounds. A 'grey lady' is sometimes encountered outside, people have remarked about 'the lady in the grey dress' and noticed that she has had no coat on because she has been seen on some very cold nights. When the Priory was used as an education centre, in 1980, the caretaker saw this same apparition.

Hitchin Priory has its very own 'anniversary ghost', said to appear every 15 June, and it is the spirit of a Cavalier called Goring. North-west of Hitchin is the village of Pirton and the ghost of a headless Cavalier is reputed to ride from Pirton to Hitchin on this particular summer's night. The Dowcras family, of Lilley village, built their Tudor mansion, High Down House, at Pirton, around 1510. During the English Civil War, in the summer of 1648, Parliamentarian troops, under the command of Colonel Scoop, called there. A Royalist supporter named Goring was visiting his lover at High Down House and he was taken by surprise at the sudden appearance of his enemies. Goring's tryst with his lady friend was a dangerous assignation, since Hitchin and the surrounding areas were crawling with Roundhead soldiers. The troops, possibly acting on the word of an informer, thoroughly searched the house. Goring was forced to make his escape via a secret underground passage and then he hid in a hollow wych-elm tree in the garden. The Roundheads discovered the hiding place, dragged Goring to the foot of the tree and ruthlessly cut him down. His murder was witnessed by his lover, who collapsed and later died from shock. Perhaps Goring had been hoping to escape to sanctuary at Hitchin Priory and so his ghost has been reportedly seen there. His lady friend has also been seen, at her former home. During the 1980s a guest was staying in a small bedroom in the attics at High Down House. The visitor was startled by the sudden appearance of a beautiful young woman, who sat on the edge of the bed before fading away from sight.

Security guards at Hitchin Priory have had numerous encounters with its ghosts. Many reports were made about talking being heard from certain rooms at night but when the rooms have been checked they have been found to be empty. Guards have seen shadowy monk-like figures but one guard had a particularly interesting encounter. He had been making his nightime rounds as usual when he opened a door to find a group of card players in old fashioned dress. He called up his colleague but when they returned together the room was deserted. The security man said later that he hadn't been frightened but he was astonished, he recalled that no one in that room had acknowledged his presence; they hadn't even looked up from their game. It was as if they were in a different time zone – had he happened on some kind of 'time slip'?

KNEBWORTH'S SPOOKY BUSINESS

Nup End, in Old Knebworth, is home to the Nup End Business Centre, where groundworks and civil engineering company A.D. Bly, owned by Tony Bly, is situated. Nearby is Nup End Farmhouse, reputed to date back to the Cromwellian era. The farmhouse and the contractors' offices are both haunted. The old farmhouse was converted into apartments by Tony Bly and there is a separate small outbuilding in the farmhouse grounds which is similarly affected. Terry Goddard leased the outbuilding from 1999-2004, and he had several strange experiences, one of which occurred at 2am in the morning. He looked up from his computer screen to see a farm worker standing in front of the desk. The man smiled at Terry before promptly vanishing. On another occasion the computer engineer saw this same worker in the corridor. Other phenomena mentioned by Terry included taps that were mysteriously turned on and off in the kitchen and the front doorbell being rung when no one was about. Terry also saw the front door handle being moved and the door then opened and closed by itself. He was equally puzzled by his abnormally high electricity bills, often the hallmark of a genuine haunting. As we have noted earlier ghosts seem able to 'tap into' any available electricity supply and to use the energy gained to produce their repertoire of anomalous phenomena. Anglia Paranormal Investigation Society was asked to mount a vigil at the farmhouse, offices and the outbuilding. We picked up some interesting impressions in the course of our researches in 2004. One of our team members, Andy Garrett, saw his first apparition, which is a landmark event in any paranormal investigator's life! Andy was standing near a window frame in the farmhouse when a man walked briskly past the side of the building, through some flowerbeds. He wore a white shirt with big cuffs and large buttons. A few team members went outside to see who the stranger was but there was nobody about other than themselves. Some people have sensed an uncomfortable atmosphere in the gardens, as though something nasty is lying in wait. Knocking sounds have also been heard downstairs, coming from above, when the upstairs apartment has been vacant. In 2002 Carol Greenall was working alone in A.D. Bly's main offices reception area when she felt unnaturally cold and she saw a hazy shape taking form by the fax machine. This misty outline then crossed the floor and went through the wall. Carol compared notes with the receptionist who confirmed that she had seen this same misty shape some twelve months previously. A number of other staff members, both men and women, came forward and admitted that they do not like working in these offices on their own and all agreed that the place has 'a funny feel to it at night'.

STEVENAGE'S UFOS AND HAUNTINGS

UFOs hit local press headlines in July 2008 when sightings were reported by a number of Stevenage residents. *The Comet* was inundated with telephone calls from witnesses who saw strange lights in the skies. On Saturday 26 July between 10pm and 11pm a number of orange lights appeared over the town. Sean Riley was having a barbecue at his Wisden Road home at the time. He commented, 'There were four very bright orange objects going from north to south, one following the other with a fair gap and then going straight up and disappearing. I had not been drinking and ten other people at my barbecue saw them, also aircraft going to Luton airport were in close proximity. We're fairly logical and reasonable people. They were travelling from north to south and the wind was going in the opposite direction so it couldn't have been Chinese lanterns (one of the usual explanations for unexplained lights). Some people look at our photos and say what we saw was the moon but there hasn't been a full moon for a long time (the moon was in its final quarter at this time). Ken Tobin was at Sean's barbecue and he stated, 'I didn't believe in UFOs until Saturday. It was quite unbelievable. The spheres were silent and travelled in a straight line. Then they got dimmer and dimmer. I have never seen anything like it.'

Another witness to the mysterious lights was Ian Sharp of Jessop Road, he stated, 'I was lying in bed when I saw two orange lights glide across the sky about fifteen seconds apart. They were following a plane that had just flown over. It was something I'd never seen before.'

The UFOs were spotted by residents on the Jackman's Estate in Letchworth Garden City and near Bancroft in Hitchin. Stephen Hague of Bearton Road said, 'I have spent twenty-one years working nights and have seen many sky items but nothing like this. Could it have been a satellite breaking up? Maybe, but it was the regularity that the items passed over that made this unlikely. They were neither planes nor shooting stars, they were way too big and you could see the flickering orange flames.'

That same evening UFO Investigations UK received a record number of reported sightings for one night and called for an official MoD enquiry. A spokesman for the investigation society said, 'More than 200 people got in touch claiming to have seen UFOs on Saturday night. Normally we receive ten to fifteen reports a day. So far we've not been able to explain all the sightings. It's time for an official enquiry.'

The previous year motorists reported a similar sighting between Baldock and Royston on the A505. They saw orange balls of light moving across the sky, but Luton Airport said they believed they were Chinese lanterns which had been lit and then released into the air. Rather conveniently they dismissed this latest mass sighting as Chinese lanterns once again. After my extensive researches into the phenomena of UFOs it is my opinion that the Stevenage reports contain all the hallmarks of a genuine UFO sighting.

When I was researching hauntings in Stevenage I was contacted by Phyllis Ayres, whose son, Ian Abernethy, and his wife Amber lived in a modern house in Forest Row, in the Roebuck district. During 2002/03 the couple were plagued by a variety of unearthly incidents. Amber's jewellery would mysteriously move itself from the bedside table and migrate to the windowsill. When the Abernethy children, Holly and Jack, were watching television they were terrified by an almighty crash from overhead. It came from their empty bedroom and it sounded as though someone had jumped off the bed but there was no one upstairs at the time. When a photograph of Jim, the family's West Highland terrier, was taken, a cloud appeared around the little dog. In the cloud a woman's face could be clearly seen. The Abernethys sometimes heard running footsteps overhead when everyone was downstairs. The ghost had an irritating habit of turning taps on in the bathroom. One of the family would turn them off again only to find, soon afterwards, that the tap had been turned back on again. This sometimes happened several times in a row. One night Ian's brother, Andrew, stayed over to look after the house while the rest of the family were away. He, too, heard the unearthly footsteps, they came upstairs and crossed the landing, and then his bedroom door was pulled open, at which point he said he ducked under the bedcovers. Another time Ian was at home alone doing some decorating when he saw a lady in a long grey dress standing at the top of the stairs. He was to see this apparition later, on several occasions. Ian suffered with a bad back and he used a special spray attachment in the bath to ease his pain. Hearing a loud bang one day, Ian ran out to investigate and discovered that his sprayer had been hurled downstairs.

One of the most well known haunted areas in Stevenage is Monkswood; many people have felt uneasy whilst walking its tree-lined pathways. It is claimed that a monastery was sited here. During the Reformation the religious order based in the area received particularly brutal treatment. This included the burning down of their buildings and the murder of many of their order, many of whom are thought to be buried beneath these very trees. What is known for sure is that apparitions of monks have been seen in this location.

Eric Hornby is a retired engineer who worked for British Aerospace in the calibration department, in 'C' building on the Gunnelswood Road. Adjacent to the calibration department was a male toilet. The policy at BAE was to employ retired personnel to clean these toilets and Eric got used to seeing one particular 'old-timer' who came in at the same time every day. This cleaner could invariably be found sitting on a box in the corner rolling a cigarette, having mopped the floor to give the appearance of cleanliness. Whenever Eric saw the cleaner, which was usually a couple of times each week, he would say 'good morning' to the older man, but he never received any acknowledgement. The engineer had not seen the cleaner for about a fortnight, then, one morning, there he was, sitting on his box as usual. Eric greeted him but was unsurprised to be ignored. The next day Eric met the cleaners' supervisor, who was mopping the floor, so he asked 'Is the usual fellow off sick today?' The supervisor's reply was unnerving, to say the least, 'He died of a heart attack two weeks ago.' Eric Hornby told me something of the site's history. Before any industrial units were built here there had been huge burial mound which ran from north to south almost to the full extent of the site. It was quite tall and had to be levelled off to accommodate the industrial units. Since then, over a period of perhaps sixty years, numerous reports were received about Roman soldiers. They were seen marching along some 3 metres above ground level down the entire length of the former burial mound.

THE GHOSTLY GROCER

Curious sightseers still used to make their way in recent times to the old National Westminster Bank (taken over by Royal Bank of Scotland in 2000) premises in Stevenage for a viewing of Henry Trigg's coffin, which was perched high up in the rafters of the building. He was certainly one of the oddest personalities who has ever lived in Stevenage, the quintessential English eccentric. Henry Trigg was a wealthy grocer who sold meat from his own twin-gabled shop in Middle Row during the 1700s. Middle Row had originally been home to market stalls in medieval times, over time it slowly it developed into a row of permanent shops and dwellings.

Trigg was well known in the locality and an important member of the community. He was a single man, owned land and property, was a churchwarden and overseer of the parish. When he died he caused his family much embarrassment due to the bizarre conditions contained in his will. Copies of this will were mass produced and sold to an eager public, who read the details with amazement. Dated 28 September 1724, it instructed his executor quite clearly that Trigg's body should be committed 'to the West end of my hovel (barn) to be decently laid there upon a floor erected by my Executor, upon the purlin (roof beam) for the same purpose, nothing doubting but that at the general Resurrection, I shall receive the same again by the mighty power of God.'

What could have caused such a clearly god-fearing man to have his coffin placed high up in the roof of a barn instead of being buried in the consecrated ground of a churchyard like everyone else? The simple answer is 'resurrectionists', the popular name given to grave robbers of England and Scotland in the nineteenth century. These individuals illicitly dug up freshly buried corpses, which they then sold, for dissection, to the medical schools in London and Edinburgh. The practise was particularly notorious in 1828-29 due to the activities of the murderers Burke and Hare. Fears aroused by the activities of the resurrectionists were out of all proportion to their real effect and led to the passing of the Anatomy Act of 1832.

Grave robbing was also happening during Henry Trigg's time, in the eighteenth century. The most famous case in this era was that of Laurence Sterne, the writer of the novel *The Life and Opinions of Tristram Shandy, Gentleman*, who died in 1768. After his death his body was 'resurrected' by grave robbers but recognised at a Cambridge anatomy lecture. Henry Trigg had a close encounter of his own with grave robbers which was to permanently leave its mark on his mind. One night, after a drinking session with a couple of friends in the Black Swan Inn, the grocer happened on some ghoulish thieves at work in a new grave at St Mary's churchyard. These 'unscrupulous vampires' (as he described them) could be dangerous people to tangle with, so Henry Trigg and his companions quietly slipped away. The idea that his own body could fall into the hands of such loathsome creatures, to ultimately end up on a dissecting table somewhere, filled Henry Trigg with horror. His solution to the problem was to create his own highly unconventional final resting place.

It must have been extremely difficult for Henry's brother, the Reverend Thomas Trigg, to accept the strange terms imposed on him. Henry had obviously anticipated opposition to his last will and testament. He had named Thomas as his executor; however, if he objected to carrying out his duties everything would go to brother George, and so on, down through the family. The estate was considerable and so it came to pass that Henry Trigg's lead-lined coffin was hoisted up into the rafters of the barn at the back of the shop. The famous coffin, which could still be seen in modern times, was neither the original casket nor did it contain the mortal remains of the ghostly grocer.

In 1774 the former Trigg house and shop became the Old Castle Inn. In the great fire of 1807 many thatched buildings in Middle Row were destroyed. The old Trigg barn (along with its coffin) situated in the northern half of the street escaped any damage when the wind suddenly changed direction. The Old Castle Inn's licence was not renewed after 1919 and the building eventually became a branch of the National Westminster Bank. Henry Trigg's coffin, however, did not lie undisturbed in all this time. Mr Bellamy, landlord of the Old Castle Inn, could not resist the temptation to check on 'Old Henry'. In 1831 Bellamy declared that, 'the hair on the skull of the deceased was in a perfect state of preservation.' The coffin was a different matter, as it was deteriorating badly. At some point in the 1800s a new one was made, bound with iron bands. Trigg's body was placed inside and the casket was returned to the rafters. The East Hertfordshire Archaeological Society later inspected the coffin and found 'about two thirds of a male skeleton'. Were grisly souvenir hunters responsible? At the time of the First World War Commonwealth troops were billeted in Stevenage. Persistent rumours circulated that they had also opened the casket and removed more of Henry Trigg's remains. The peace that Trigg sought was not to be. Did the soldiers in transit for the front line perhaps imagine that, like a latter day saint's relics, the grocer's bones might afford them some sort of protection in the coming conflagration? It was also alleged that the soldiers had sold all the bones for ready cash. When they were, at last, all gone the resourceful recruits made up the deficiency by restocking with animal bones, obtained through one of the town butchers.

One Stevenage resident admitted in a letter to the local press that she had, along with some army friends, raided the coffin, but the bones that they found turned out to be horses' bones! The fact that the coffin no longer contained any part of Henry Trigg was kept quiet as long as copies of his will were selling steadily at sixpence per copy. Revenue might well have suffered if it became public knowledge that there was only an empty coffin in the barn rafters. It is most ironic that a man who went to so much trouble to ensure that his dead body was kept intact at all costs did not have it stolen and dissected, as he had feared, but instead had it stolen piecemeal.

In 1964 renovation work was carried out on a building in Middle Row – a building that backed onto the barn that had once belonged to Henry Trigg. During the course of the project workman Fred Usher went into the storeroom one morning to fetch a crowbar. Usher said he met a 'shabbily dressed' old man, 'in an overcoat and gaiters' coming through the doorway. 'He must have been about 5ft 8in tall', so real did the apparition seem to be that the workman called out to him but as is the way with ghosts there was no reply. The figure 'seemed to drift past me', but what happened next really shook Usher. 'I turned and nearly collapsed when I saw him disappearing through a solid brick wall.' Older residents who had lived in the area for a long time told Fred Usher that what he had seen was the spirit of Henry Trigg.

THE STEVENAGE 'POLTERGEIST'

The most interesting investigation that APIS has had in Stevenage is the 'Stevenage Poltergeist' case. It began when a medium called Lesley phoned me one Monday evening in November 2008, sounding quite distressed. She had never had any trouble with her mobile phone reception but as soon as she started talking with me about this poltergeist case the line became crackly and she couldn't hear me at all. She was forced to leave the house and went out to her car to try and phone again, strangely this time the line was crystal clear. Lesley told me that she'd been contacted by another medium friend from Harlow who told her about a family that had been experiencing poltergeist activity in their home in the Chells area of Stevenage and they were now desperate for help. The family had been tormented with all kinds of phenomena. The freezer was mysteriously unplugged many times and the cooker tampered with, the internet connection was found in the garden, writing had appeared on the bathroom mirror, five alarm clocks were smashed, a new phone just purchased was later discovered down a toilet, the heating had been turned off and sink plugs were taken from the sinks and thrown at the family. Taps were turned on in the downstairs toilet and sometimes the taps were turned completely around. Lesley told me that she had successfully cleared haunted houses many times, both in this country and abroad. In this case, however, she had been unsuccessful and had decided to call in APIS. She visited the affected house on Sunday, the day before she phoned me, and had stayed there for four hours. There was an initial burst of activity, when a phone went flying through the air and a knife landed on the settee. All was calm for a while as the medium talked with the family, a boy of fourteen called John (not his real name) and his grandparents, who were both in their seventies. John was living at his grandparents' home because his mother just could not cope any more. His grandfather was forced to keep his pockets full of things like glue, tweezers and scissors that could easily have been used as missiles by the poltergeist. Numerous items from the bedrooms and even the garage, no matter if they were in cupboards or locked drawers, were hurled about the living room by the unseen force. This intense poltergeist activity had just been too much for his mother to cope with when John had been living at home with her, so John's grandparents had offered to look after him.

Leslie walked around downstairs, checking for cold spots but could find none, then, before she left she gave everybody some healing. John's grandmother was concerned that there would be activity after the medium had gone, she said, 'They will be angry you have been here and we will have to pay for this.' It was a telling remark, which clearly showed the level of intimidation that had been suffered by this family over many days. Leslie had personally witnessed some of the destructive haunting for herself. She had seen spoons flying through the air (there wasn't a straight spoon left in the house) and much of their cutlery had gone missing. A knife had smashed a cup while it was in the grandmother's lap. This was also witnessed by the medium who had heard the noise of scissors impacting on the kitchen door. Pairs of gloves and socks were missiles favoured by the unseen forces, twice Leslie was hit in the back of the head. (The grandmother wasn't so lucky; she was hit in the back of the head by a battery). All seemed to be quiet when the medium returned early the next morning (Monday) so that John wouldn't be late for school. At this time John was only allowed to go to school for an hour each day and his place on the school coach, to take him to college, had been withdrawn. The previous night it turned out that the grandmother's worst fears had been realised. The grandparents and their grandson all had to sleep downstairs, on two settees and an armchair, as past poltergeist activity had been so intense in the bedrooms. On that Sunday night, soon after the medium left, knives went flying about (a frequent event) and a mug of water was splashed on John's duvet as he tried to sleep on the settee. Activity continued through the night, right up to 4am the next morning. This included black paint being splattered across one of the settees and beads (which were transported from one of the bedrooms) being scattered across the living room floor.

I visited the house on the Tuesday morning, the day after receiving Leslie's phone call requesting my help. I was shocked at the damage done by this particular poltergeist infestation. That very morning the electric kettle had been smashed twice against the back door causing a hole in the hardboard covering which had been masking previous damage. The back door had been rendered unusable. The family's toaster was dashed against the floor. The portable TV that they had been using had several gouges out of it and nicks out of the screen in two places. As I drove up to the neat, detached property, the first thing I noticed was a broken front window, a whole double glazed pane had been damaged. Inside the house I saw a flat screen TV that was smashed. I learned from the grandparents that these damages had occurred in one particularly violent night. That same evening another front window had been damaged and a table, from a nest of tables, had been hurled with such force that it embedded itself into the glass in a back door. The police had been called in on that occasion and they had removed the table. Other items damaged included two glass ashtrays which were completely shattered, the light bulbs from every single upstairs room were all smashed and a conservatory window was broken. One door had fifteen small glass panels shattered with extreme force. The damage was done by spanners, which had somehow been transported from John's mother's house! The police noted the severe damage and three black plastic sacks of broken glass were removed.

I settled down with the grandparents and they completed my paranormal questionnaire about the events that they had been experiencing. The trouble had started a year ago, in November 2007. John's paternal grandmother died then and a few days later the poltergeist activity had begun, on 3 December. It continued until February. During this time money, both coins and notes, would rain down on John, wherever he went. On one notable occasion £200 came down and many people were consulted about the case, including Professor Richard Wiseman of Hertfordshire University and Spiritualist healer and medium Bill Parkins. John's school were very supportive and saw John as a model pupil, he was willing to learn, always in his uniform and his homework was always in on time.

I discovered that in the past there had been animosity between John's mother and her mother in law, over access to John. It was interesting that activity was breaking out again, on the anniversary of the mother in law's death. It seemed that it was more disturbing and destructive this time. There were no inconsistencies in the grandparents' story and many of the hallmarks of a genuine poltergeist infestation were revealed. It was my duty to help these people; they didn't deserve the misery that they had been subjected to. Not only were they being deprived of sleep but they weren't eating properly, food would go flying off their plates, so they had been living on sandwiches for the past fortnight. If they went to a restaurant to eat something would happen either there or in the car. Days before my visit John's grandfather was driving when John's iPod flew off the rear parcel shelf, past the driver's head and struck the windscreen. The family were anxious about going out because when they did so there would be repercussions in terms of destructive phenomena when they got home again. I considered that all of this was quite intolerable. I liked them; John seemed like any normal fourteen year old, probably brighter than most, and I felt great sympathy for the family's plight. The boy, as well as his grandparents, was a victim in all this, his inhalers had been destroyed and on numerous occasions his cross and chain were taken from him. Pieces of pyrite, brass ornaments and other small pieces of metal would fall out of thin air to land beside him. Articles regularly disappeared, in some cases permanently, at other times they turned up in a new location. One visitor's trainers were taken, so he had to borrow a pair from the family. After he'd gone his trainers turned up separately in different parts of the house. The poltergeist did its best to disrupt communications; no less than five telephones either had their lines cut, were ripped out or just would not work. Mobile phones were similarly affected; three of them had their SIM card taken, then the battery removed (one battery was broken in half) and finally the phones were used as missiles. The phones were damaged every time the family were going to talk to someone about what was happening in the house.

I put together an APIS 'clearance team' in double quick time, these folk needed our support, and quickly. We returned the very next night (Wednesday). We all saw the black paint that was daubed on two walls; it was also put on the settee and on John. When the boy had been preparing to leave the house that morning acrylic paint was splashed down the front of his uniform from head to foot. He had to go to school like that and the staff there were most sympathetic. They weren't too pleased, however, when John was left alone in the school office and damage happened there too.

There were seven of us in the APIS team, including my good friend Margaret Rolph, an extremely gifted psychic healer and medium. We went from room to room and used our combined concentrated energies to rid the house of any unwanted entities. I was uncomfortable, however, because I couldn't detect any 'presences', not that I lay any claim to being psychically developed. Margaret advised me that I might be more 'sensitive' than I thought because she, too, could feel no negative energies in the house. My intuition was telling me that John was the focus of the poltergeist activity; he himself was inadvertently causing the phenomena experienced both at his mother's house and now at his grandparents' home. Margaret started working with John to help him to try and control the energies that were 'leaking' out of him. My own line of investigation leads me to believe that John's case is actually a case of RSPK rather than a poltergeist case. What is RSPK? The acronym stands for recurrent spontaneous psychokinesis. Psychokinesis comes from the Greek: *psyche* (or mind) and *kinein* which means 'to move'. It is the ability to move objects without applying any physical or other scientifically explainable force. The recurrent spontaneous part of RSPK refers to the fact that it happens over and over again but without conscious effort or focus on the part of the 'energy supplier', John in this instance. At time of writing I'm working closely with a parapsychologist friend to try and unravel this fascinating case. I'm sure that we haven't heard the last of the 'Stevenage Poltergeist'...

FURTHER READING

Paranormal Bedfordshire
Damien O'Dell

ISBN: 978-1-84868-119-4
Price: £12.99